# REMAPPING WORLD CINEMA
## identity, culture and politics in film

# REMAPPING WORLD CINEMA
## identity, culture and politics in film

edited by Stephanie Dennison and Song Hwee Lim

 **WALLFLOWER PRESS** LONDON & NEW YORK

First published in Great Britain in 2006 by
Wallflower Press
6a Middleton Place, Langham Street, London W1W 7TE
www.wallflowerpress.co.uk

A catalogue for this book is available from the British Library

ISBN  1-904764-62-2 (pbk)
ISBN  1-904764-63-0 (hbk)

Book design by Elsa Mathern

Printed by Replika Press Pvt Ltd., India

cover images:
*Beau travail* (Claire Denis, 1999)
*Audition* (Takashi Miike, 1999)
*Crouching Tiger, Hidden Dragon* (Ang Lee, 2000)
*Sex and Lucia* (Julio Medem, 2001)
*City of God* (Fernando Meirelles, 2002)
*Ten* (Abbas Kiarostami, 2002)

# CONTENTS

## PERFORMING STARDOM AND RACE

## INTERROGATING GENDER

## HOLLYWOOD'S OTHERS

# ACKNOWLEDGEMENTS

The inspiration for this edited volume came from an international film conference held in June 2002 at the University of Leeds entitled *World Cinemas: Identity, Politics, Culture*. As well as specially-commissioned pieces, a number of chapters have been based on papers delivered at the conference. The editors are thus grateful to the conference organising committee in particular and University's School of Modern Languages and Cultures in general for their support in the organisation of the event.

The following people have offered insightful comments on the manuscript at different stages in its production: Paul Cooke, Diana Holmes, Ananya Jahanara Kabir, Rachel Killick, Robert J. Miles, Mark Morris, Jay Prosser and Kamal Salhi.

Finally our thanks to the following individuals: Yoram Allon at Wallflower Press, Kenneth Hargraves at the School of Modern Languages and Cultures, and on a more personal note, Fernando Barbosa and Mme Tan Geok Kiang.

ACKNOWLEDGMENTS

# NOTES ON CONTRIBUTORS

**Dudley Andrew** is Professor of Film Studies and Comparative Literature at Yale University. His various publications include *Mists of Regret, Culture and Sensibility in Classic French Film* (Princeton University Press, 1995) and, as co-author, *Popular Front Paris and the Poetics of Culture* (Harvard University Press, 2005).

**Guy Austin** is Senior Lecturer in French in the Department of French at the University of Sheffield, and Director of the AHRB-funded online bibliographical database of modern French film stars. His publications include *Contemporary French Cinema: an introduction* (Manchester University Press, 1996), *Claude Chabrol* (Manchester University Press, 1999) and *Stars in Modern French Film* (Arnold, 2003).

**Kaushik Bhaumik** is Research Fellow at the Ferguson Centre for African and Asian Studies, Open University, UK. He is co-editor of *Visual Cultures: An Alternative Reader* (Berg, 2005) and *The BFI Indian Cinema Book* (British Film Institute, 2006). He is also finishing an as yet untitled monograph on Bombay cinema between 1896 and 1936.

**Michael Chanan** is Professor of Cultural Studies at the University of the West of England, Bristol. He is a filmmaker, author, editor and translator of books and articles on film. He is the author of *The Dream That Kicks: The Prehistory and Early Years of Cinema and Britain* (Routledge, 1996) and his seminal study of Cuban cinema, *The Cuban Image*, has recently been updated and reprinted by the University of Minnesota Press (2005).

**Stephanie Dennison** is Senior Lecturer in Brazilian Studies in the Department of Spanish and Portuguese and Co-Director of the MA in World Cinemas programme in the School of Modern Languages and Cultures at the University of Leeds. She is co-author of *Popular Cinema in Brazil* (Manchester University Press, 2004) and co-editor of *Latin American Cinema: Essays on Modernity, Gender, and National Identity* (McFarland, 2005). She is currently co-authoring a volume on Brazilian national cinema for Routledge.

**Hideaki Fujiki** is Assistant Professor in the Graduate School of Letters at Nagoya University, Japan. His recent publications have appeared in *ICONICS*, *Cinema Journal* and the *Encyclopedia of Documentary Films* (Routledge, 2005). His monograph on the formation of the Japanese film star system is forthcoming from Nagoya University Press.

Mark Goodall is Lecturer in Electronic Imaging and Media Communications at the University of Bradford. He is co-coordinator of the National Museum of Photography Film and Television's annual 'Crash Cinema' symposium and is the lead singer in rock band Rudolf Rocker. His *Sweet and Savage: The World Through the Shockumentary Film Lens* is published by Headpress (2006).

Rachael Hutchinson is Assistant Professor of Japanese Studies in the Department of East Asian Languages and Literatures at Colgate University and co-editor of *New Cinemas: Journal of Contemporary Film*. Her work on Occidentalism has appeared in *Japan Forum* and the co-edited volume *Representing the Other in Modern Japanese Literature: A Critical Approach* (Routledge, 2006).

Song Hwee Lim is Lecturer in Chinese in the Department of East Asian Studies and Co-Director of the MA in World Cinemas programme in the School of Modern Languages and Cultures at the University of Leeds. He is also the General Editor of *New Cinemas: Journal of Contemporary Film*, and the author of *Celluloid Comrades: Representations of Male Homosexuality in Contemporary Chinese Cinemas* (University of Hawai'i Press, 2006).

Rosanna Maule is an Assistant Professor in Film Studies at the Mel Hoppenheim School of Cinema, Concordia University, in Montreal. She is a member of GRAFICS, a research group on early cinema, and is on the editorial of *CinemaS*. She has published several articles on contemporary European film authorship and edited three special issues of international film journals on early cinema. She is currently completing a monograph on new developments in authorial film practices in French, Italian and Spanish cinema since the 1980s, and a co-edited anthology on the cinematic work of Marguerite Duras.

Lúcia Nagib is Centenary Professor of World Cinema at the University of Leeds. She is the author of *Werner Herzog – o cinema como realidade* (Estação Liberdade, 1991), *Em torno da nouvelle vague japonesa* (editora da Unicamp, 1993), *Nascido das cinzas – autor e sujeito nos filmes de Oshima* (Edusp, 1995) and *O cinema da retomada – depoimentos de 90 cineastas dos anos 90* (Editora 34, 2002). She has also edited books on Ozu and Mizogucki and *The New Brazilian Cinema* (I. B. Tauris, 2003). She is currently completing a monograph entitled *Brazilian Screen: Cinema Novo, New Cinema, Utopia*.

Evelyn Preuss is a doctoral student in the Department of Germanic Languages and Literatures at Yale University. Her publications have appeared in *Perspecta 036: The Yale Architectural Journal* and *Focus on Literature*.

Keith Richards teaches Latin American literature at Universidad Mayor de San Andrés in La Paz, Bolivia. He has published several articles on Latin American cinema, literature and popular culture, as well as two books on Bolivian literature: *Lo Imagi-*

*nario Mestizo* (Plural, 1999) and *Narrativa del trópica boliviano* (La Hoguera/Center for Amazonian Literature and Culture, 2004).

**David Robb** is Senior Lecturer in German Studies at The Queen's University of Belfast. His edited book *Clowns, Fools and Picaros: Popular Forms in Literature, Drama and Film* is forthcoming with Rodopi/At the Interface. His book *East and West German Political Song since the 1960s* is forthcoming with Camden House.

**Rob Stone** is Senior Lecturer and Head of the Department of Media and Communication at the University of Wales, Swansea. He is the author of *Spanish Cinema* (Longman, 2002), *The Flamenco Tradition in the Works of Federico García Lorca and Carlos Saura* (Edwin Mellen, 2004) and *Julio Medem* (Manchester University Press, 2006), and co-editor of *The Unsilvered Screen: Surrealism on Film* (Wallflower Press, 2006).

**Louise Williams** received her PhD from the Department of East Asian Studies, University of Leeds, working on 'Masculinity on the Run: History, Nation and Subjectivity in Contemporary Mainland Chinese Cinema'. She is currently a post-doctoral fellow affiliated to the University of Leeds and funded by the Chiang Ching-Kua Foundation for International Scholarly Exchange, working on modern Taiwanese cinema.

# INTRODUCTION

## Situating world cinema as a theoretical problem

Stephanie Dennison and Song Hwee Lim

'What is world cinema?' This is a deceptively simple question that has proved to be a challenging theoretical problem. In his book *Cinemas of the World*, James Chapman wonders 'whether any general model can adequately account for the many different filmmaking practices, genres, styles and traditions that have arisen in the global context' (2003: 33). In a volume entitled *Remapping World Cinema*, it might be expected of us, the editors, to provide a definition, if not a definitive answer, to the question. However, perhaps that is not the right question to ask in the first place. In an article entitled 'Discourse', Paul A. Bové argues that an essay like his 'not only does not but *cannot* provide definitions, nor can it answer what come down to essentialising questions about the "meaning" or "identity" of some "concept" named "discourse"' (1995: 53; emphasis in original). For Bové, questions such as 'what is discourse?' or 'what does discourse mean?' 'imply a norm of judgement: meaning and essence are better and more important than a discussion of "how things work" or "where they come from"' (ibid.). Whilst the questions 'What is world cinema?' and 'What is discourse?' may not share an entirely similar epistemological premise, we do agree with the post-structuralists in Bové's essay that 'these essentialising questions emerge from the very interpretive models of thought which the new focus on "discourse" [and in our case, "world cinema"] as a material practice aims to examine and trace' (ibid.).

What we will attempt to do below, therefore, is not so much to provide an answer to the question 'what is world cinema?' but to trace the processes by which it has been discussed and conceptualised, to examine how these conceptualisations work and where they come from, to account for their embedded contradictions and tensions, and, perhaps most importantly, to underscore the situatedness of each discourse in its specific context, including that of our own. It is futile, if not hypocritical, to pretend that a loaded phrase such as 'world cinema' can be value free, and it is in bringing into play the power structures inherent in discourses on 'world cinema' that one could paradoxically begin to throw light, however elliptically, on the question 'what is world cinema?'

### Situating analogies: world cinema, world music, world literature

The first thing to note about the concept of world cinema is its situatedness: it is, in this book at least, the world as viewed from the West. In this sense, world cinema is analogous to 'world music' and 'world literature' in that they are categories created in the Western world to refer to cultural products and practices that are mainly non-Western. While the historical trajectories of their origins and developments may not have been totally identical, their relationships to non-Western cultural products and practices in terms of consumption and reception of the latter in the Western world bear striking similarities that lend themselves to a comparative study. On the most mundane level, in music and video shops (and in the public library in Leeds), world cinema and world music occupy separate sections from mainstream film and music, with both signifying non-English-language products. In an academic institutional context, world cinema (if it exists at all) is peripheral to film and cinema studies whilst world literature often resides within English departments, with both sharing an investment in the Third World and the postcolonial. The politics embedded in the concepts of world literature and world music can thus be illuminating to our understanding of world cinema.

Definitions of world literature have traditionally been influenced by Goethe's formulation of the term *Weltliteratur*, which concerns itself with the discussion of literature in a global context at least since the 1820s. Central to Goethe's early fascination with obscure literatures is the notion that these works offer the (Western) reader a window into foreign worlds. In an essay entitled 'What is World Literature?', David Damrosch writes:

> World literature is ... always as much about the host culture's values and needs as it is about a work's source culture: hence it is a double refraction, one that can de described through the figure of the ellipse ... A work changes in nature when it moves from a national sphere to a new worldly context; works become world literature by being received into the space of a foreign culture, a space defined in many ways by the host culture's national tradition and the present needs of its own writers. Even a single work of world literature is the locus of a negotiation between two different cultures. (2003: 14)

What is missing from the above account is the acknowledgement that, for the literary work to attain any meaningful cultural capital, the host culture's ability to confer prestige and recognition is paramount: an obscure world literature might as well be non-existent. In his discussion on 'the formation of a creature that never existed before: "world poetry"', Stephen Owen illustrates the role of the Nobel Prize in shaping 'world poetry', particularly the poetry of the Third World. For Owen, the lure of the Prize 'can sometimes be immense: it is "international" (that is, Western) recognition that casts glory on one's nation and promises a moment when the provincial can stand in the global centre of attention' (1990: 28). The negotiation between two different cultures in Damrosch's account is, of course, an unequal one as, according to Owen, 'to write in the dominant language of the age [English] is to have the luxury of writing with unshaken faith in the permanence of a culture's hegemony', whereas world poetry 'turns out, unsurprisingly, to be a version of Anglo-American modernism or French modernism, depending on which wave of colonial culture first washed over the intellectuals of the country in question' (ibid.).[1]

Whilst highlighting the continuing effects of colonialism in an age of globalisation, Owen also shores up the implications for the production and reception of non-Western cultural products – and thus questions about authorship/auteurship and readership/spectatorship (as well as the site of exhibition) – with a 'world' label. In world cinema, for example, it has already become quite ubiquitous to suggest that non-Western cinemas are sought out and selected to be viewed beyond their home markets only when they defy the notion of cultural uniformity implied by globalisation.[2] On the other hand, filmmakers from non-Western cultures are often accused – by critics both at home and abroad – of self-exoticisation and courting controversy in their bids to attain global recognition.[3] Complicate these with issues of marketing and distribution attending the site of exhibition, the forces of demand and supply, the politics of multiculturalism in the Western world – to name just a few – and what we are faced with is a web of power relations and at times conflicting ideologies that defy any simplistic account on the definition or meaning of world cinema.

For some people, the label 'world' has become almost a derogatory term in light of the power dynamics delineated above. David Byrne, the well-known American singer-songwriter and promoter of 'other musics', took umbrage at the use of the term in an article entitled 'I Hate World Music'. For Byrne, 'the term is a catchall that commonly refers to non-Western music of any and all sorts, popular music, traditional music and even classical music. It's a marketing as well as a pseudo-musical term – and a name for a bin in the record store signifying stuff that doesn't belong anywhere else in the store' (1999). Byrne continues: 'In my experience, the use of the term world music is a way of dismissing artists or their music as irrelevant to one's own life … It groups everything and anything that isn't "us" into "them" … It's a none too subtle way of reasserting the hegemony of Western pop culture. It ghettoises most of the world's music' (ibid.).

What Byrne forgets, however, is that the reasons for the hegemony of Western pop culture (and by analogy, the Hollywood film industry) and the ghettoising of world music (or cinema) are more numerous and complex than the use of a specific terminology. What he also fails to recognise is the potential of using such marketing tools in the goal of increasing interest and exposure of these other cultural forms, as ghettos can also provide opportunities. In an article entitled '*Baraka*: World Cinema and the Global Culture Industry', Martin Roberts notes the 'break-up of the domination of First World movie screens by Hollywood and the European cinemas' to include more global (which he uses interchangeably with 'world') varieties:

> For consumers in such [First World] cities, going to the movies and eating out have become more or less equivalent activities, with choosing a movie, like choosing a restaurant, a matter of selecting from a repertoire of available ethnic options. While the audience for these multicultural cinemas is no doubt in large part white and middle class, it would be mistaken to assume that they cater solely to Euro-American exoticism. Indeed … the audiences for multicultural films may be as transnational as the films themselves, and watching them may be as much a way of reconnecting with one's own culture as of indulging a touristic curiosity about someone else's. (1998: 66)

The mechanics of consumerism and identification are arguably more subtle than Byrne's account as the mere availability of non-Western cultural products does not guarantee greater cross-cultural understanding. Indeed, one could question if these film-viewing experiences only serve to reinforce one's identity vis-à-vis, or one's stereo-typical image of, an Other by virtue of the latter's pre-packaged, ready-to-consume, exotic quality. However, what is significant about Roberts' account is the revelation that the film-viewing subject is not homogenous. In an age of globalisation and increased migration, spaces ranging from the geographical (such as national boundaries) to sites of cinematic exhibition (such as international film festivals) are invariably hybrid and plural, and distinctions between dichotomies such as Western and non-Western, self and other, although entrenched in the popular imagination, are beginning to dissolve.

Perhaps as a result of the legacies of Britain's history of splendid isolation and US non-alignment, and of the global reach of the English language, both nations have a habit of locating themselves beyond the boundaries of geographical groupings, whereby Britain refers to Europe as 'the continent' and both countries see 'the world' as the rest of the planet. There is clearly a need in the UK and the US (and other English-speaking countries) to encourage a greater interest in and consumption of music, literature and cinema from other parts of the world, with a certain notion of 'education for the English-speaking audience'.[4] This, nevertheless, should not obscure the fact that such instincts are not unique to the English-speaking world, its cultural hegemony notwithstanding.[5] Indeed, one could argue that where there is Orientalism, there is also Occidentalism, even though the latter is only beginning to gain recognition in the Western world and may still be stubbornly denied elsewhere.[6] This is particularly important because any account of Western hegemony can unwittingly confine non-Western cultures only to ghettos (as seen above) and relegate their position to one merely of resistance,[7] while there needs to be a concomitant acknowledgement that, precisely because of the legacy of colonialism and neo-imperialism, essentialised notions of both the West and the non-West have become increasingly untenable as their histories, cultures and peoples become inextricably intertwined.

## Resisting resistance: world cinema and Third Cinema

Rey Chow has argued persuasively on the blind spots embedded in the discourse of resistance:

> If there is a metanarrative that continues to thrive in these times of metanarrative bashing, it is that of 'resistance' ... As an imaginary appealing especially to intellectuals, 'resistance' would have to come from somewhere. It follows that resistance is often lodged in something called 'the people' or one of its variants, such as 'the masses', 'the folk', or, at times, 'the subalterns'. What is implicitly set up, then, is a dichotomy between the pernicious power on top and the innocent, suffering masses at the bottom, whose voices await being heard in what is imagined as a corrective to the abuses of political power. (1998: 113)[8]

Chow's account does not serve to deny the existence of actual forces of oppression and resistance in the world; rather, she wishes to highlight the 'crucial notion of a mediating apparatus, a specifically defined public space, that would serve to regulate the relationship between those who have political power and those who do not' (ibid.). Chow's reconceptualisation of the political relationship between the powerful and the powerless can illuminate issues in world cinema, especially those pertaining to the notion of Third Cinema.

In the chapter entitled 'Issues in World Cinema' in *The Oxford Guide to Film Studies*, Wimal Dissanayake suggests that we must see non-Western cinemas not as 'expressive of some unchanging "essence"' but instead as 'sites of discursive contestations, or representational spaces, in which changing social and cultural meanings are generated and fought over' (1998: 527–8). However, Dissanayake does not define what the 'World Cinema' in his title is and refers to 'non-Western cinemas' in the text throughout. More suggestively, he begins his interrogation via the concept of Third Cinema, which he claims 'addresses a number of issues related to non-Western cinemas' (1998: 528). While he goes on to show the limits of Third Cinema to provide a complete account of non-Western cinemas (presumably meaning world cinema), the boundary between the two cannot be clearly demarcated.

Coined in the late 1960s by Argentine filmmakers Fernando Solanas and Octavio Getino and influenced by the revolutionary struggles against neo-colonialism, Third Cinema theory arose in Latin America in response to worldwide liberation struggles and decolonisation movements, and represented a tri-continental (Asia, Africa and Latin America) call to arms against social injustice and post-imperialism (Guneratne 2003: 3–4). It was thus revolutionary in origin, nature and intent. According to its theorists, First Cinema is cinema made in Hollywood, Second Cinema is the *auteur* cinema of the *nouvelle vague* or *cinema novo*, and Third Cinema is a cinema of liberation: films 'that the System cannot assimilate and which are foreign to its needs, or … films that directly and explicitly set out to fight the system' (Solanas & Getino 1997: 42–3). With moves towards redemocratisation in Latin America in the 1970s and 1980s, and a recognition, perhaps, of the unrealistic demands made on filmmakers of the original definition afforded Third Cinema by its proponents, it is hardly surprising that it never really took off as a film theory or practice.

However, Teshome Gabriel returned to the concept in 1982 in *Third Cinema in the Third World*, which he redefined as films that contribute to a universal 'decolonisation of the mind' (1982: 3). In the introduction to a recent study on the impact and legacy of Third Cinema, *Rethinking Third Cinema*, Anthony Guneratne denies a place in the ranks of Third Cinema for 'commercially-orientated postcolonial cinemas', which he sees as 'immature relics of imperialism and neo-colonialism' (2003: 1). At the same time, he authorises the entry of First World-based directors 'who address the very issues of First World dominance and Third World abjection which concern the more politically sensitive Third World filmmaker' (2003: 14). This inclusion of First World directors in Third World struggles echoes Chow's idea of mediating apparatus regulating the relationship between the powerful and the powerless. This idea is more fully formulated by Ella Shohat and Robert Stam in their excellent book, *Unthinking Eurocentrism*, which Dudley Andrew describes as a 'first and crucial "World Cinema" textbook' in his chapter in this volume. Calling for a polycentric filmmaking, Shohat and Stam envision overlapping circles of denotation, whereby the core circle is occupied by Third Cinema produced by and for the Third World, the next wider circle by Third World films in general, the third circle by Third Cinema made by First or Second World people and the final circle by diasporic hybrid films imbued with Third Cinema properties (1994: 28).

While Shohat and Stam's book is undoubtedly one of the most useful texts produced on the subject, Andrew raises a valuable point which reminds us of why Third Cinema as theory and practice failed in the first place: he charges Shohat and Stam's approach with being 'moralistic' which 'upholds a set of smart, politically correct films standing against Eurocentric global media forces' but does not account for 'popular genres and failed heritage films as well as critical successes'. For example, Shohat and Stam might not have envisaged that, at the turn of the twenty-first century, Mexican cinema was going to be so popular both at home and abroad, and that Alfonso Cuarón, the director of *Y tu mama también* (*And Your Mother Too*, 2001) would also direct a Harry Potter film. Indeed, one of the problems with definitions of Third Cinema, and to a certain extent this also applies to world cinema, is the denial of pleasure, particularly for the home audiences. The implicit dichotomy set up between popularity and integrity often goes unquestioned, as does the one between oppression and resistance.

Hence, the discourse of resistance should not be one of empty slogans but an examination of actual processes of resistance, the forces at work, the aim and the realistic prospect of achieving it. Shohat and Stam's call to unthink Eurocentrism acts as a starting point in recognising that crucial cinematic issues such as point of view can vary from nation to nation, and from culture to culture,[9] and that not all cinematic influences and referents can be traced back to Hollywood and post-war Europe.[10] On the other hand, it is also important to move beyond the discourse of resistance to place more focus on the interconnectedness of cinematic practices and cultures in the age of globalisation, particularly in terms of the conditions of production and consumption, and theorise world cinema not in terms of 'the West vs. the rest' but in relation to notions such as hybridity, transculturation, border crossing, transnationalism and translation. These concepts should be subjected to the same process of interrogation about 'how they work' and 'where they come from', so that they may hopefully provide invigorating ways of reconceptualising 'world cinema'.

## World cinema: discipline, methodology, perspective

There are currently two popular ways of understanding world cinema. The first regards it as the sum total of all the national cinemas in the world, and the second posits it against US or Hollywood cinema. Both are problematic in different ways, and they also raise different sets of questions.

In the former case, to regard world cinema as the sum total of national cinemas is to presuppose and privilege an entity known as the nation or the nation-state. To view the world as a collection of nations (as in the United Nations) is to marginalise if not deny the possibilities of other ways of organising the world, whether by economic power, gender, sexuality, and in a more general sense, other identities or formations that cannot be defined by a geopolitical boundary or by race and ethnicity. In terms of cinema, this take on world cinema risks overlooking modes of film practices that include, among others, Third Cinema, women's or feminist cinema, queer cinema, and many regional, sub-state, transnational, diasporic and nomadic cinemas. One therefore cannot but challenge the foregrounding of nation, ethnicity and race in this construction, and question at what cost it imposes upon identities based on gender, sexuality, class, (dis)ability and others.

In the latter case, the imperative to oppose world cinema against US or Hollywood cinema is perhaps understandable given the often unquestioned and at times unspoken US-centrism even within works on world cinema. For example, in the organisation of Geoffrey Nowell-Smith's *The Oxford History of World Cinema*, US cinema does not feature as a 'national cinema' but occupies a central position against which all national cinemas must somehow define themselves. Whilst it may be 'a fact that, from the end of the First World War onwards, one film industry – the American – has played a dominant role, to such an extent that much of the history of cinema in other countries has consisted of attempts by the indigenous industries to thwart, compete with, or distinguish themselves from American ("Hollywood") competition' (Nowell-Smith 1998: xx–xxi), some questions remain unasked: to what extent is this narrative accounted from a US-centric perspective, and would it be possible, the 'fact' notwithstanding, to construct a narrative that de-centres US domination, challenges its hegemony, and uncovers examples of cinemas that have developed in total oblivion to Hollywood?[11]

However, to posit world cinema as an antithesis of US or Hollywood cinema is also to disregard the diversity and complexity within both cinema in the US as well as cinemas from the rest of the world. Whilst this opposition is often premised upon the reaction against US or Hollywood film aesthetics or modes of production and distribution, it tends to gloss over the independent, underground and avant-garde cinemas with the US itself, and fails to give adequate recognition to cinemas from other parts of the world which share similar film aesthetics or modes of production and distribution as Hollywood. As Chapman eloquently argues, the tendency to describe other modes of film practices as 'alternatives' to Hollywood implies that, in the study of world cinema, those cinemas 'which set out to differentiate themselves from Hollywood have been privileged' and the fact that some of these so-called 'alternatives' are actually dominant modes of film practices in their own cultures has been ignored (2003: 35, 37).

In our attempt to venture beyond the two existing models, we propose to rethink world cinema in three ways: as a discipline, a methodology and a perspective. This is not, however, an attempt to fix disciplinary boundaries, dictate research methodologies or to impose politically correct perspectives. Rather, using the three as tools, we hope to articulate the complexities embedded in the process of such a theorisation, and to highlight issues that have troubled us and should continue to cause us unrest even as we seek to problematise and establish world cinema as a theoretical concept.

Firstly, what does it mean to think of 'World Cinema' as a discipline? As an academic discipline, film and cinema studies are still primarily Euro- and US-centric in their orientation, often with scant attention paid to other forms of cinemas, and even if so, the latter only occupy a peripheral position. The study of other cinemas, if defined by nation, chiefly resides in area studies departments, where it also assumes an emerging but still marginal role. While both claim a common interest in film and cinema studies, in practice there is a lack of interaction and cross-fertilisation between scholars in both disciplines. More importantly, the establishment of World Cinema as a discipline promotes a truly global perspective upon a seemingly universal one (film studies) and a decidedly regional one (area studies). This will hopefully lead to a rethinking of how film and cinema studies may be studied, taught and researched within academia.

Take, for example, the MA programme in World Cinemas at the University of Leeds, which rather than being taught exclusively by staff in Communication Studies, taps into the expertise in film and cultural studies of academics from a large number of language and area studies departments, such as Middle Eastern and East Asian Studies as well as Francophone and Hispanic Studies. Such departments in Leeds and elsewhere have been steadily incorporating the study of cinema into their programmes in response to an increased interest shown by both staff and students, and have begun to challenge the hegemony of Film and Communication Studies departments in terms of offering programmes on cinema. As departments gradually become subsumed into Schools and Faculties, and as pressure mounts to create ever more interesting, cutting-edge and financially viable undergraduate and postgraduate programmes, the trend is to move towards greater interdisciplinarity in terms of programmes and courses.

Interdisciplinarity, however, seems only to be paid lip service as a buzzword in institutional policy statements but seldom practised – and more importantly, recognised – in research terms. Whilst academics working in English departments may have conventionally encompassed topics in their research that can be variously identified as 'belonging' to the disciplines of comparative literature, cultural studies and film studies, such a luxury is not usually afforded to those working in disciplines whose boundaries remain rather strait-jacketed. The implication and effect of outmoded disciplinary divides is that certain kinds of intellectual inquiry, such as that epitomised by and germane to world cinema, are precluded, discouraged or unrewarded. Until and unless the processes of research assessment to which departments are subjected in the United Kingdom catch up with these developments along the road to interdisciplinarity, scholars will be disinclined to look beyond their disciplinary boundaries, and the development of World Cinemas as a discipline will be impeded as a result. Reversing this logic, we want instead to promote World Cinema as a vital way of challenging – and hopefully, in time, of breaking down – disciplinary divides so that new and interdisciplinary kinds of research can begin to flourish.

The relationship between film studies and area studies invariably impinges upon the second question, that of World Cinema as methodology. Whilst it may be too generalised to describe film and cinema studies scholars as paying more attention to text and area studies scholars to context, and whilst scholars in both disciplines have always employed diverse methodologies, fostering an interaction between the two under the umbrella of World Cinema can undoubtedly produce exciting and imaginative ways of studying films and cinemas that are at once sensitive to the operation of the cinematic apparatus as well as the milieu in which it operates.

In the past few decades in Western academia, the rise of critical theory – a body of work originating from continental Europe and which can be described broadly as post-structuralist in outlook – has forged a common language among scholars in the fields of humanities and the social sciences.[12] More importantly, the challenge and modification to this body of work, whether from a postcolonial, feminist, subaltern or queer perspective, have revitalised critical theory. By bringing the specific historical, socio-political and cultural conditions to bear on the common currency of theory, the discipline of World Cinema can provide innumerable illuminations to the processes of negotiation at the site of cinematic practices. The contribution of scholars such as Robert Stam, Hamid Naficy and Rey Chow – and we hope also the chapters in this volume – attest to the potential that World Cinema can bring to research methodologies and critical approaches.

These new research methodologies will bring to the fore the third and final question, that of perspective. From whence do we view, visualise and theorise world cinema, and what impact does this have on cinematic discourses and practices around the world? How does one's perspective limit one's view, and is it possible to develop a multifarious perspective that takes into account concerns of our own as well as that of the others? Is it possible for one to adopt a different or even multiple perspectives, and if so, how, and what does it take to do so? We might even ask: why is it important to not only lay bare one's perspective but also attempt to assume another?

This is where our earlier suggestion pointing towards notions such as hybridity, transculturation and border crossing may fulfil its promise. In the age of globalisation and increased migration, not only do people physically travel more, but both theory (to recall Edward Said's idea of 'travelling theory') and perspective also interpenetrate. It can be argued that subjectivity and identity in the twenty-first century are inescapably hybrid and multiple, so that one invariably embodies at once knowledge and perspectives from multifarious sources, which lend themselves easily to the study, and benefit from the insights of World Cinema.

In the final analysis, World Cinema as a theoretical concept is destined not to definition and closure but to ceaseless problematisation, always a work-in-progress, its ground beneath one's feet forever shifting even as one attempts to pin it down. To situate World Cinema as a theoretical problem is to question not just what world cinema is but also to/for whom it is a problem, in what contexts, how and why; to interrogate to what purposes does it serve, under what kinds of mechanisms of power does it operate, and what audiences does it seek to address or perhaps empower. Indeed, why theorise, problematise, or even promote World Cinema as a theoretical concept? We hope we have begun the process of answering these questions by raising the right ones.

## Remapping world cinema

This volume represents an attempt to remap the concept of World Cinema for an Anglophone readership. Part One, 'Remapping World Cinema in a Post-World Order', redraws the theoretical terrain of World Cinema by radically reorienting the map away from the hegemony of the world system that privileges Hollywood. Dudley Andrew's chapter provides an atlas of world cinema that highlights the political, demographic, linguistic, orientation and topographical aspects of mapping. Written with American students of film studies in mind, Andrew stresses that world cinema is not about coverage but displacement, and that it should place students in unfamiliar conditions of viewing while providing them with coordinates for navigating the world of world cinema. Lúcia Nagib's chapter calls for a positive definition of World Cinema, one that is not defined negatively as 'non-Hollywood' and that moves away from the iron grip of hierarchised binarism. Rather, echoing Ella Shohat and Robert Stam's idea of polycentric multiculturalism, Nagib calls for an understanding of world cinema as a way of cutting across film history according to waves of relevant films and movements that create flexible geographies with no particular cinema occupying a central position. Michael Chanan's chapter offers an illustration, by way of Latin American cinema, of how a renewed concept of World Cinema would acknowledge the plurality and diversity of film products and their conditions of production not just across the globe but also within seemingly homogenous continents. Using Latin American theories of underdevelopment, Chanan demonstrates that filmmaking in the region has been motivated more by political rather than economic forces, and yet, manifested as postmodernism, Latin American cinema is contemporaneous with rather than 'behind' Europe, despite the asymmetrical relation between the two.

'Remapping' world cinema also entails the acknowledgement of the interconnection of cinematic practices beyond the national boundary. The chapters in Part Two, 'Crossing boundaries', draw our attention to the politics of representation in such attempts at cinematic travelling in the postcolonial world. Citing filmic projects by Pier Paolo Pasolini, Dennis Hopper and Werner Herzog, Keith Richards' chapter serves as a reminder of the pitfalls and tension in such cross-cultural representation, in which mythology is (re)produced and exported, however unwittingly, in neo-colonial terms. Rob Stone's chapter compares two propaganda films and shows that, in both post-revolution Cuba and the Basque Country during the Francoist dictatorship, film was central to reclaiming each nation's identity, while invariably producing national myths that lent themselves to revolutionary aims. In contrast to Stone's chapter exploring the imagining of national identities with the aid of a foreign model, Rosanna Maule's chapter illustrates that identities are necessarily transnational in a context where the legacies of colonialism traverse to postcolonial spaces. Maule argues that Claire Denis' gendered position as a female director and the multicultural perspectives in her films complicate the master/servant dialectics underlying cinematic representation in the West. Precisely because we live in transnational and postcolonial times, spaces within national boundaries are already hybridised and crossed, though this does not in any way undercut the imperative to continue crossing boundaries of all kinds, including national, political and gender. Insofar as cinematic practices and representations are interpenetrable, the study of World Cinema has to be remapped to fully recognise this hybridity and boundary crossing.

Popular film genres are often omitted from the canon of World Cinema, as we have suggested, because they are traditionally understood to offer no real form of ideological resistance, and for the belief that they are rarely viewed outside their place of origin because they do not travel well. The three chapters in Part Three, 'Carnival and Transgression', bring together scholarship on popular film from four different regions (Hollywood, the Weimar Republic, East Germany and Italy), and consider in particular the extent to which each set of films discussed makes use of a carnival aesthetic to engage with issues relating to modernity. David Robb's chapter offers a comparison of the films of two comedic performers, the German Karl Valentine and British-born Hollywood legend Charlie Chaplin. Here, Robb avoids the all-too-pervasive tendency to judge the less familiar performer Valentine, whose work is barely known outside of Germany, by the standards set by the more famous, Hollywood-based Chaplin, arguably the first international screen star. Like Robb, Evelyn Preuss reveals in her chapter, through her detailed study of East German cinema of the 1960s and 1970s, how cinema has translated and re-established the carnivalesque in modern society because cinema, as a medium of the modern era, operates against a background of political ideologies that borrow heavily from the carnival spirit. Both Robb and Preuss show us that within a remapped world cinema, there is also space for discussion of films whose challenge to dominant ideology is much more covert than, say, the overt challenges presented by Third Cinema filmmaking. To complete this section Mark Goodall's chapter offers an analysis of the woefully neglected 'mondo cycle', a series of hugely popular 'perverse' documentaries produced in Italy in the 1960s. The transgressive nature of mondo films, Goodall argues, has resulted in their almost complete absence from film histories, given the traditional film canon's insistence in dismissing commercial films that jar with political and cultural climates. But the extent to which the mondo films can be read as harbingers of many aspects of globalising media production and consumption justifies their re-evaluation in the context of World Cinema today.

The study of stars has until relatively recently centred around actors and actresses working within the so-called Hollywood star system, and even when foreign stars are afforded space in such discussions, these tend to concentrate on the trajectories of foreign actors in Hollywood. This is particularly noticeable in the case of Hollywood stars from the Hispanic world.[13] In an attempt to break with the tradition of privileging the study of stardom within the Hollywood context, in Part Four, 'Performing Stardom and Race', both Stephanie Dennison's and Guy Austin's chapters deal exclusively with the national star texts of two actresses with international profiles, concentrating on their 'problematic' whiteness, and how this was inflected in their public personae and the roles they played on screen. Austin exposes how the star text of Isabelle Adjani, doyenne of French cinema screens in the 1980s, underwent a (temporary) seismic shift and unleashed a wave of racist abuse when she revealed her own mixed-race origins. In contrast Dennison argues that Sônia Braga, of mixed race but perceived beyond question as white, at the height of her career in Brazilian cinema in the 1970s stood in for the mixed-race or black woman who was everywhere to be seen in popular culture but noticeable by her absence from the big screen. Both chapters highlight the dangers of reading star texts through an overly Anglo-Saxon prism, thus raising a question that is important in the study of World Cinema: whether theories of both race and stardom apply across all cultures.

Similarly, we must ask if theories of gender and sexuality are universal, a question central to the chapters in Part Five, 'Interrogating gender'. Echoing the performance of stars in the previous section, Hideaki Fujiki's chapter looks back historically at the performance of stardom in early Japanese cinema, in which the practice of male actors playing female roles was a mainstay until it was supplanted by the overflowing images of female actresses in American films. Replacing an indigenous form of (trans)gender performance with female actresses playing female roles in the name of 'naturalism', this shift was, for Fujiki, fundamentally concerned with the definition and management of gender and sexuality. Louise Williams' chapter interrogates the representation of gender and sexuality in a country where it remains highly charged and often taboo. Through her analysis of the protagonist in a mainland Chinese film, *Nannan nünü* (*Men and Women*), Williams sees the indeterminate sexuality of Xiao Bo as posing a challenge to established identity categories, including homosexuality and heterosexuality, masculinity and femininity, as well as men and women.

The final part, 'Hollywood's others', brings our remapping of world cinema full circle with its focus on the 'other' two powerhouses of film production: Japan and India. As Rachael Hutchinson clearly demonstrates, the popular reception of Akira Kurosawa as either a mostly universal or an essentially Japanese director betrays the dynamics of Orientalism and Occidentalism. Rather, Hutchinson proposes that Kurosawa appropriates elements from all kinds of sources, and that the intertextuality of his oeuvre offers new ways of overcoming problems of binarism and cultural essentialism in the study of World Cinema. Similarly, Kaushik Bhaumik argues that, rather than seeing Bollywood cinema as hermetically sealed, it in fact raises uncomfortable questions not just about Occidental Orientalist exoticisation but also about the place of genre and value within world cinema. Bollywood has become a sign mobilised by different agents for their own purposes, from reconfiguring the economic framework of the film industry in India to the stirring up of nationalistic sentiments by rejecting the term itself as a poor copy of Hollywood. As Bhaumik asks at the end of his chapter, Bollywood may become world cinema, but for which world(s)?

## Notes

1   For a rebuttal of Owen's arguments, see Rey Chow (1993), chapter 1.

2   For example, Michael Chanan argues in his chapter in this volume that, in the case of Latin American cinema, nation-states are not individualised merely by the inclusion of background decoration but 'instead what you get is a continuing imperative to bear witness to local histories which takes us to the interstices, the margins and the peripheries'.

3   For example, Yingjin Zhang suggests that 'oriental *ars erotica* as a mythified entity is fixed or fixated at the very centre of Western fascination' with Chinese cinema and lists the 'essential' or 'magic' ingredients in the formula for satisfying Western aesthetic tastes: primitive landscape, repressed sexuality, gender performance and a mythical or cyclical time frame in which the protagonist's fate is predestined (1998: 116, 118). In his discussion of the Chinese filmmaker Zhang Yuan, Geremie Barmé also formulates

a detailed 'formula for success', suggesting that all Zhang needed to secure success for his films was an official ban in China (1999: 188–98).

4   Pamela A. Genova cites the example of the important journal *World Literature Today*, founded in 1927 (called *Books Abroad* until 1977) which tried 'to offer non-ideological commentary on a variety of foreign literatures as a means of aiding America to move away from what he [the founder] saw as a dangerous trend towards isolationism' (2003: xvii).

5   For example, there is a journal in China called *Shijie wenxue* (*World Literature*) and another in Taiwan called *Shijie dianying* (*World Cinema*), both serving a similar function of a window to the (rest of the) world.

6   On Occidentalism, see Xiaomei Chen (2002), and Ian Buruma and Avishai Margalit (2004).

7   As Lydia Liu notes, 'I am struck by the irony that, in the very act of criticising Western domination, one often ends up reifying the power of the dominator to a degree that the agency of non-Western cultures is reduced to a single possibility: resistance' (1995: xv–xvi).

8   See also Yuriko Furuhata (2004).

9   As Dudley Andrew argues in his chapter in this volume, 'in cinema something as technical as "point of view" asserts an ideological and political claim, literally orienting a culture to a surrounding world'.

10  Dissanayake, for example, has warned against judging melodramas produced in Latin America, Africa and Asia in terms of Western conceptualisations of melodrama (1998: 532).

11  For example, this 'fact' is disputed in Lúcia Nagib's chapter in this volume as she points out that both Japan and India have, at different periods in the twentieth century, produced more films than the US, thus debunking the myth of US cinematic domination.

12  It should be qualified, however, that the surge of critical theory has not gone uncontested in academia as not only has there been what Paul de Man terms 'the resistance to theory' (1986) but more recently, Terry Eagleton has published a book entitled *After Theory* (2004) while David Bordwell and Noël Carroll edited a film theory book entitled *Post-theory* (1996).

13  See, for example, López (1993), Ríos-Bustamante (1991) and Rodríguez (1998).

## Works cited

Barmé, G. R. (1999) *In the Red: On Contemporary Chinese Culture*. New York: Columbia University Press.

Bordwell, D. and N. Carroll (eds) (1996) *Post-theory: Reconstructing Film Studies*. Madison: University of Wisconsin Press.

Bové, P. A. (1995) 'Discourse', in F. Lentricchia and T. McLaughlin (eds) *Critical Terms for Literary Study* (second edition). Chicago and London: The University of Chicago Press, 50–65.

Buruma, I. and A. Margalit (2004) *Occidentalism: The West in the Eyes of Its Enemies*. London: Penguin Books.

Byrne, D. (1999) 'I Hate World Music', *The New York Times*, 3 October. Available online: http://www.luakabop.com/david_byrne/cmp/worldmusic.html (accessed: 30 October 2004).

Chapman, J. (2003) *Cinemas of the World: Film and Society from 1895 to the Present*. London: Reaktion.

Chen, X. (2002) *Occidentalism: A Theory of Counter-Discourse in Post-Mao China* (second edition). Lanham, MD: Rowman and Litterfield.

Chow, R. (1993) *Writing Diaspora: Tactics of Intervention in Contemporary Cultural Studies*. Bloomington and Indianapolis: Indiana University Press.

_____ (1998) *Ethics after Idealism: Theory-Culture-Ethnicity-Reading*. Bloomington and Indianapolis: Indiana University Press.

Damrosch, D. (2003) 'What is World Literature', *World Literature Today*, 77, 1, 9–14.

de Man, P. (1986) *The Resistance to Theory*. Minneapolis: University of Minnesota Press.

Dissanayake, W. (1998) 'Issues in World Cinema', in J. Hill and P. Church Gibson (eds) *The Oxford Guide to Film Studies*. Oxford: Oxford University Press, 527–34.

Eagleton, T. (2004) *After Theory*. London: Penguin Books.

Furuhata Y. (2004) 'Desiring Resistance in the Age of Globalization', *New Cinemas*, 2, 2, 91–106.

Gabriel, T. H. (1982) *Third Cinema in the Third World: The Aesthetics of Liberation*. Ann Arbor, MI: UMI Research Press.

Genova, P. A. (2003) 'Introduction' to P. A. Genova (ed.) *Twayne Companion to Contemporary World Literature: From the Editors of* World Literature Today. New York: Twayne Publishers, xvii–xxxiii.

Guneratne, A. R. (2003) 'Introduction: Rethinking Third Cinema', in A. R. Guneratne and W. Dissanayake (eds) *Rethinking Third Cinema*. London and New York: Routledge, 1–28.

Liu, L. H. (1995) *Translingual Practice: Literature, National Culture, and Translated Modernity – China, 1900–1937*. Stanford, CA: Stanford University Press.

López, A. (1993) 'Are All Latins From Manhattan?: Hollywood, Ethnography and Cultural Colonialism', in J. King, A. López and M. Alvarado (eds) *Mediating Two Worlds: Cinematic Encounters in the Americas*. London: British Film Institute, 67–80.

Nowell-Smith, G. (ed.) (1997) *The Oxford History of World Cinema*. Oxford: Oxford University Press.

Owen, S. (1990) 'What is World Poetry?', *New Republic*, 19 November, 28–32.

Ríos-Bustamante, A. (1991) *Latinos in Hollywood*. Encino, CA: Floricanto Press.

Roberts, M. (1998) '*Baraka*: World Cinema and the Global Culture Industry', *Cinema Journal*, 37, 3, 62–82.

Rodríguez, C. (ed.) *Latin Looks: Images of Latinas and Latinos in the U.S. Media*. Boulder, CO and Oxford: Westview Press.

Shohat, E. and R. Stam (1994) *Unthinking Eurocentrism: Multiculturalism and the Media*. London and New York: Routledge.

Solanas, F. and O. Getino (1997) 'Towards a Third Cinema: Notes and Experiences for the Development of a Cinema of Liberation in the Third World', in M. T. Martin (ed.) *New Latin American Cinema, Vol. 1*. Detroit: Wayne State University Press, 33–58.

Zhang, Y. (1998) 'Chinese Cinema and Transnational Cultural Politics: Reflections on Film Festivals, Film Productions, and Film Studies', *Journal of Modern Literature in Chinese*, 2, 1, 105–32.

# PART ONE

# Remapping World Cinema in a Post-World Order

# CHAPTER ONE

# An atlas of world cinema

Dudley Andrew

The term 'world cinema' is now permanently with us: in our classes, our textbooks, the popular press. It names the global reach of Hollywood, beginning with *Jaws* (1975) and *Star Wars* (1977), and it names the resistance to Hollywood evident in the GATT debates over a decade ago. Sometimes postcolonial critics mobilise the term, as nations vie for recognition at film festivals. 'World cinema' replaces the 'foreign art film' which first slipped through heavily guarded university doors in the 1960s. We used to teach foreign films as autonomous masterworks in 'film as art' courses or as addenda to the sanctioned national literatures. Today national literature departments are shrinking while the number of films begging for study and the places they come from increases. The old ways do justice neither to this variety, nor to the international interdependence of images. The rubric that I, like so many others, employed for years, 'Survey of film', does an injustice to the situation and to students. For a 'survey' suggests a distant gaze, panoptically monitoring the foreign for our convenience and use. A course of study in world cinema, however, should instead be ready to travel more than to oversee, should put students inside unfamiliar conditions of viewing rather than bringing the unfamiliar handily to them. This is the pedagogical promise of a discipline such as World Cinema, a manner of treating foreign films systematically, transcending the vagaries of taste; taking the measure of 'the foreign' in what is literally a freshly recognised global dimension. Such an approach examines overriding factors, then zeroes in on specific 'cinema sites' – provides coordinates for navigating this world of world cinema. No need to dock in every port as if on a *tour du monde* with some 'Michelin guide' textbook. Displacement, not coverage, matters most; let us travel where we will, so long as every local cinema is examined with an eye to its complex ecology.

My approach might best be conceived as an atlas of types of maps, each providing a different orientation to unfamiliar terrain, bringing out different aspects, elements and dimensions. Each approach, or map, models a type of view: hence, the *Atlas*. Film festivals long ago came up with a basic map as they sought top products to be put in competition each year as in a Miss Universe contest. For a long while the cognoscenti did little more than push coloured pins onto a map to locate the national origin of masterpieces. This appreciation of cut flowers adorned film study in its first years but required a more systematic account (call it botanical or ecological) of the vitality of privileged examples. What political and cultural soil nourished these films and their makers? Today's impulse – more ambitious because more dynamic and comparative – would track a process of cross-pollination that bypasses national directives. To begin to encompass all this material in this confusing 'field' of study an historical atlas would seem a sensible first step. Yet my course is neither a gazetteer nor an encyclopedia, futilely trying to do justice to cinematic life everywhere. Its essays and materials model a set of approaches, just as an atlas of maps opens up a continent to successive views: political, demographic, linguistic, topographical, meteorological, marine, historical.

## Political maps

Pushing pins onto a spread of countries marked by borders has its uses. In high school all of us poured over successive shapes of world power: the Greeks, the Romans, various barbarian kingdoms, Islam's arms reaching through Africa and girdling Europe. What would a map of cinematic power show? With global feature film output at around three thousand titles a year, we might indicate filmmaking hotspots, using a gray-scale of production density that could be keyed to Hollywood – a dark constant. Competitors would be variably less dark: since 1930 France has put out over a hundred features a year except during the German occupation. Japan, more like three hundred. And India, at least since the 1950s has increased from three hundred to its current eight hundred. The surprise would be Egypt, Turkey and Greece, all making hundreds of films each year after World War Two until television undercut them in the 1980s. Were one to graph world output at ten-year intervals, significant pulsations would appear: Brazilian production, for instance, phases in and out with shifts in government; Hong Kong emerges with Run Run Shaw's operation in the 1950s, then dominates East Asia after the 1970s; and of course there is Iran. Like Mali and Burkina Faso in West Africa, Iran in the 1980s surges ahead of surrounding nations.

Iran and Burkina Faso remind us, however, that national prestige in cinema comes more by way of critical assessment and festival performance than by sheer quantity of titles. It was Abbas Kiarostami and Idrissa Ouedraogo who put these nations on the map at Cannes. Similarly Edward Yang and Hou Hsiao-Hsien raised Taiwan to a par with Hong Kong (they receive equal space in the *Encyclopedia of Chinese Film* and in *The Oxford History of World Cinema*) despite Taiwan's lesser output and popularity. Nor can we forget Denmark, which in the past decade or so has become a European colossus compared to Germany despite being out-produced annually by a factor of three. As a first clarifying step, we need to analyse production and prestige across the century, with particular attention to the years since 1975, when 'world cinema' came to attention.

## Demographic maps

Apportioning the world's annual three thousand feature films by place of origin makes the globe appear to spin more smoothly than it really does. For Hollywood's lopsided economic mass (bags of box-office receipts returning to it from nearly everywhere but India) pulls it out of true. Such domination of distribution includes both theatrical exhibition and video dissemination (except for the black-market economy rampant particularly in Africa and China). To represent not the production, but the availability of images region by region, the grayscale no longer suffices. These displays must be chromatic: red daubs for Hollywood films playing in theatres and taking up space on video shelves, blue for indigenous images. Speckles of yellow and green would suggest diversity – yellow for images imported from neighbouring countries, green for those coming from afar. Take Ireland, the European country with the highest per capita attendance. Lately Hollywood has colonised some 76 per cent of its screen space and time; local productions (over 20 films a year) garner 3–4 per cent. The rest come mainly from the UK (15 per cent) and European Union countries. Now in France, Hollywood last year dipped below 50 per cent for the first time in two decades. The French have a taste for Italian and Asian films, but mainly their own products prevail, set up by intensive promotions and economic incentives.

Since the real film wars have been waged less over production than competition for audiences, demographic studies serve as military maps in strategy sessions at the boardrooms of CEOs or of cultural ministers. Nation-states have frequently protected their workforce and the minds of their citizens from carefully calculated foreign invasion. Unlike literary fiction where the native product has been provisionally secure behind the Great Wall of the native language, films from the outset invaded foreign screens. The Lumière brothers dispatched camera crews around the world before their invention was two years old, showing films shot in one place to audiences in another. And Pathé, as Richard Abel (1999) has shown, was a feared imperial image power by 1913, with offices everywhere. Taken to be an international concern, Pathé provoked local competitors to call upon loyalty to 'national cinema'. Critics were enlisted to invent and uphold something newly baptised, 'the American cinema', 'the Japanese cinema', and so forth. By 1920 Hollywood had replaced France as the Emperor of Images. The tables now turned, the Parisian press of the 1920s invented a national tradition of French cinema that demanded (as it does today) the support of the government and of citizen-spectators.

Nationalists imagine a simple competition between *our* images and *theirs*. However, following Fredric Jameson, we should be alert to a dialectic that often produces a synthetic form combining both (1993: xiii). For example, the name of the key compromise form in France of the 1920s is 'narrative avant-garde'. 'Narrative' signals the common shape given to films everywhere by D. W. Griffith and Thomas Ince, while 'avant-garde' announces the native aesthetic impulse that made France the centre of successive movements in fiction and the fine arts from impressionism to symbolism, cubism and beyond. The overall study of French cinema of the 1920s, then, should take imports into account, because Hollywood films constituted 50 per cent of the images occupying the country's screens, that is, occupying the minds of those who made and watched films. It should also consider other imports, German expressionism in this case, which provided the French an alternative model to that of Hollywood. By triangulating French cinema in relation to America and Germany, the presumed singularity of a national movement can be much more accurately plotted.

No study of French cinema, my own on the 1930s included, has attended to imports in this way. To use Franco Moretti's analogy, national cinema studies have by and large been genealogical trees, one tree per country (2000: 67). Their elaborate root and branch structures are seldom shown as intermingled. A 'world systems' approach, on the other hand, demands a different analogy, that of 'waves' which roll through adjacent cultures whose proximity to one another promotes propagation that not even triangulation can adequately measure. Moretti's term attracts one of world cinema's best examples: for the New Wave that buoyed French film in 1959 rolled around the world, affecting in different ways and under dissimilar circumstances the cinema lives of Britain, Japan, Cuba, Brazil, Argentina, Czechoslovakia, Yugoslavia, Hungary and later Taiwan. As we know, its so-called original undulation in Paris owed much to the Hollywood films that came ashore behind the Normandy invasion of 1944, literally rejuvenating a tired French culture. The New Wave passed first through youth fads in fashion, design and the novel before cresting at Cannes in 1959 where its effects were patently international.

Demographic studies of box-office and video-store statistics can devolve quickly into assessments of audience predilection. Important for some questions, such sheer sociology generally results in predictable stereotypes. In a survey of 46 countries, called 'Planet Hollywood', Moretti (2001) finds what we would expect: that Asians are drawn to action films, that wealthier nations watch a lot of children's films, that comedies are more often home-grown, and so on. Overviews like this do not begin to give us the feel for the varieties of cinematic cultures on the planet; one might as well study breakfast cereals. Fortunately, Moretti, a brilliant literary historian, has invented far more intricate maps.

## Linguistic maps

In his *Atlas of the European Novel 1800–1900* (1999) and the five-volume history of the 'World Novel', Moretti explicitly puts into play a Darwinian hypothesis that should apply to feature films as well. To map the growth and withering of novelistic trends around the globe, he employs a law he gleaned from Fredric Jameson: 'In cultures that belong to the periphery of the literary system, the modern novel first arises not as an autonomous development but as a compromise between a Western formal influence (usually French or English) and local materials' (2000: 58). Moretti maps the flow of translations and booksellers from an English/French power source to literary hotspots springing up later in Russia, India, and so on. This dialectical law nicely accounts for Hollywood's dominance of the form of films made everywhere, especially after Moretti rightly complicates this crude 'form/content' binary with a third factor, indigenous local narration (ibid.).[1] For novelists and filmmakers may have learned a successful formula from Charles Dickens or D. W. Griffith, but they adapt it to their culture's experience in a homegrown manner. This 'manner' inflects the standard form with the register of traditional oral or theatrical storytelling. In West African film, in the Korean hit *Chunhyang* (Im Kwon-Taek, 2001), in Kenji Mizoguchi's long-take 'theatrical' *mise-en-scène*, the cinema grafts rather than mulches cultural roots. The cohabitation of this (European) medium and local traditions produces compromise film forms that are often as hybrid and ambivalent as the subjects that such movies represent.

Moretti's hypothesis for the novel upholds the colonialist map of cinema attacked by Ella Shohat and Robert Stam in *Unthinking Eurocentrism* (1994). This first and crucial 'World Cinema' textbook, alerted us all to cultural wars fought with the weapon of style and theme. But their rather moralistic approach upholds a set of smart, politically correct films standing against Eurocentric global media forces. As proper as this may be, an evolutionary map of film history requires a larger view, one capable of accounting for popular genres and failed heritage films as well as critical successes. This is precisely what Miriam Hansen has proposed in a far-reaching article on 'Classical Cinema as Vernacular Modernism' (2000). Classical Hollywood, the dominant and dominating force in the entertainment world from World War One at least through the Korean conflict, was always both 'international' and 'vernacular' in promoting a modernist sensibility that derived from popular rather than official or elite origins. All films minted in Hollywood have been ubiquitously accepted as legal currency, stamped with the logo of 'Universal Pictures' or of Paramount's mountain (which dissolved into the Andes in the first frames of *Indiana Jones and the Temple of Doom* (Steven Spielberg, 1984)). That currency underwrites a stock market of stars and a narrative economy that the entire world has apparently bought into, aside from the fringe market where Shohat and Stam's alternative films trade. But buying into classical cinema does not mean digesting its values whole, for its universal language breaks apart on national or regional shorelines into a Babel of varied receptions.

I am inclined to take Hansen's vocabulary rather more literally than she does. Classical cinema would thus be the medium's classical language, that is, Latin. By 1920 Hollywood was, first of all, unapologetically imperial, literally colonising countries and continents and setting up administrative institutions to govern these. Latin preceded vernacular languages that were formed through its contact with local ways of speaking, including residual tribal languages. In a similar way, and as Moretti has noted, most national cinemas came into existence through a process of differentiation from an already well-situated Classical Hollywood. Hansen would call Shanghai melodramas of the 1930s and Mexican cinema of the 1940s 'dialects' of a universal vernacular modernism whose cinematic centre was Hollywood. Because I have my eye on more recent developments, on the achievement of putatively homegrown cinemas after 1975 in Africa, Ireland and Mainland China, I am inclined to call them actual vernaculars, related to, but set against the one universally recognised language of the movies, Classical Hollywood's Latin, no longer spoken purely today in the post-classical age, but still fondly remembered.

Hansen properly inflates the importance of Hollywood as 'vernacular modernism', since this allies it to the power of the high modernism of Proust, Joyce, Picasso and Le Corbusier, while trumping all these through its popular appeal. Uncredited, Hollywood participated in the momentum we attribute to the privileged discourses of art, and it did so internationally as metropolitan peoples around the globe responded immediately to its attractions: speed, narrative disjunction, primacy of the visual, surveillance, excessive stimulation, negotiated ethics, and more. Hollywood, more than the intellectual pioneers we always adulate, brought modernism into the world. But Moretti's study of the novel alerts us to watch for the way each country both read and rewrote (in their own productions) this classical form. A close analysis of key films from any locale should reveal a conflicted cinematic vocabulary and grammar, as my recent examination of East Asian cinemas is revealing. Where Hansen insists on a dyadic pattern involving Hollywood with each of innumerable peripheral cinemas, I would complicate the map by tracing the regional interaction that is particularly visible when storytelling traditions are in focus. Thus a description of Hong Kong and Taiwanese cinema today must include not just their obvious ways of adopting and transforming Hollywood; it must account for the presence of various Asian characters in their plots and of Chinese and Japanese theatrical forms in their style. Vernaculars alter each other. Just look at *Crouching Tiger, Hidden Dragon* (Ang Lee, 2000). Better still, look at it from the perspective of Mainland Chinese audiences who had the pleasure or annoyance of rectifying three distinct acting styles and accents, which came across the subtitles in such a unified way for us in the West, ignorant of the sounds of the language.

## Orientation maps

Thus the idea of the atlas aspires to totality through an accretion of multiple yet differentiated maps that apportion objects and views. Even an immense sum of maps does not afford that captious, final perspective one relishes when spinning a globe at arm's length. Still, the atlas' thwarted totalisation encourages a dialectical understanding of culture and of one's place in it. This makes historicity possible, according to Jameson, since every view is local and, thereby, partial; and an acknowledgement of partiality underwrites the historical struggle over 'the territory' one inhabits. Moretti gave us just the ocular tool needed when he added 'indigenous narration' to Jameson's dialectical process of hegemonic form meeting local material. For is not narration precisely the mechanism by which totality is imagined and managed from such and such a place? In cinema something as technical as 'point of view' asserts an ideological and political claim, literally orienting a culture to a surrounding world.

And yet Moretti backs away from the analysis of point of view in texts, backs away from texts altogether, retreating to the distance demanded by the protocols of social science (2000: 56).[2] How odd, when he has in front of him Jameson's plea for 'cognitive mapping' (1988). Should not the next shift in the dialectic take him from the sociological perspective to precisely the 'perspective of *perspective*', that is, to the interior map that the text itself can be said to draw? All films by definition – and ambitious works by design – contain and dramatically coordinate the various forces that the social scientist plots on graphs. Why not examine the film as map – cognitive map – while placing the film *on* the map. How does a fictional universe from another part of the world orient its viewers to their global situation?

Every film implies a geopolitical orientation, even if some Hollywood films assume that this question is obviated by their putatively universal perspective. But in other places – in Ireland, for instance – orientation is exactly what is at stake in representation. To account for the local/global *transfocus* that so many Irish films employ, I have invented the term 'demi-emigration' (see Andrew 2002), trying to point to the complex way in which a culture can be itself without turning in on itself. Whether or not Irish films deal explicitly with global issues, the place of the culture in the world is visible to the careful analyst. Look at the recent film *The Mapmaker* (Johnny Gogan,

2001), set at Ireland's interior border, separating off the six counties. In fact it concerns a single county, Leitrum, which, with its divided populace, becomes a figure of the nation. At whatever level, the border literally contains the forces that mount up against and amongst one another under the centripetal pressure borders naturally exert. Those forces and pressures may often be uncomfortable, even repressive, and today they may be (or seem) arbitrary and dismissible, but borders provide constant orientation; for most citizens within them, they are like the walls of a house, reassuring rather than confining. You can usually open a window or walk out the door in times of stress. Most important, the continuity and definition they give to an otherwise unlimited space, trades extension for depth. There is an Irish atlas that marks an amazing number of distinctive features, county by county, district by district (Aelen, Whelan & Stout 1997). Natural and man-made marks atop the landscape are openings that allow local people and historians to tunnel into a past, in what amounts to a historical dictionary of the Earth. The same holds true for ways of speech and behaviour; restricted in space for generations, these ingrained habits absorb history in each performance of them, lending its weight to the everyday. Natural borders such as the sea-girdle surrounding the two Irelands make this obvious; historical borders, like the one between those Irelands are only 'marginally' different. The fact is that every citizen knows what it feels like to arrive on the other side of passport control coming back from a trip. The sense of freedom abroad, the observations of differences and similarities, recede as we sink again into 'being back home', with all the conflicts included. We can recognise the habits of our home as a 'habitus', appreciating or mocking their peculiarities, understanding their connection to time and place. Films make palpable collective habits and a collective sensibility. In their inclusions and exclusions, in their scope and style, films project cognitive maps by which citizens understand both their bordered world and the world at large.

## Topographical maps

What do we do with the nomadic refusal of maps? The Nomad, at least as he has been famously figured by Gilles Deleuze and Felix Guattari (1987), snaps the tether tied to the tree of history, and skips along the surface toward a fluctuating horizon. Protean and quick, he evades the mapping prowess of the colonialist, the tax collector and the academic researcher who would position him; he loses himself in unmappable terrains, a force outside representation. Raised on postwar art cinema, Deleuze prized 'deeply foreign' films for these qualities, for resisting the imperial administration of audio-visual entertainment that goes under the flag of Hollywood.

The term 'world cinema' vibrates with this nomadic energy; many of us sidle close, curious, tempted to try it out. Usually we demand the best films brought to us conveniently. Metropolitan connoisseurs, we cultivate alluring, sometimes aggressively dangerous species of exotic films. How to give back to such films the force to disturb us? Can films refuse to be mapped, refuse representation in the way nomads are said to do? Can films still strike with the force of the unexpected the way Akira Kurosawa, Satyajit Ray and Jerzy Kawalerovicz did in the 1950s? Relief maps suggest uneven contours on the globe, including layers. When we add to these the geological and marine dimensions, topographical maps represent the struggle to represent depth, that which is hidden. Deleuze's notions of 'smooth nomadic space' founder when one looks at deeply 'rooted' cultures, including those that have escaped our attention.

Since 1990 hundreds of Nigerian scripts (over 500 last year) have been shot direct-to-video in Yoruba and Ibo; VHS tapes (their sole mode of existence) are traded in the urban market, then bicycled along old trading routes to villages throughout the country. No festivals feature these films; no critics review them. Their reputation travels by word of mouth, and within national, often tribal borders. This, the most successful image market on the entire African continent, has been invisible to us ... unrepresented on our screens and until a few years ago unmentioned in our scholarly literature. One of the only viable non-subsidised image industries in the world, Nigerian video films are off the map. They have not sought our interest, not yet at least; however, they must concern anyone who scans screens for a different vision of the world or a different function of the medium. Not long ago, I concluded a long discussion of African cinema and its rapport with Deleuze's 'nomadology' by mentioning these films as precisely unmentionable, unviewable, unmappable (Andrew 2000). I saw this phenomenon as the proper but self-negating conclusion of Deleuze's flight of thought, a limit that contested his ideas. But that was before copies of such videos began to appear in London and other diasporic communities, and before Nigerian scholars touted their indigenous success. Now California Newsreel, a counter-culture distributor in the US, has picked one example, *Thunderbolt* (Tunde Kelani, 2001), the most complex they could find of course. They expect to market it to professors of African Studies and anthropology and to those film scholars ever on the lookout for a different cinema, whether in the hope that a purer vision may be available, or a purer people. Many of us will be racing to examine this vibrant phenomenon, to be the first to tell our peers about it, the first to explore its (hopefully idiosyncratic) use of the medium, its special cultural function – in short, the first to map it.

## Conclusion

Let me not be coy. We still parse the world by nations. Film festivals identify entries by country, college courses are labelled 'Japanese Cinema', 'French Film', and textbooks are coming off the presses with titles such as *Screening Ireland, Screening China, Italian National Cinema*, and so on. But a wider conception of national image culture is around the corner, prophesied by phrases like 'rooted cosmopolitanism' and 'critical regionalism' (Andrew 2002). Such terms insist upon the centrifugal dynamic of images, yet without surrendering the special cohesion that films bring to specific cultures.

In this perpetual push-pull between local conditions and broader cosmos, I throw my slight weight behind the latter for strategic reasons, certain that American students are primed to celebrate identity far too uncritically, applauding its certitudes wherever they may be found, as a guarantee for that most important identity, their own as Americans. Behind the acclamation accorded recently exported Indian films, for example, you can hear overtones of relief from critics and spectators, who welcome the chance to cheer for the local, even the familial. It is hard not to get behind music, genre, dance and custom, particularly when hundreds of millions of people celebrate exactly these things far from the clutches of Hollywood. Yet, given the treatment of the British in *Lagaan* (Ashutosh Gowariker, 2003) and of those outside the bride's family in *Monsoon Wedding* (Mira Nair, 2001), the politics of Bollywood seems exclusionary. A larger globe may surround these dramas, but it does so nefariously – with wicked England in the first case, immoral America in the second. Propriety remains with family, to which one belongs by birth and to which one owes allegiance. Without dismissing the communal feeling such films foster, should we empathise with the way they bask, so self-satisfied, in this unapologetic promotion of self-identity? A larger vision would place communal allegiance within a social and geographical landscape accessible to other points of view. Take the legendary, though hotly-debated, *Sholay* (1975) which uses song and local ritual to build community from a spectrum of villagers, bandits and government officials, even foreigners.[3] In *Sholay*, the India one belongs to is more inclusive than that of *Lagaan*; its characters relate to each other less as family members than as fellow citizens. Their negotiations, compromises and even juridical conflicts represent a self-differentiated India to which all characters feel conflicted allegiance, but allegiance all the same. Such an India operates and cooperates more dextrously and critically in a highly differentiated world than would a unified and self-satisfied nation-family.

Or take *Amélie* (Jean-Pierre Jeunet, 2001), which has endeared itself to the public and to so many critics. The comfort it undeniably offers is the comfort of the known. No foreigners muddy the 'ethnically cleansed' Paris of Montmartre and of the quintessential corner café, whose little people enjoy their distinctive French likes and dislikes. By contrast, *Jules et Jim* (François Truffaut, 1961), an image of which is directly cited in *Amélie*, announces a tension in its very title. Its classic love story has a geopolitical dimension. Catherine has an English mother, we are told, and studied in Munich. World War One splits the action in half, while Austria and France comprise its two epicentres. Indicatively, the *détente* Jules, Jim and Catherine have brought forward from *la belle epoche* comes to an end once all three characters watch a newsreel of Germans celebrating national unity by burning books, cleansing the dirt of difference.

Permit me one final look back at Irish cinema where you can readily calculate the extent to which each product turns inward or outward. Homecoming films like *Far and Away* (Ron Howard, 1992) or *This is My Father* (Paul Quinn, 1998) figure Mother Ireland as a tribe if not a family. On the other hand, *The Crying Game* (Neil Jordan, 1992), no matter what one thinks of it, can claim to look out from a distinctly Irish view onto a multi-dimensional world, a world troubled by class, religion, sexuality and national obsession. Neil Jordan is a demi-emigrant, Irish but worldly.

My preferences are clear: American students need continually to be alerted to the international dimension implied in, or smothered by, the films they are shown from abroad. The same may not be true for spectator-citizens from those foreign countries. Citizens of India, France and Ireland instead may need to maintain a focus on the distinctiveness (that is, the nationality) of the international perspective implied by films made within their borders. Borders are thresholds as much as walls. National cinema studies should take account of what borders make possible, as well as how films enter and exit. Hence Ireland's border, like the glass of a hothouse, retains the heat of all films projected and discussed within the nation, most of which have entered from outside. Indigenous productions may take only a small percentage of the box office, but the critical attention they receive in addressing local issues increases their heat coefficient to a potentially incendiary level. Even so, such a thing as Irish national cinema, whether studied in the US or in Irish universities, must be seen from a geopolitical perspective that takes in not just Hollywood and Britain but Continental Europe as well. And Asia too. For images trade in a global currency even when they represent a restricted neighbourhood of characters and situations, like Cathal Black's drama set in the 1950s in a Donegal village, titled *Korea* (Cathal Black, 1995). Under the pressure of national borders, strong films reach toward and respond to an international gaze. Such is the dialectic of cinema these days, and I would argue such it has always been.

Brian Friel's rich play, *Translations* (1980), names in its title and models in its plot just this give and take. It is set in Ireland in 1833, when for reasons of taxation and military security the British commissioned the very first complete land survey ever undertaken. The dialogue between British surveyors and Irish citizens over what constitutes a place, a name, a geological feature, a boundary or a value directly dramatises questions that concern world cinema: the struggle over language, education, land, religion, literal surveillance and identity. Friel's play effectively maps attitudes toward mapping, and in a highly contested space. Each party knew the territory differently.

The study of world cinema should let us *know the territory differently*, whatever territory it is that the film comes from or concerns. Today, amidst digital confections tempting filmmakers and audiences to escape to the land of the virtual, world cinema brings us back precisely to Earth, on which many worlds are lived and perceived concurrently. A certain cinema continues to remind us of the intricate rapport, both tactile and relational, that makes up 'Life on Earth', the title, by the way, of an African film worthy of starting or concluding any study of this immense and tempting subject.

## Notes

1   See especially footnote 25 relating to African oral traditions.
2   Moretti calls for 'distant reading', as a necessary and desirable concomitant attitude that his sociological mapping project brings about (2000: 56).
3   Even when this film occasions animosity, the terms of the debate are large. See Z. Saddar (1998) 'Dilip Kumar made me do it', in A. Nandy (ed.) *Secret Politics of Our Desires: Innocence, Culpability, and Indian popular cinema*. New York: Zed Books, 19–91.

## Works cited

Abel, R. (1999) *The Red Rooster Scare*. Berkeley: University of California Press.
Aelen, F. H. A., K. Whelan and M. Stout (eds) (1998) *Atlas of the Irish Rural Landscape*. Cork: Cork University Press.
Andrew, D. (2000) 'The Roots of the Nomadic: Gilles Deleuze and the Cinema of West

Africa', in G. Flaxman (ed.) *The Brain is the Screen*. Minneapolis: University of Minnesota Press, 215–49.

\_\_\_\_ (2002) 'The Theater of Irish Cinema', *Yale Journal of Criticism*, 15, 1, 24–58.

Deleuze G. and F. Guattari (1987) 'A Treatise on Nomadology', in *A Thousand Plateaus*. Minneapolis: University of Minnesota Press, 351–423.

Hansen, M. B. (2000) 'The Mass Production of Senses: Classical Cinema as Vernacular Modernism', in C. Gledhill and L. Williams (eds) *Reinventing Film Studies*. London: Arnold, 332–50.

Jameson, F. (1988) 'Cognitive Mapping', in C. Nelson and L. Grossberg (eds) *Marxism and the Interpretation of Culture*. Urbana: University of Illinois Press, 347–58.

\_\_\_\_ (1993) 'In the Mirror of Alternate Modernities', in K. Kojin (ed.) *Origins of Modern Japanese Literature*. Durham, NC: Duke University Press, vii–xxii.

Moretti, F. (1999) *Atlas of the European Novel 1800–1900*. London: Verso.

\_\_\_\_ (2000) 'Conjectures on World Literature', *New Left Review*, 1, 54–68.

\_\_\_ (2001) 'Planet Hollywood', *New Left Review*, 9, 90–102.

Shohat, E. and R. Stam (1994) *Unthinking Eurocentrism: Multiculturalism and the Media*. London and New York: Routledge.

# CHAPTER TWO

# Towards a positive definition of World Cinema
Lúcia Nagib

Over the past decade or so film theory has been subjected to a recycling process, of-ten indicated in book titles by words such as 'rethinking', 'unthinking', 'reinventing' or 'reconstructing' (see, for example, Shohat & Stam 1994, Bordwell & Carroll 1996, Gledhill & Williams 2000 and Guneratne & Dissanayake 2003). There is a perceived exhaustion of traditional theoretical assessment of cinema, which some authors, such as David Bordwell and Nöel Carroll (1996), ascribe to petrified models based on psy-choanalysis and cultural studies. As a contribution to the debate, I would like to sug-gest that the exhaustion may well reside above all in the object that has inspired such models, that is to say Hollywood cinema. One way of reflecting on this exhaustion is to elaborate on how Hollywood relates to 'world cinema', an increasingly popular term highlighting the global aspect of film production. Indeed, as communication nets spread and cinema transcends national and continental borders, world cinema issues proliferate in bibliographic output and academic syllabuses, where they articulate with a wider perception of culture in the postcolonial era.

However common it has become, the term 'world cinema' still lacks a proper, posi-tive definition. Despite its all-encompassing, democratic vocation, it is not usually employed to mean cinema worldwide. On the contrary, the usual way of defining it is restrictive and negative, as 'non-Hollywood cinema'. Needless to say, negation here translates a positive intention to turn difference from the dominant model into a vir-tue to be rescued from an unequal competition. However, it unwittingly sanctions the American way of looking at the world, according to which Hollywood is the centre and all other cinemas are the periphery.

Such a binary division of the world, a convention particularly cultivated in Anglo-phone countries, has been widely adopted by critics and historians as a way of organis-ing and structuring film history and geography. An example is *World Cinema: Critical Approaches*, edited by John Hill and Pamela Church Gibson (2000). This pioneer at-tempt to look at world cinema as an independent theoretical subject does not include American cinema, to which a separate volume of the Oxford University Press series is devoted, likewise called *American Cinema and Hollywood: Critical Approaches*. The procedure is justified by Hill with the argument that 'since the end of World War One, the US film industry has been the dominant cinema in the world and this has also meant that it has enjoyed a pre-eminent position within film studies' (2000: xiv).

Indisputable though it may sound, the argument contains a few questionable gen-eralisations. It does not specify, for example, whether 'dominant cinema' refers to box-office revenues or number of viewers. It also fails to spell out the exact time and place of this dominance. To counter it, one could point out the fact that in the late 1930s and again in the mid-1950s, Japan was the most prolific film producer in the world, reaching the mark of five hundred feature films a year. In the early 1970s, it was surpassed by India, which remains the world's leading film producer up to today, attracting annually over one billion viewers and being enormously influential within and beyond South Asia. However, Indian and Japanese cinemas deserve just one chapter each in Hill and Gibson's book, under the heading 'Case-studies: cinemas of the world'.

Hill's argument goes on to reinforce the idea that Hollywood is the centre not only of world film practice but also theory. The result is that other cinemas of the world are of interest insofar as they adopt 'a different aesthetic model of filmmaking from Hollywood' (ibid.). The Hollywood aesthetics is thus confirmed as the general paradigm for the appraisal of all other cinemas even though, as one would expect and is acknowledged by the author himself, they 'do not constitute a homogeneous filmmaking practice' (ibid.).

Of course, this and other similar approaches are always meant for the benefit of world cinema, which is then identified with art as opposed to commerce, or with progressive as opposed to conservative cinema. This goes back to a tradition of the 1960s and 1970s, when critics such as Guy Hennebelle (2004), in his famous book *Cinémas nationaux contre Hollywood*, qualified national cinemas of the world according to their degree of rejection of American imperialism. This was also the pattern once established by Third Cinema movements, which, in the 1960s, had turned the concept of Third World into a political weapon against Hollywood.

Indeed, the tripartite worldview derived from Third Cinema conceptions – according to which America produces first and Europe second cinemas – seems to enjoy an easy currency among film critics and historians. The recent book *Rethinking Third Cinema* (Guneratne & Dissanayake 2003), for example, fervently advocates Third Cinema as the most adequate theoretical approach to 'alternative' (or non-mainstream) cinemas of the world. Likewise, *Cinemas of the World* by James Chapman (2003), apart from the introductory and concluding parts, is divided into 'Hollywood Cinema', 'European Cinemas' and 'World Cinemas'.

The result of viewing world cinema as 'alternative' and 'different' is that the American paradigm continues to prevail as a tool for its evaluation. Authors are not short of arguments to justify such procedure. For Geoffrey Nowell-Smith, the editor of the comprehensive *The Oxford History of World Cinema*, the dominance of American cinema has been 'so extensive', that 'much of the history of cinema in other countries has consisted of attempts by the indigenous industries to thwart, compete with, or distinguish themselves from American ("Hollywood") cinema' (1997: xxi). Hill strikes the same note, arguing that 'the dominance of Hollywood has meant that other cinemas have often had to define themselves by differentiation from, or opposition to, Hollywood norms' (2000: xv). Fair as they may sound, such statements are not immediately applicable to actual cases. What are exactly the cinemas that define themselves by opposition to Hollywood? Third Cinema films, for example, go far beyond this confrontation, if you just think of Glauber Rocha, whose films combine a multiplicity of influences, from Sergei Eisenstein to Luchino Visconti, with the central aim of re-elaborating local (or national) myths and storytelling traditions. Hollywood could contribute little to the understanding of such an oeuvre.

The inevitable result of such conceptions is the reinforcement of the binary division of the world, according to which Hollywood deserves a different treatment from all other cinemas. In Nowell-Smith's book, American cinema occupies 'a central position throughout the "general" sections [and] there is no separate consideration of American cinema as a "national cinema" along with the French, Japanese, Soviet, and other cinemas' (1997: xxi). A similar viewpoint is adopted by Miriam Hansen in her famous article on 'Classical Cinema as Vernacular Modernism'. For her, the very category of national cinema 'in many cases describes defensive formations shaped in competition with and resistance to Hollywood products' (2000a: 340). Does this mean that many national cinemas would not have existed if it were not for the overwhelming presence of Hollywood? Whatever the case, the fact remains that seeing Hollywood, with all its stars and stripes, as the only really international cinematic current denies a positive existence to all other world cinemas, which are thus made incapable of originating independent theory.

Analysing world cinemas through the American perspective is nevertheless a deeply-engrained habit among writers. The obvious explanation for this, at least in the Anglophone world, is that American cinema is the best known among authors of film history and criticism. Chapman points out that 'one of the reasons why American cinema is the most heavily researched in the world is because it is also the best documented' (2003: 21). In addition, I would mention the commercial reason, as America's massive presence on Western screens opens up a profitable market for a corresponding bibliography. However, this produces an overblown image of Hollywood's influence that is badly in need of correction.

Such a corrective perception is now being expressed, even on the part of those who most contributed to the shaping of the 'Classical Hollywood cinema' idea. Kristin Thompson and David Bordwell have recently released the second, updated edition of what is probably the best informed and structured film history in a single volume. In it, they deconstruct several myths about American cinema that they used to support themselves, such as the belief in D. W. Griffith's sole invention of 'virtually every important technique for film storytelling' (2003: 51). However, when explaining the filming techniques of someone as great as Yasujiro Ozu, they still mechanically apply the American paradigm, saying, for example, that Ozu's strategies 'consistently violated Hollywood's traditional 180-degree continuity editing' (2003: 249). Contradicting Hollywood, however, was certainly one of the least of Ozu's worries, when he had to deal with an immense Japanese heritage in need of translation into cinematic language. Here, as much as in Noël Burch's old Japanese film book, *To the Distant Observer* (1979), Japanese films are turned into unconventional, rebellious forms of expression just because they differ from the Hollywood model, regardless of the fact that, as in the case of Ozu, they are hegemonic at home.

## Escaping binarism

On the other hand, less conventional approaches have been attempting to forge a positive concept of world cinema. An example is Dudley Andrew's imaginative proposal of 'An Atlas of World Cinema', included in this volume. Its aim is to 'model a set of approaches, just as an atlas of maps opens up a continent to successive views: political, demographic, linguistic, topographical, meteorological, marine, historical'. Andrew's method has the immediate merit of relativising Hollywood's importance as a mainstream cinema and showing how peaks of production, popularity and artistic input are attained in different times and places across the globe. However, the distinction between Hollywood and the rest of the world still reverberates in his approach when he qualifies world cinema as 'foreign' and 'unfamiliar' – something that sounds at odds with the highly mixed audiences of today's film theatres and courses both in Europe and the US.

Andrew's 'Atlas of World Cinema' derives in its substance from Franco Moretti's polemical essay 'Conjectures on World Literature', published in the first issue of the re-launched *New Left Review* in 2000. Moretti applies to world literature the dialectics between centre and periphery imported from political economy, with particular emphasis on the 'foreign debt', a term coined by Brazilian critic Roberto Schwarz to signify the large use made by colonised countries of models provided by the colonisers, especially France and Britain. Andrew translates Moretti's ideas from literature into film via Miriam Hansen's above-cited theory of 'vernacular modernism'. In Hansen's view, Classical Hollywood cinema caused a huge impact on cinemas all over the world, changing them all of a sudden into modern cinemas and giving birth, for example, to the Soviet montage cinema and the Shanghai cinema of the 1920s and 1930s.

Of course Andrew, as much as Moretti, is aware of, and concerned about, the reduction and simplification entailed by the binary approach. Moretti tries to correct views such as Fredric Jameson's, for whom modern Japanese literature, for example, is nothing more than Western form applied to local raw material. To that end, Moretti introduces a third element, which he calls the 'local narrative voice'. Andrew also tries to complicate Hansen's binary pattern by shifting the emphasis from Hollywood, whose role, according to him, is overestimated by her, to 'the regional interaction that is particularly visible when storytelling traditions are in focus'.

However, the introduction of a third element or the shift of focus still falls short of solving the epistemological problems caused by the binary division. For example, in her extremely insightful article 'Fallen Women, Rising Stars, New Horizons', Hansen does acknowledge that Sun Yu's *Tianming* (*Daybreak*, 1933) 'achieves a translation, hybridisation, and reconfiguration of foreign (and not just American) as well as indigenous discourses on modernity and modernisation' (2000b: 19). However, because her essay draws entirely on the Hollywood paradigm, she attributes the construction of the extraordinary female protagonist exclusively to the Hollywood influence, and not at all, for example, to Chinese theatre traditions, which are so striking in the film. There are important questions here: Can one really isolate foreign from local components of an art work? Could not the imported form itself be the result of multiple influences, often originating in the same regions that now import them back? On what basis is modernity considered an exclusively Western attribute, when Western modernist artists were constantly looking at Africa and Asia?

A truly encompassing and democratic approach has to get rid of the binary system as a whole. In this respect, I tend to side with Ella Shohat and Robert Stam, who have been consistently attacking the binary system since their groundbreaking book *Unthinking Eurocentrism* (1994). Shohat and Stam dismiss as unnecessary and ultimately wrong the world division between 'us' and the 'other', 'centre and periphery', 'the West and the Rest'. Their approach champions a 'polycentric multiculturalism' as an alternative to 'liberal pluralism' (1994: 8). Thus they expect to 'decentre the discussion by calling attention to other traditions, other cinemas and other audio-visual forms' (1994: 7). Indeed, their method of film analysis is particularly attractive for their intimacy not only with local productions but also with local theories. Stam has always insisted, for example, on the pioneering character of the Brazilian modernist movement of the 1920s, and he was the first to acknowledge Ismail Xavier's allegories of underdevelopment as an important branch of postcolonial theory (Stam 2000; Miller & Stam 2004).

In my view, the belief in a centre is as mythic as the quest for origins. Although cinema is a technological medium with a more or less precise date of birth at the end of the nineteenth century, pre-cinema theories have already pushed its true beginning much further back (see, for example, Charney & Schwartz 1996). Even if authors such as Jacques Aumont dismiss such theories as 'confused' and reassert Lumière's cinematic primacy as 'the last impressionist painter' (1995), I tend to side with German filmmaker and philosopher Alexander Kluge, for whom 'cinema has existed for over ten thousand years in the minds of human beings' in the form of 'associative currents, daydreams, sensual experiences and streams of consciousness. The technical discovery only made it reproducible' (1975: 208). Thus, a real search for the origins of cinema should take us far beyond Hollywood and Lumière to the remote times of the early humans, who already strove to depict dynamic figures on the walls of caves. Hollywood and the modern experience would be more adequately comprehended if seen not as the origin but as an aspect of film history.

Therefore, I would favour a method in which Hollywood and the West would cease to be the centre of film history, and this would be seen as a process with no single beginning. The advantage of such an approach is that, once the idea of a single centre is eliminated, nothing needs to be excluded from the world cinema map, not even Hollywood, which, instead of a threat, becomes an element or a cinema among others. It can receive major, minor or no attention depending on the object in question. Against the exclusive method based on Hollywood, be it pro or anti, I propose, following Shohat and Stam's suggestion, the inclusive method of a world made of interconnected cinemas.

The natural question derived from such an approach would be how to define the cinemas, periods or aspects to be looked at. Here Dudley Andrew provides insightful answers. The first of them relates film history to 'waves, which roll through adjacent cultures whose proximity to one another promotes propagation that not even triangulation can adequately measure'. The obvious example here is the French New Wave, which, according to Andrew, 'buoyed French film in 1959 and rolled around the world, affecting in different ways and under dissimilar circumstances the cinema lives of Britain, Japan, Cuba, Brazil, Argentina, Czechoslovakia, Yugoslavia, Hungary and later Taiwan'. To approach world cinema through its waves is all the more attractive for the fact that waves have peaks in different places and times. As regards the French New Wave, for example, one could see a previous crest of a wave a little earlier in the mid-1950s with the films made by the so-called Tribe of the Sun in Japan, which had a decisive influence on François Truffaut. One could also look at the New German Cinema of the 1960s and 1970s in relation to how it re-elaborated elements of the Brazilian *cinema novo*.

Another of Andrew's important suggestions is the study of single films, as opposed to Moretti's defence of 'distant reading'. As Andrew quite rightly argues, 'all films by definition – and ambitious works by design – contain and dramatically co-ordinate the various forces that the social scientist plots on graphs. Why not examine the film as map – cognitive map – while placing the film *on* the map'. To read a film as a map entails the discovery of new territories and the tracing of new geographies across the history of world cinema.

Thompson and Bordwell's film history book must be acknowledged as a great achievement in terms of braving the complexities and overlapping events in cinemas worldwide. Alongside the necessarily chronological parts, the book evolves in the form of a hypertext, opening boxes to decisive technological inventions, cinematic currents, important single films or outstanding auteurs, and making room everywhere for queries and notes which often deconstruct the Hollywood myth. They even frankly recognise that 'many of the basic principles of the system [of so-called "Classical Hollywood cinema"] were being worked out before filmmaking was centred in Hollywood, and, indeed, many of those principles were first tried in other countries' (2003: 43). Films all over the world are thus not confined into tight compartments of their own nationalities, but interconnected with each other according to their relevance at a given historical moment, regardless of whether they originate in the first, second or third worlds.

## Conclusion

By way of conclusion I would like to propose the following definition of world cinema as a first step for discussion:

- World cinema is simply the cinema of the world. It has no centre. It is not the other, but it is us. It has no beginning and no end, but is a global process. World cinema, as the world itself, is circulation.
- World cinema is not a discipline, but a method, a way of cutting across film history according to waves of relevant films and movements, thus creating flexible geographies.
- As a positive, inclusive, democratic concept, world cinema allows all sorts of theoretical approaches, provided they are not based on the binary perspective.

World cinema needs to be assessed through new theories – and this is a key issue. Any film criticism becomes instantly richer when patterns of realism, genre, authorship and dramatic construction emerge from the analysed object itself and not from an alien (usually American) paradigm. Bordwell and Carroll have already defended what they call 'middle-level research' (Bordwell) or 'piecemeal theory' (Carroll), which, not accidentally, relates chiefly with cinemas other than the American mainstream, as the examples they draw from Latin American, Arab and African film studies abundantly confirm (1996: 34–5).

The hardest aspect of developing new theoretical models is the necessary knowledge of the cultures generating the works of art in focus. With regard to the Anglophone world, there is not only a lack of translations of fundamental foreign works (such as the books on Italian Cinema by Lino Miccichè, the world film criticism by Glauber Rocha, the monumental Japanese film history by Tadao Sato, or even some key essays by André Bazin), but also a need on the part of scholars and students to learn foreign languages (it is not an accident that so many outstanding film specialists come from language departments). Contextual knowledge of films has already produced a great number of original theoretical approaches and is certainly the best way of escaping the traps of binarism.

## Works cited

Aumont, J. (1995) *L'Oeil interminable: cinéma et peinture*. Paris: Séguier.

Chapman, J. (2003) *Cinemas of the World: Film and Society from 1895 to the Present*. London: Reaktion.

Charney, L. and V. Schwartz (eds) (1996) *Cinema and the Invention of Modern Life*. Berkeley: University of California Press.

Bordwell, D. and N. Carroll (eds) (1996) *Post-Theory: Reconstructing Film Studies*. Madison: University of Wisconsin Press.

Burch, N. (1979) *To the Distant Observer: Form and Meaning in Japanese Cinema*. Los Angeles: University of California Press.

Gledhill, C. and L. Williams (eds) (2000) *Reinventing Film Studies*. London: Arnold.

Guneratne, A. R. and W. Dissanayake (eds) (2003) *Rethinking Third Cinema*. New York and London: Routledge.

Hansen, M. B. (2000a) 'The Mass Production of Senses: Classical Cinema as Vernacular Modernism', in C. Gledhill and L. Williams (eds) *Reinventing Film Studies*. London: Arnold, 332–50.

____ (2000b) 'Fallen Women, Rising Stars, New Horizons: Cultural Influence of Hollywood Film in Shanghai, China, in the 1920s and 1930s', *Film Quarterly*, 54, 1, 10–22.

Hennebelle, G. (2004 [1975]) *Cinémas nationaux contre Hollywood*. Paris: Le Cerf.

Hill, J. and P. Church Gibson (2000) *World Cinema: Critical Approaches*. Oxford: Oxford University Press.

Kluge, A. (1975) 'Kommentare zum antagonistischen Realismusbegriff', in *Gelegenheitsarbeit einer Sklavin: Zur realistischen Methode*. Frankfurt am Main: Surhkamp.

Miller, T. and R. Stam (eds) (2004) *A Companion to Film Theory*. Malden and Oxford: Blackwell.

Moretti, F. (2000) 'Conjectures on World Literature', *New Left Review*, 1, 54–68.

Nowell-Smith, G. (ed.) (1999) *The Oxford History of World Cinema*. Oxford: Oxford University Press.

Shohat, E. and R. Stam (1994) *Unthinking Eurocentrism: Multiculturalism and the Media.* London and New York: Routledge.

Stam, R. (2000) *Film Theory: An Introduction.* Malden and Oxford: Blackwell.

Thompson, K. and D. Bordwell (2003) *Film History: An Introduction* (second edition). New York: McGraw-Hill.

# CHAPTER THREE

## Latin American cinema: from underdevelopment to postmodernism
Michael Chanan

There is nothing film critics love more than discovering an unheralded masterpiece. At the end of the 2002 Cannes Film Festival, a critic in the *Guardian*, Andrew Pulver, wrote about an out-of-competition Brazilian film, *Cidade de Deus* (*City of God*, 2002) by Fernando Meirelles and Katia Lund, a story of children and violence in the favela. He called it 'a dazzling display of both photographic and editing technique … culled from a background in Latin American music video and commercials', and this, he continued, 'belies any idea that we are looking at some kind of dispatch from a primitive movie-making backwater'. He went on to speak of 'a resurgent Latin American film movement termed *la buena onda* – "the good wave" – that takes in everything from Fabián Bielinsky's Argentinian thriller *Nueve Reinas* (*Nine Queens*, 2000), Walter Salles' *Central do Brasil* (*Central Station*, 1998) and *Abril Despedaçado* (*Behind the Sun*, 2001), Alfonso Cuaron's record-breaking *Y tu mama también* (*And Your Mother Too*, 2001) to Alejandro González Iñárritu's *Amores Perros* (*Life's a Bitch*, 2002).

Doubtless well-meaning, these comments nevertheless reveal something about the reviewer's dispositions, or *habitus* in Pierre Bourdieu's word, and the place occupied within it by Latin American cinema, and this provides a useful entry point to a series of observations about the trajectory of Latin American cinema over the last few decades.

Two things in particular in Pulver's remarks draw my attention. First, he feels he has to affirm that Latin America is not a cinematic backwater, which suggests that the history of Latin American cinema has been forgotten, in particular the movement that grew up in the 1960s to be known as *el nuevo cine latinoamericano*. Second, how impressed he is by the diversity of *la buena onda*, by the fact it has no 'house style' (as there is or was, for example, in contemporary Iranian cinema, or in the British New Wave at the start of the 1960s). This again suggests the same loss of memory, because in *el nuevo cine latinoamericano*, it was *never like that* – on the contrary, the movement thrived on its diversity ('*el uno en el diverso*', unity in the diverse, as Fernando Birri described it in my 1983 film for Channel 4, *New Cinema of Latin America*). Both these positions of Pulver's represent distinct problematics which I shall try to identify and place in historical perspective.

Forty years ago, after decades of low-level commercial production, Latin American cinema underwent an astonishing rebirth as a vanguard film movement with objectives both political and aesthetic. The 1960s was the moment when Latin American cinema plunged into modernism, in a process in which, country by country, the representational space of the screen was reconfigured and the whole continent re-envisaged. We might speak of an entirely new visual discourse, but not in a singular sense.

Starting off from the emulation of Italian neorealism, which they used to wipe the slate clean, filmmakers across the continent began to experiment, taking off in quite different directions, arguing and sparking off each other in equal measure. It was completely unlike what is called an artistic movement in European culture, which is usually grouped around a common stylistic model, often expressed in the form of a manifesto or a group exhibition or a literary journal which plays the role of incorporating or excluding. Here, the criteria of inclusion were not aesthetic but political – adherence to anti-imperialism, and one or other form of socialist ideology.

This movement – which called itself *el nuevo cine latinoamericano* – embodied an analysis of its own conditions of production in terms of the theory of underdevelopment. Underdevelopment was seen as a condition of oppression which is due to the continuous economic exploitation long imposed by the metropolitan centre on the countries of the periphery. The process operates through unequal terms of trade to deform the economy, society, the state and culture. Modernisation is forever promised and never fully delivered, as if the underdeveloped country can never catch up with the metropolis. The wish to create cinema in these circumstances was considered the same as the struggle for national liberation; the movement's philosophy acknowledged Frantz Fanon as a kindred spirit, and was cousin to the emergent theology of liberation.

Fanon maintained that a nation's sense of itself can be colonised as well as its territory, and this is exactly what the new cinema set out to tackle. Imperialism must be combated on all fronts, including cinema itself, which therefore needs a new language in order to testify to the truths of national – social, cultural, political – identity. But if

Cuban cartoon of the 1960s

cinema could do this, then it would represent a powerful contribution to the struggle for liberation. This is the position advanced in the initial, combative form of Third Cinema first presented by Fernando Solanas and Octavio Getino in Argentina in 1969, by the manifestos of Glauber Rocha in Brazil and Jorge Sanjinés in Bolivia, and in Cuba, in the idea of imperfect cinema, formulated around the same time by Julio García Espinosa.

From Havana to Santiago de Chile, the new filmmakers of the 1960s saw no contradiction between art and militancy. On the contrary, they put film forward as a strategic site in the battle for hegemony in a war in which the cultural worker was an enlisted soldier, and the camera, in a favourite metaphor, was likened to the gun of the guerrilla fighter. At any rate, it was always more of a political movement than an artistic one, making no call for any kind of stylistic unity, but eager to take positions that repudiated models imposed by the hegemony of Hollywood. In short, it invoked an avant-garde spirit of iconoclasm which could be accomplished in many different ways, and was therefore, in aesthetic terms, radically pluralist. This was one of the key features in its continent-wide appeal, as a movement which operated within national boundaries but imagined a community of nations called Latin America which shared a common destiny.

For all the factors that have been traditionally advanced to explain Hollywood's world domination, which mostly centre on its successful populism, the appeal of the star system, and the efficiency of the studios' methods of production, from the Latin American point of view the central issue was cultural imperialism, which was seen as part and parcel of underdevelopment. Indeed underdevelopment was a key factor in the history of cinema in Latin America from the very beginning. In Brazil, for example, according to Paulo Emílio Salles Gomes (1997), if cinema failed to take root for about a decade after its introduction, it was due, he said, to underdevelopment in electricity. Once energy was industrialised in Rio de Janeiro, exhibition halls proliferated like mushrooms – and production soon reached a hundred films a year. And of course the intimate link between economic and cultural imperialism crops up in Gabriel García Márquez's *One Hundred Years of Solitude* (1967), where film arrives in the town of Macondo with the same trains that bring the United Fruit Company.

Exhibition thrived but production was condemned to cycles of boom and bust. The opportunities for local producers were undercut by Hollywood's aggressive overseas marketing techniques. As Hollywood advanced across the globe, local film industries in third world countries were able to take root only on condition that the home market was large enough to allow the producer to break even – as long as budgets were kept low enough. Since this is always an uncertain equation to achieve, what we find in Latin America is that film production has often only survived because, from as early as the 1930s, governments have been prepared – in recognition of cinema's social power, or persuaded of its cultural prestige as a badge of a modern nation – to give it special treatment, and they thus engaged in what were usually piecemeal and ill-conceived systems of subsidy or support or tax breaks. That this nevertheless made a difference is shown by what happens when these schemes are withdrawn, like the collapse of production in Argentina and Brazil in the 1980s. (Both countries later relented. In Brazil, *la buena onda* is based on a novel scheme of investment funding by tax breaks; more recently, Argentina has extended protection for domestic production in the cinemas.)

The transformation of Hollywood from the home town of the great film studios into the hub of the global entertainments industry has had little effect on these basic conditions in countries of the periphery, which remain artisan by comparison, and whose practical results were described to me a few years ago by the Argentinean director Eliseo Subiela when he explained Argentina's three-budget system of production. Budget number one is the official budget in local currency; two is the official budget in dollars, for the foreign co-producer (without whom practically no films are nowadays made); but the real budget is the third one, which no one else ever sees, where all the currency deals and backhanders are worked out. This is a description of the everyday life of underdevelopment. As a result of which (*pace* Salles Gomes) the production that is readily stimulated by exhibition *cannot* be satisfied at the local level, which is prevented from developing its potential. Since local filmmakers also have very little access to foreign markets, even within Latin America, in order to make up the difference, making movies thus remains throughout the continent a highly uncertain field of employment where people have both day jobs and night jobs. It is consequently also prone to self-exploitation, because, on the other hand, it is well supplied with a wealth of talent, imagination and determination, as well as a proud and inspirational – though always uneven – history. Thus, according to a film union official from Argentina talking to a sympathetic North American observer at the beginning of the 1990s, 'Making movies is not an economic decision in Latin America. It's a political decision' (Jorge Ventura, quoted in Aufderheide 2000: 241). This is much the same now as it ever was, and not yet altered much by such developments as international co-production, or Spanish investment in new multiplex cinemas. These things may expand a few opportunities but how should they alter the basic situation, since they are also its symptoms?

Fredric Jameson has pointed out how the history of cinema recapitulates over a shorter period the stages or moments of cultural development which correspond to the evolution of capitalism: the realism dominant at the stage of national or local capitalism; the stage of monopoly capitalism (Lenin's 'stage of imperialism') which seems to have generated the various modernisms; and the multinational era which accounts for the developments now known as postmodernism (1992: 156–7). In the passage from its artisan beginnings to industrial enterprise controlled by national capitals, cinema develops the classical realism associated with Hollywood's subsequent worldwide hegemony. In the 1920s came the first signs of modernism, especially in Europe and Soviet Russia, a development which was set back by the coming of sound, to resurface after World War Two under new conditions, only to be subsumed, however, or as we used to say, recuperated, by the cultural transformation of the last quarter century, the aesthetic mutation which is generally spoken of as postmodernism and linked to globalisation. This is very general and we need to tread carefully, since cinema was transnational from the very start, and global in reach and operation by the 1930s, before postmodernism; this makes the link in cinema between globalisation and post-modernism, and the question of when it began, a slippery one.

Underdevelopment theory holds that different regions in the periphery are held back to a greater or lesser extent by their particular histories of colonialism. But because film culture is a globalising force from its very first stages, the pattern of its aesthetics also runs in broad parallel across all sorts of economic and political boundaries, and Jameson draws a comparison between imperfect cinema and the contemporaneous practices of First World oppositional filmmakers like Jean-Luc Godard – he cites their use of handheld cameras, their deliberately sloppy and foregrounded editing, their ostentatious valorisation of amateurishness in place of Hollywood sheen (1992: 218–19). But this is only the surface. In both of them the dominant codes of generic realism were challenged and subverted to produce a different set of representational values, in which – evidence the eager reception given to Latin American cinema in the vanguards of film culture in Europe – each, at least to some extent, recognised the other; a moment symbolised by the scene in Godard's *Le Vent d'est* (1970) where Rocha appears at the crossroads of cinema.[1] In short, when one compares these two cinemas, it cannot be said that Latin American cinema was in any way 'behind' Europe in the aesthetic domain, in the development of cinema as a (political) art, as communicative expression. (Pulver's review from Cannes suggests that this is another lesson which has been forgotten, like much else from the 1960s and 1970s, and we now live in a (screen) world where striking films from Latin America are like exotic rarities, orchids in a world of postmodernism.)

For the Latin Americans, whose relationship to their audience at home was much more tenuous, the recognition they found in Europe as ambassadors of the aesthetics of anti-imperialism helped to affirm their sense of identity as a vanguard of revolutionary cultural politics, but it left open the possibility that they still served for the European as an imaginary other. From the metropolitan perspective, it was a shock to discover that the periphery does not stand still, and nor was it correct to imagine that those who live in a condition of colonial or post-colonial deprivation were 'behind the times', since in these films they turn out to be the contemporaries, in every sense, of those who have what they lack (which they would not lack if the others did not have it).

Under favourable conditions, the new cinema was able to reach very large audiences, especially in Cuba, for reasons that I have rehearsed elsewhere (Chanan 2004). But this is also true, for example, in Chile before the overthrow of President Allende, and with individual films like Jorge Sanjinés' *Yawar Mallku* (*El Sangre del Condor/ Blood of the Condor*, 1968) in Bolivia, or in the film club circuit in Brazil which by the early 1980s included some five hundred locales. These examples point to a critical factor: this was a cinema which flourished at the margins of the market and beyond its confines, where cultural voluntarism was more important than commercial viability and cinema could make direct contact with the community. This applies to alternative forms of distribution in countries like Argentina, Bolivia and Brazil, and also to Cuba, which was pushed to the edge of the international market by the US blockade and thus found itself free to develop cinema on a cultural rather than a commercial basis. The different character of the audiences reached in this way is reflected in the films, which

stylistically develop in quite different directions in dialogue with their own local audiences and histories. In Argentina, the combativity of Solanas and Getino's *La hora
de los hornos* (*The Hour of the Furnaces*, 1968) addressed an urban underground. In
Sanjinés, it responded to the subaltern discourse of the Andean *indígena*. In Brazil, the
film club movement drew on a young urban intelligentsia, and *cinema novo* evolved
into the *udigrundi*, or underground.[2]

What is common to these instances is first of all their stance of defiance, which
came from the political conditions in which they had to operate: right-wing military
dictatorships (the most extreme of which, as in Chile, put a stop to all forms of cinema,
as if they were all equally liable to breed opposition). Secondly, their insistence on
alternative narratives and different representational logics which fracture the imaginary unity of society conjured up by the hegemonic norms of the creole bourgeoisie.
In the name of a more authentic national cultural aspiration, the new cinema throws
the nation as an imagined community into disarray by giving image and voice to the
marginal and subaltern who has previously only received the most derisory representation, and who has been systemically excluded from the public sphere. As José Joaquin Brunner puts it, 'in situations of extensive cultural heterogeneity, the very notion
of national collectivity finds itself questioned' (1995: 49). If this is one of the primary
themes of *el nuevo cine latinoamericano* from Glauber Rocha onwards, it is because
cinema inevitably constitutes a site of ideological contestation over definitions of nation, state, people and country.

Warners bites the dust: Cuban newsreel on the expropriation of the distributors

When this movement found itself in growing crisis in the 1980s – a crisis of both confidence and identity – there were several contributory factors which echoed (unevenly) across the region, including a crisis in production, a declining audience and a major shift in the political climate.

Economic crisis hit the major industries of Argentina and Brazil, as the state turned towards austerity measures and withdrew even its paltry forms of support. In Argentina, production fell dramatically from 46 films in 1982 to four in 1989. In Brazil in the same year, it had fallen to twenty from nearly a hundred a few years earlier. In Mexico, it was different: a record-breaking 128 features in 1989, but most of them, says Pat Aufderheide, 'were low-budget romances and action films for a US Hispanic market' (2000: 241). The crisis of Mexican production will come later, when the country's accession to NAFTA will unleash a flood of American pictures into the domestic market and local production would be 'driven to the wall', as Alex Cox wrote in 2000, 'unable to compete with a massive influx of gringo movies that distributors could pick up cheaply'.

Aufderheide says that the blame for the loss of the cinema audience lies partly with new technologies, especially the domestic VCR. In fact, there was a double shift in the very ground of film's relation to its public. First came the loss of the cinema-going audience to television, which in Latin America like everywhere else, overtakes it numerically as a mass medium. Despite the widening divide between rich and poor, television spread to even the poorest *barrios* and *favelas*. There were *poblaciones* around capital cities like Lima which had no sanitation but the inhabitants tapped into electricity supplies and were able to enjoy television. In Brazil, TV Globo became a major ideological player through demonstrating the capacity of television to recreate the imaginary community of the nation in its own (that is, television's) image. Then came the transformation of television by the VCR into a new means of distribution, and therefore consumption, of films. But neither of these developments reduced the demand for films as such. On the contrary, in Latin America, again like everywhere else, television and video have expanded the market through the recapitalisation of cinema by means of new technology, leaving cinema to demonstrate its cultural power in retaining, despite intensified competition with rival forms of entertainments, the highest cultural prestige for all its main audiences – popular or aficionado, urban youth, or the media world itself.

But perhaps the most critical and binding element in the crisis, for a cinema founded on a political conception of itself, was the transformation of the political space in which it operated, through the democratic turn of the 1980s. This, according to the more astute commentators, was a process supervised by Washington in which the neo-fascist counter-revolutions of the 1970s were replaced by the normalisation of their right-wing policies under the guise of democratisation – as exemplified by the career of Bolivia's dictator General, later elected President, Hugo Banzer. In short, dictatorships have come and gone, leaving governments mostly beholden, despite contrary signs here or there, to neo-liberal doctrines of the free market which only exacerbate unequal exchange and underdevelopment. Crippling foreign debt became a permanent factor; ecological damage has reached crisis proportions; communications and entertainment have been transformed by the spectacular growth of informatics, in a new phase of uneven development. Already in 1991, an Argentinian film by Miguel Pereira, *La última siembra* (1991), traces the arrival of these tendrils in the rural hinterland, where the son of an ageing landowner returns to the estate from studying in the US to modernise the business and introduce the latest techniques, a process which begins when he sets up a mast, affixed to the church spire, to link his communications – telephone, fax and computer – to his hoped-for partner back in the States. In the end, these changes amount to the passage from the older economic imperialism of what Eric Hobsbawm has called the short twentieth century, which ended with the collapse of the Soviet Union in 1991, to the unhindered globalisation of the transnational capitalist economy following the end of the Cold War. The moment of postmodernism has definitely arrived.

Like everywhere else the first effects of postmodernism are to sow confusion, and the urgent need to rethink became the theme of the seminar at the Havana Film Festival in 1987, which had meanwhile become the movement's most important annual gathering. A central strand of debate, according to Aufderheide's useful account (2000), was the loss of relationship to the audience. The effects of television and democracy on a cultural politics nurtured on revolutionary resistance to dictatorship was seriously disorienting (except in Cuba, where the revolution was in power, leading to different sorts of problems) – because audiences were no longer engaged in the same ethos of resistance as before, and without it, the movement's self-declared mandate for radical aesthetic innovation was weakened. Indeed, despite the fillip of the Sandinista victory in Nicaragua in 1979, the overall trend of the 1980s was inexorable – and even in Cuba, which was not immune to wider cultural shifts, the new cinema was becoming more populist.

For some, the source of the crisis was clearly political, or rather, the loss of the political. When the founder of the Cuban Film Institute, Alfredo Guevara, began by speaking in the same old way of 'the sacred nexus between militancy and poetics', Mexican producer Jorge Sánchez immediately objected: 'But the political vanguard doesn't even exist now' – *nota bene*: this is still two years before the Sandinistas lost the elections in Nicaragua, and three years before the collapse of communism in Eastern Europe – 'Not only is it not like 1967, but there is no coherent left vision in Latin America, except in Cuba' (Aufderheide 2000: 244). Nevertheless, for some of the original members of the movement, this did not invalidate the original aims. As García Espinosa asked, 'Why did we call it *New* Latin American cinema? Because we were disappointed in what the old cinema was doing, creating a vernacular version of the worst codes of Hollywood, and opening the doors to the worst kind of pseudo-culture' (quoted in Aufderheide 2000: 250). This target was still the same, if anything, even more so. However, this was not the mantra of someone caught in the past, trying to hold on to outdated verities – García Espinosa, the proponent of imperfect cinema, was in the thick of it, transforming the Cuban Film Institute of which he was then president. If they had lost their link with the audience, he said, they needed a new language. But others saw the situation more starkly. In the blunt words of the Venezuelan filmmaker Carlos Rebolledo, 'For aesthetic, moral and historical reasons, we cannot continue deceiving ourselves with an alternative, sporadic and unequally national cinema. Either we definitively enter the world of the Spectacle, or we are stuck lagging behind in a trivial farce' (quoted in Aufderheide 2000: 245). (In 2006, García Espinosa is still fighting his corner, but now as the head of the International Film and Television School at San Antonio de los Baños, near Havana.)

The Spanish film critic Manuel Pérez Estremera took the more sober view that whatever the advantages and dangers, Latin American cinema was identified abroad with the New Latin America Cinema movement, which was deeply characterised by its dignity and humanist realism. There was a danger that the search for a bigger public and foreign markets was taking this cinema 'away from its thematic and narrative roots'. Moreover, the effort was destined to failure, because the big foreign commercial markets were effectively closed. What Latin American films could do, however, was offer the smaller niche-markets 'variety, imagination, history, original and popular literary achievements, political and ethical engagement, youth, self-criticism, expressive rigour, analysis of one's own identity and low costs' (quoted in Aufderheide 2000: 246–7). One could argue with Pérez Estremera's reading of the market. The Spanish critic avoids the difficult question of the growing Hispanic audience in the United States. On the other hand, from the perspective of 2006 it seems very prescient. And there is no argument that the process operates internationally and has serious implications for the kinds of films that get made. This is the reality of the global economy. As if the only markets that the transnational corporations have not carved up between them are niche markets, but these too are highly competitive, where none of the qualities you have to sell are good enough if you cannot keep it cheap.

Clearly Latin American cinema was shifting ground, and by the turn of cinema's first century and then the millennium, talk of liberation, along with the experimentalism of the 1960s, were both highly attenuated. The sense of political urgency which exploded on the screens in the 1960s has gone, along with the iconoclasm of its visual and narrative language. The visual style – with marked exceptions like *Amores Perros* – is much smoother and more controlled, as in the cinematography of Walter Carvalho for the films of Walter Salles. At the same time, Latin American cinema has taken up a number of genres more or less repudiated by *el nuevo cine latinoamericano* as ideologically suspect, such as melodrama, science fiction and even horror (like, respectively, Arturo Ripstein's *Profundo Carmesí* (*Deep Crimson*, 1996), Eliseo Subiela's *Hombre mirando al sureste* (*Man Looking South-East*, 1986) and Guillermo del Toro's *Cronos* (1991)). At the same time, given the nature of today's international film market (more about this in a moment), co-productions are the order of the day, in which Latin American filmmakers have often turned, willingly or unwillingly, to trading on the exotic.

However, none of this indicates quite the kind of *volte face* it seems to imply. There are certain continuities. Twenty years ago, for example, Jameson (1986) spoke of third world films as 'necessarily allegorical', because even when narrating apparently private stories they turn on metaphors of the inextricable links between the personal and the political, the individual and the national, the private and the historical. The thesis was controversial and certainly needs certain qualifications, but in many examples since then, this allegorical function remains very much to the fore, and even reproduces itself within the new generic framework. Here I am thinking of the use of science fiction in a number of recent Argentinian films – *Hombre Mirando al sureste*, Gustavo Mosquera's *Moebius* (1996), Fernando Spinner's *La Sonámbula* (1998) – which all function to create allegories of the disappeared, or the seeming amnesia which followed the dirty war.

There are also several examples of films which announce their cousinhood to the styles associated with postmodernism in first world cinema. *Amores Perros* has been compared by various critics in North America and Europe with Quentin Tarantino, although in that case it is the latter who comes off much the worse. Pulver alludes to this question in referring to techniques 'culled from a background in Latin American music video and commercials' (he also mentions that Katia Lund, co-director of *City of God*, previously worked on a Michael Jackson video, *You don't care about us*). This cousinhood of style is implicitly taken to confirm the passage of Latin American cinema to the postmodernism associated with globalisation. The question is, if this is indeed so, can it be the same postmodernism as in the North?

In Perez Estremera's comments in Havana in 1987, we can recognise an early reading of the characteristics of the globalised market place in cinema. If this is not in fact so very different from before, that is because cinema had globalising tendencies from the very start. If you compare the economic conditions of the 1960s with today, then from the point of view of the individual film producer, they are not so different either. Take Carlos Sorín's wonderfully bathetic film, *La película del rey* (*A King and His Movie*, 1986), ostensibly about a French visionary of the nineteenth century who, supported by several indigenous tribes, makes himself King of Patagonia, but which actually recounts a young filmmaker's desperate attempt to make a costume drama while struggling against an inhospitable location, the desertion of the cast and no money. A kind of dramatised documentary of the everyday life of filmmaking in Argentina – the pre-title sequence is the director making his pitch to a couple of producers, then they are holding auditions for the male lead, and so it proceeds – it is not only a very good demonstration of why the epic is not a well-developed genre in Latin American cinema, but at the same time serves as an allegory of underdevelopment. The final irony is that despite winning an award at the Venice Film Festival, the film failed to cover its costs.

Sorín's film exemplifies the situation of cinema which still obtains today throughout Latin America, that of a series of medium to small, sometimes tiny, national film industries, all of them plagued by structural weakness and small markets, condemned to marginalisation by global distributors. If these distributors wield power in the cultural field, their habitus is quite different from that of the critics, with whom they nevertheless have a symbiotic relationship. The latter are among the targets of the industry's public relations activities, but some of them have a penchant for challenging the industry's norms and seeking to expand the distributors' acceptable range of possibilities – if only because the critic increases their symbolic capital, and therefore their cultural power, by picking out winners.

As long as this world of public relations is centred on film festivals like Sundance in the US and Cannes, Berlin or Venice in Europe, both critic and distributor are tied to an ethos dominated by a North American/European axis, which leaves Latin American cinema marginalised yet again. Nonetheless, they keep coming. There is a constant and complex need, on both sides of the North Atlantic, for films that break the mould, for example through aesthetic beauty or novelty, always combined in suitably digestible form with social awareness and human concern. Hence the succession of critical enthusiasms for various other cinemas, what Pulver calls the jostling for 'the international cinematic crown held in recent years by Iran, Hong Kong and China', which goes back to the 'discovery' in the 1950s of directors like Satyajit Ray and Akira Kurosawa, followed in the 1960s by *el nuevo cine latinoamericano*. And now, *la buena onda*.

Underdevelopment theory posited that underdevelopment hinders the process of modernisation and causes uneven development, a formulation which can all too easily support assumptions about third world backwardness. This is particularly misleading when it comes to the cultural field, which positively encourages the expression of historical contradictions.

For example, as Nestor García Canclini (1995) sees it, from a Mexican perspective, Latin American culture is shaped by contradictions between cultural traditions with different forms of rationality (the indigenous, Catholic colonial Hispanicism, modernising liberalism) which end up, through uneven development, as different historical temporalities that coexist in the same present (Fredric Jameson has a similar reading of magical realism), whose result has been to generate hybrid formations in all social strata. Indeed popular religion and culture in Latin America are themselves hybrids, in which symbolic discourses from different origins – pre-Colombian, European and African – are blended in different combinations in syncretistic fusion. As every self-respecting radio presenter of world music nowadays explains, this is what accounts for the richness and variety of popular and so-called folkloric musics of the entire continent, north as well as south.

There is an affinity between the idea of cultural hybridity in Canclini and Teshome Gabriel's (1982) interpretation of the evolution of third cinema and his interest in the interstices between the categories; the mixing of genres across boundaries both aesthetic and territorial; the expansion of impure genres; the break-up and renewal of symbolic representation and discourse through the constant interaction of the local with the national and the transnational. All these factors have come to the fore with postmodernism, but which Canclini argues are inherent in the Latin American condition.

This is why we find other cultural critics in Latin America, like José Joaquin Brunner, speaking of the continent's cultural heterogeneity as a kind of postmodernism *avant la lettre*, and already present within modernism; or why Fernando Calderón believes that the 1960s (which he calls 'years of a tragic and lucid schizophrenia') gave rise not only to modernist, but even postmodernist, impulses (1995: 40, 59). Carlos Rincón goes further: speaking of the writing of García Márquez, Julio Cortázar, Carlos Fuentes and others, he suggests that not only were they rapidly incorporated into the international canon of literary postmodernism, but they represent a constituent element of the postmodern condition, through the force of their alterity, their de-centred and de-centring relationship to the metropolis (1995: 224). All these perspectives raise critical questions about the cultural relations implied by underdevelopment theory, insofar as the conventional picture is a route that always leads from the centre to the periphery, which is consequently always a step behind. It is more as if, in the effort to catch up, the periphery starts moving ahead of itself, which gives rise to what Santiago Alvarez once called 'accelerated underdevelopment'.

Apologists for globalisation are given to argue that the world economy is now so integrated that the particularities of the local and the framework of the nation-state are increasingly irrelevant; place, on this reading, is a matter of the reduction of difference to background decoration. This is not what you see in Latin American cinema. Instead what you get is a continuing imperative to bear witness to local histories which takes us to the interstices, the margins, and the peripheries – I am thinking of films like Solveg Hoogerstein's *Macu, la mujer de policía* (Venezuela, 1987), Víctor Gaviria's *Rodrigo D: No futuro* (Colombia, 1990) and *La vendedora de rosas* (Colombia, 1998), Sergio Cabrera's *La estrategia del caracol* (Colombia, 1993), or again of course, *Amores Perros*, all of which take us into the urban interstices.

. In the same way but in a different vein are a number of films of internal exile, in the judicial, not the psychological sense, where an individual who has offended against the dictatorship is banished to some remote part of the country. The prime examples, not surprisingly, come from Chile, like Pablo Perelman's *Archipiélago* (1992) and Ricardo Larraín's *La Frontera* (1991); films where the spatial discourse encompasses an existential drama which serves as an allegory of the country's enforced political silence. In Argentina, a similar preoccupation turns up in films about the amnesia of the dirty war, like Alejandro Agresti's *La boda secreta* (1989). In each case, these are films located in remote and marginal zones, the most peripheral regions within the national territory; zones of underdevelopment within underdevelopment (which of course is nothing new in Latin American cinema). Even a film like Alfonso Arau's *Como agua para chocolate* (*Like Water for Chocolate*, 1992) which rehearses Mexican nationality through the exotic combination of magical realism, food and revolution, is at the same time a film of the borderlands, like another recent Mexican film, Maria Novaro's *El jardín de Edén* (1994). Above all, I think of Adolfo Aristarain's *Un lugar en el mundo* (*A Place in the World*, 1992). Here the narrative is realist and perfectly explicit, but the eponymous place is profoundly allegorical. Its location within representational space – that amalgam of space and place which is constituted by the screen – functions as a social microcosm, as a character in the drama, and as the crossroads of a certain set of geographies, a space which gains its resonance because the world in which such a place is located is multi-layered and multi-dimensional.

What comes to light from this brief and very incomplete survey are certain trends which seem to be shared by filmmakers across the continent, a highly variegated output which shows an unfolding of tendencies already present in the paradigm of a cinema of radical difference which preceded the present phase. If this is postmodernism, it is something like the realisation of a project which began in the moment of modernism, in which the imaginary Latin Americas of screen representation were constantly and repeatedly fractured and split, a cinema which would represent images and voices of what was previously forbidden territory, the heterogeneity below the surface of underdevelopment, an ethos which meant that on principle no one could rule out in advance any propensity which might arise in the attempt to constantly develop cinematic language. But in that case there would be no break between the moments of modernism and postmodernism but an extension of immanent tendencies, and Canclini is right to speak of a sociological continuity in Latin America between the modernist vanguards of the past, and the postmodern art that only appears to reject them.

This consciousness of multiplicity is indeed a crucial part of what we mean by postmodern sensibility, but it takes on different aspects according to where you are seeing it. In the metropolis it spells de-centring and loss of conviction in the old history, but in the third world, it re-inscribes the periphery as a site of counter-narrative, or to borrow a phrase from Jameson, a new type of historicism. Rincón has criticised Jameson on the grounds that he operates with an overarching concept of 'the experience of colonialism and imperialism', which represses differences within the cultures of the periphery. But the difference between these two commentators is complementary – it comes precisely from looking at the same set of phenomena from opposite sides. This would be the answer, then, to my leading question, whether the postmodernism of contemporary Latin Cinema is the same postmodernism as ours in the North. The answer is ... the same, but also different ('diversity in unity'). The same because it is a constitutive part of the contemporary world; different because this world remains asymmetrical, both in economics and in cultural positioning, and this asymmetry is an integral part of the same postmodernism. It is a quality of difference in which the viewer discovers the deep humanity which makes these films so compelling. Or in Jacques Derrida's word, *différance*.

## Notes

1   See 'Wind from the East', in *Weekend and Wind from the East* (1972), trans. M. Sinclair and D. Adkinson. London: Lorrimar Publishing, 164–5.
2   A similar dynamic is at work today in Argentina. In the wake of the *Argentinazo* of December 2001, when the banks put up shutters, the country defaulted on its international debt, and then got through five presidents in twelve days, a new video documentary movement known as *cine piquetero* has grown exponentially.

## Works cited

Aufderheide, P. (2000) *The Daily Planet*. Minneapolis: University of Minnesota Press.
Brunner, J. J. (1995) 'Notes on Modernity and Postmodernity in Latin American Culture', in J. Beverley, M. Aronna and J. Oviedo (eds) *The Postmodernism Debate in Latin America*. Durham: Duke University Press, 34–54.
Calderón, F. (1995) 'Latin American Identity and Mixed Temporalities; Or, How to Be Postmodern and Indian at the Same Time', in J. Beverley, M. Aronna and J. Oviedo (eds) *The Postmodernism Debate in Latin America*. Durham: Duke University Press,

55–64.

Chanan, M. (2004) *Cuban Cinema* (second edition). Minneapolis: University of Minnesota Press.

Cox, A. (2000) 'Lights, camera, election', *Guardian*, 26 February.

Gabriel, T. H. (1982) *Third Cinema as the Third World: The Aesthetics of Liberation*. Ann Arbor, MI: UMI Research Press.

García Canclini, N. (1995) *Hybrid Cultures: Strategies for Entering and Leaving Modernity*, trans. C. L. Chappari and S. L. López. Minneapolis: University of Minnesota Press.

Jameson, F. (1986) 'Third World Literature in the Era of Multinational Capitalism', *Social Text*, 15, 65–88.

_____ (1992) *Signatures of the Visible*. London and New York: Routledge.

Pulver, A. (2002) 'Follow that chicken', *Guardian*, 24 May.

Rincón, C. (1995) 'The Peripheral Center òf Postmodernism: On Borges, García Márquez, and Alterity', in J. Beverley, M. Aronna and J. Oviedo (eds) *The Postmodernism Debate in Latin America*. Durham: Duke University Press, 223–40.

Salles Gomes, P. E. (1997) 'Cinema: A Trajectory within Underdevelopment', in M. Martin (ed.) *New Latin American Cinema, Vol. 2*. Detroit: Wayne State University Press, 263–71.

Solanas, F. and O. Getino (1997) 'Towards a Third Cinema: Notes and Experiences for the Development of a Cinema of Liberation in the Third World', in M. T. Martin (ed.) *New Latin American Cinema, Vol. 1*. Detroit: Wayne State University Press, 33–58.

# PART TWO

# Crossing Boundaries

# CHAPTER FOUR

# Export mythology: primitivism and paternalism in Pasolini, Hopper and Herzog
Keith Richards

In the context of relationships between metropolitan centres of production and peripheral potential markets, cinema has long been a vehicle for cultural and economic penetration. The invasive quality of film is, of course, most clearly demonstrable in commercial cinema, its domination of distribution networks and crafting of seductive imagery. Studies of imperialism in cinema range from technical through psychological and political elements. Daniel Dayan (1999: 129) has referred to classical cinema as a 'ventriloquist of ideology', alluding to the concealment of codes in the creation of the narrative film as a replica of reality. Frantz Fanon (1986: 152–3) has acknowledged the importance of film as part of a cultural 'constellation of postulates' reinforcing subliminal notions of race. Fredric Jameson (cited in Bordwell & Carroll 1996: 481) is among those to have attested to the hegemonic role inherited by cinema from literature. Metropolitan film exercises a dual function, bolstering dominance in both economic and cultural terms.

But a rather different set of questions is raised by cinema that involves location filming in previously colonised lands. At issue here are the effects of conspicuous opulence and the complex paraphernalia of filmmaking upon local populations, as well as the discourse conveyed in the final product. Christine Bolus-Reichert (1998), for instance, talks of a paradoxical tendency in late twentieth-century French films made in former colonies, offering critiques of colonialism whilst still subscribing, albeit knowingly, to its discourse and iconography. The work of Claire Denis, Bertrand Tavernier and Jean-Jacques Annaud in Africa can also be understood as a form of postcolonial self-examination:

> In all of these postcolonial representations of the colonial period, there is a strong tendency to revert to familiar aesthetic and cognitive patterns – an imaginary geography which still locates identity in the landscape or power relations figured in the tales of travellers. All seem to be ironically aware of their own nostalgia ... or reactionary position. It is from this precarious position that each of these postmodern directors criticises the colonial narrative and at the same time displays that which made it so appealing and sustaining for more than five hundred years. (1998: 184)

Moreover, the question of neo-imperialist filmmaking is not limited to relationships between former masters and slaves, a former power returning with a neo-colonial cinematic project. Travel-based films can reassert latent myths of European supremacy without overt reference to any particular colonial presence. Unlike the French instances mentioned above, none of the three films I will discuss here (made by Italians in Central Africa, North Americans and Germans in Peru) emanate from former colonial masters of the lands chosen as locations, yet all display clear neo-colonial precepts.

Of course, a foreign presence is not necessarily pernicious: Ana López considers that 'the figure of the traveling filmmaker – and the foreigner's gaze – as a site for tracing the mediation of nation is potentially a key for opening up a space for transnational analyses of the classic Latin American cinema' (2000: 35). López refers to practices of the 1930s to the 1950s but her focus is on the value of outside perspectives in dealing with local conditions and the questionability of an overly national paradigm. As will be seen below, there is the possibility of a form of Bakhtinian cultural interaction in which mutual enrichment occurs between foreign filmmakers and local imaginaries.

Cultural intrusion, though, demonstrably exists and can be at its most conspicuous when unintentional: in experimental auteur projects shot in remote locations, particularly those inhabited by indigenous or tribal peoples. Hollywood, like other metropolitan centres of production, propagates social models and rationalises neo-imperialist positions recognisable even through their encoding. As Robert Young (1990) reminds us, Europe was formed by the experience of empire at least as much as the colonies themselves, and European thinking is inextricably linked to that reality. Young quotes Fanon's observation that 'Europe is literally the creation of the Third World' (1990: 119). Nonetheless paternalism can unconsciously surface in the work of independent filmmakers who may profess sympathetic, or even revolutionary, sentiments towards their subject. As with the writings of early chroniclers in the Americas, Third World film locations often become a *tabula rasa* upon which the cineaste's pet concerns may be explored – sometimes with minimum attention paid to the reality of the area visited. This applies more often to cultures that do not display material sophistication and visible infrastructure. If the generally accepted (material, sedentary) manifestations of civilisation do exist, then an ethnocentric template is laid over them and distortion may still proceed with impunity. But what happens when the filmmaker's project makes clear reference to itself as artifice, and even openly acknowledges the medium's intrusive potential?

This chapter investigates three productions, all of which display some form of consciousness of the effects of filmmaking upon the environments they visit. One is a documentary partly concerned with this very problem, whilst another is a 'work in progress' for a proposed later project and the third a metafictional film-within-a-film. All, moreover, are shot in locations that present numerous pitfalls: the temptation to exploit their exoticism is strong, and genuine understanding of local conditions difficult to acquire. Remote 'Third World' locations offer various forms of escape from the constraints of filming at home, undeniably compensating for logistic difficulties by offering the filmmaker a certain licence to fabricate, particularly as regards a home audience untutored in anthropology, or predisposed towards some suspension of disbelief. 'Exotic' or 'primitive' landscapes and peoples can provide a backdrop far enough removed from metropolitan reality to become neutral, a colourful but circumstantial frame for the film's concerns.

This chapter was suggested by a viewing of the 1975 film *Appunti per un'Orestiade africana* (*Notes for an African Orestes*) by Pier Paolo Pasolini, a filmmaker widely admired for his uncompromising cinematic strategy and radical efforts towards a poetics and politics of film. My own subscription to this view was shaken by what revealed itself as an example of 'unthinking eurocentrism' (to borrow Ella Shohat and Robert Stam's phrase) that is well intentioned, certainly accentuated by changes in our perceptions during the intervening years, but nonetheless transparent. This film followed two other efforts by Pasolini at filming the Third World realities for which his concern is at first sight undeniable: *Sopraluoghi in Palestina per il vangelo secondo Matteo* (*Locations in Palestine for The Gospel According to St Matthew*, 1964) and *Appunti per un film sull'india* (*Notes for a Film on India*, 1969). He also nursed the idea of a Third World film cycle that would have embraced Asia, Africa and Latin America but was never realised. As Sam Rohdie (1995: 85–7) has pointed out, the three films on Palestine, India and Africa deploy classical analogical texts that are intended to comment upon contemporary realities. But whilst Pasolini uses Matthew's Gospel for Palestine, and a sub-continental fable for the Indian film, the Aeschylus trilogy is far less immediately applicable to an African setting. This transposition of Greek tragedy to Africa smacks of a set of cultural assumptions curiously at odds with his declared internationalism and filmic celebrations of tribal cultures. His project, to transpose the play in the newly independent states of Uganda and Tanzania, was never brought to fruition, but what remains is a puzzling and self-contradictory array of disparate images and oddly incoherent voiceover commentary. Here the cinematic medium, allied with Pasolini's cultural preconceptions, results in a palpably alienating mechanism. Africans are filmed not for themselves, but for what resemblance they suggest to Aeschylus' characters. Similarly the African situation is forced into the mould of Greek political development.

This is reminiscent of a number of other cinematic efforts at resolving or at least exploring the contradictions presented by filmmaking in non-industrialised countries. The two films to be discussed alongside Pasolini were made by foreigners in Latin America. Whilst the vast differences between these two continents are undeniable, there are certain parallels between Pasolini's *Notes for an African Orestes*, Dennis Hopper's *The Last Movie* (1970) and the Les Blank documentary *Burden of Dreams* (1982). Whilst only Hopper's film is what Robert Stam (1992) would call 'reflexive', in that it calls attention to its own processes of production and reception (as well as those of film itself), all three deal in some way with other cinematic projects, whether unfinished (Pasolini), fictional (Hopper) or observed (Blank). All are evidence of the difficulties of filmmaking in the context of indigenous cultures remote from the metropolis, which presents problems both logistical and ethical. Whether these cultures are used as thematic background or as object of study, film appears doomed by its very nature to misrepresent and even betray its chosen other. Is this necessarily the case? The mythical element in all three films belongs to two types: firstly, the individual and cinematic mythology generated by flamboyant personalities and extravagant projects and the demands of genre. Secondly, there is the cultural paraphernalia introduced to incongruous settings: Greek tragedy to Africa (Pasolini); the western to Andean Peru

(Hopper); opera and the German Romantic tradition to the Amazon rainforest (Werner Herzog, examined by Blank). Mythology in various ways provides the impetus for each of the projects and largely explains the considerable efforts undergone by each filmmaker. In each case myth is a kind of cultural mirage, simultaneously drawing the filmmaker into a far-flung location and insulating him from its reality.

The voiceover commentary of *Notes for an African Orestes* anticipates the full realisation of a vision destroyed with the brutal murder of Pasolini in 1975. Instead we are left to judge the film as it stands, comprising four interdependent but distinct strands. Firstly there is the material filmed on 16mm by Pasolini himself in Africa; then a series of newsreel clips taken from footage of the Biafran war; thirdly a debate between the filmmaker and a group of African students at the University of Rome; and finally a musical performance featuring two African-American singers and a three-piece jazz band fronted by the Argentine saxophonist Gato Barbieri.

There are a number of possible objections to Pasolini's approach to Africa. Some of these, it must be said, are redundant in that he conceives of Africa as part of a political and aesthetic universe rather than in any real or documental sense. Nonetheless, it is striking that he quite unapologetically imposes a European paradigm, the Orestes tragedy being presented as analogous to the so-called birth of democracy in the African continent. Ancient Greece is presented unquestioningly as a model for political and cultural development, a discursive position not very far removed from that of the European imperialists he abhorred. Furthermore, as Edith Hall (1991: 204–10) has pointed out, the tragic genre was instrumental in defining Greek identity through differentiation from the Barbarian, a crucial contribution to the imperialist imaginary. Maurizio Viano (1993: 255) asserts that Pasolini was before his time in attempting to blend mythology and ideology, refusing Marxist orthodoxy. But the mythology used in this case is misplaced, serving only to bolster a poetics that opposes reality with representation. It is an imperialist mythology placed at the service of an ostensibly revolutionary ideology. Rohdie argues that 'fundamentally, Africa is superfluous to Pasolini's films about Africa'. He sees the Third World essentially as in metaphorical opposition to the consumerist world he despised, as a repository of the instinctual, irrational states he prized (but sought, paradoxically, to civilise). Hence the historical factors ignored in the conception of his *Orestiade*, such as the existence of advanced civilisations in ancient Africa and the African contribution to Greek culture.

Pasolini's voiceover commentary glibly 'casts' passers-by and onlookers who have little apparent contact with the outside world and are never consulted about either their experience of African 'democracy' or their reaction to his project. These subjects, seen and not heard, are as much part of the general landscape as the windswept trees that, according to Pasolini's narration, evoke the 'solitude of Africa', or the lions that might be cast as the Furies. The filmmaker's assertion that the spectacle must be 'profoundly popular' elides the issue that the Africans filmed here would not know Aeschylus' play and could have had only the most peripheral role in producing it. This brings to mind Alberto Moravia's description, given in an interview with Renzo Paris, of Pasolini's Marxism as 'absolutely non-scientific but curiously Christian' (quoted in Pasolini 1990: 118); a messianic conception of political development and a populist rather than horizontal outlook. Pasolini's stress upon the popular is contradicted also by his choice of interlocutor: rather than interview the people filmed on location, he consults a group of middle-class African students at the University of Rome. The debate takes place after a screening of his material rather than before embarking on the project. This need for reassurance as to the validity of his film is at odds with the non-documental, poeticised approach he has taken. When the Africans express misgivings over such points as the viability of the democracy left behind by the Europeans, or the filmmaker's focus on tribalism, they are either humoured or simply misunderstood. Moreover, Pasolini expects the students (mainly from Northeast Africa) to be able to speak of the continent as a whole – a generalisation compounded by the inclusion of scenes from the Biafran war as though these were directly relevant to Uganda and Tanzania. There is a sequence in which Pasolini's words are dubbed into English but not those of his African interlocutors whose Italian and French is left in the original. If this oversight can be attributed to the distributor, no such excuse applies to the musical sequence in which the African-American singers are drowned out almost completely by Barbieri and his rhythm section.

Attilio Coco (1995) speaks of the utopianism of Pasolini's poetic-political vision, a term that could also apply to the questionable practicality of some of his suggestions for filming. Orestes is also Utopian in the sense of pertaining to 'no place', since it wilfully bypasses all manner of geographical, cultural and historical factors in presenting a composite Africa bereft of any cultural specificities. That the 1960s saw the first instance of democracy in black Africa is questionable, and surely indefensible even as part of a poetic construct. Africa is dehistoricised in much the same way as that denounced in Edward Said's *Orientalism* (1979); for example Pasolini sees the Ugandan city of Kigoma as 'still close to prehistoric times', yet its buildings are 'recent, there was probably only a little market here before'. In his effort to allegorise and celebrate African independence, he falls into almost every trap provided by the colonial legacy; stripping Africa of its own heritage he attributes both the concept of social order, and the means by which it is achieved, to Europe.

Film in Latin America has long been prone both to suffer and inflict what Stephen Hart (2002) in his discussion of Jorge Sanjinés' film *Para recibir el canto de los pájaros* (*To Receive the Birds' Song*, 1995) has termed 'cultural invasion'. As Hart points out, Sanjinés set out partly to counteract the effects of misrepresentation of the indigenous in film, seeking a film language that would faithfully render Andean culture by using elements of native aesthetics. Sanjinés is entirely aware of the pitfalls, and if arguably not able fully to resolve them with this film he nonetheless shows a cultural sensibility rare amongst even today's Latin American filmmakers. Rather than discussing native-born but non-indigenous outsiders, though, I have chosen to focus on those from other continents seemingly attracted either by picturesque and exotic locations or the political and cultural significance of the region. There are numerous other cases of filmmakers from Europe or the USA working in Latin America. The following examples do not interrogate the process of filmmaking itself, but do provide insights into various attitudes. *Orfeu Negro* (*Black Orpheus*, 1958), made in Brazil by the Frenchman Marcel Camus, was based on a play by Vinicius de Morães but panned for exploiting the picturesque qualities of Rio's *favelas*. Sergei Eisenstein's *¡Que viva México!*, as Laura Podalsky (1993) has demonstrated, was an example of a foreign filmmaker being enriched by working abroad and drawing influences from the experience. Luis Buñuel's work in Mexico also had a galvanising effect upon the film culture he visited, but as Michael Wood (1993) has shown here too the influence was largely reciprocal.

However there are numerous films that have merely plundered their location as colourful and exotic context, and Dennis Hopper's *The Last Movie* certainly belongs to this category. The Andes here are turned into a backdrop not only for the western action but for the 'offscreen' antics of the cast and crew. *The Last Movie* also renders the natives mute, apart from the non-translated scraps of conversation in Quechua heard during their rituals and processions and non-verbal forms of expression such as music and dance. The most striking performance seen from the Indians, though, is one that has been required of them for the purposes of the script. The 'shadow' filmmaking undertaken as a response to the 'real' western is a response entirely invented by the scriptwriters (Hopper and Stewart Stern) and with no anthropological or ethnographical foundation. It is instigated by an individual, rather than resulting from the collective action common to Andean communities. The response appears to be suggested by the Pacific Island Cargo Cults of World War Two, when local peoples reacted to the activities of Allied troops and their supply planes by building their own propitiatory airstrips in the belief that air cargo would then be brought to them. Similarly the indigenous people portrayed in *The Last Movie* imitate their ostensibly more sophisticated visitors/invaders, assembling replica cameras and other equipment from bamboo.

Whatever their intentions, Hopper and Stern crassly confuse two distinct types of society. Cultures extremely remote from the West and with relatively little experience of contact cannot be equated with Andean societies and their long and traumatic acquaintance with the materialistic values of Europe and the US. Hopper explains that the natives' imitation filming is due to their desire to make a better version of the film, rather than a ritual practice aimed at emulating the *gringos'* wealth and glamour. The Indians, presented as remote and primitive, know about and are fascinated by the legend of Billy the Kid. Perhaps familiarity with this Hollywood staple is taken for granted. This assimilation of western/Western mythology may be seen as an inversion of the decision made by Kansas (the stuntman played by Hopper) to stay on and live in Chinchero. He uncritically adopts the locals' 'unspoiled, elemental' values just as they ape his profession. Kansas becomes a sacrificial victim in the 'bamboo' western, despite attempting to convince the Indians that film violence is pure sham. This is the 'last' film, not just for him but, presumably, ever: the debunking of film artifice is allegedly Hopper's chief aim in this film, accompanying the entrapment of his protagonist. Repetitive cutting of the 'filmed' execution of Kansas implies that his death is interminable, a condition of his existence in this environment. But Kansas does not die, and Hopper refused to 'kill' him off even when it was demanded of him by Universal Studio executives anxious to salvage at least some of their financial investment. Hopper fails to de-mystify cinema, descending instead into a narcissistic maelstrom of self-representation. Thus the sacrificial aspect of Kansas echoes that of the Christ statue carried in the local processions, whilst other archetypes include Billy the Kid himself and, by implication, James Dean. Film becomes as much a ritual activity as the parading of saints at Corpus Christi (accompanied, of course, by the bamboo cameras). A full exposition of the use of religious imagery is explained by Dan E. Burns (1979), as congruent with Hopper's preoccupation with structure, self-realisation resulting from the reconciliation of opposites.

This device of layered narrative, then, adds a further layer to the dimension of the locals and their imitative 'shooting' through the use of religious imagery, and a role-playing scene in the local whorehouse provides another instance of an enactment as parallel or parody of life. Curiously though, the Indians' cultural servility is not entirely passive; rather than simply consuming a finished product (in fact they never see projected images) they are blurring reality and representation. This suggests, again erroneously, that they have little or no experience of fictional representation whereas Andean theatre and storytelling are ancient cultural practices.

As a meditation on the nature of filmic representation and violence (as Hopper claims it to be) *The Last Movie* misses a number of possible targets. The parallel, in terms of self-referential and almost incestuous ritual, between the Catholic religion and the practice of Hollywood-style filmmaking is one example. The use of Peru as a location, after permission to film in Mexico was refused, is another. An exploration of the incongruities thrown up by this situation might have provided some crucial insights and, given that Mexican actors are used regardless, could have helped inject a badly needed dose of irony. The humourlessness of the film doubtless contributed to its lack of critical and commercial success, and invites comparison with *Blazing Saddles* (1974), Mel Brooks' comic yet far more thorough interrogation of the western genre. If Hopper is concerned, as Richard Combs argues (1982: 219–20), with criticising film practice from within rather than from the outside – yet his exegesis uses as backdrop a culture which, despite some attentive photography by Laszlo Kovacs, is essentially disregarded – Hopper's wilful myopia towards the indigenous other amounts to a denial of their culture's very existence in any autonomous or active manifestation. The Indians simply react to what is visited upon them from outside. Whilst Hopper does question film from the inside, he nonetheless does not engage in any worthwhile fashion with the outside. The egocentricity of Hopper's film extends from his own endlessly repeated image to a representation of cinema as necessarily and inevitably narcissistic, not a self-sufficient and open medium but one that is hermetic, contemptuous of external reality.

Les Blank's *Burden of Dreams* contrasts with the efforts of Pasolini and Hopper, not simply because of its relationship with the local Amazonian peoples and their environment. It also deals with the production of a real film, albeit one so fraught with bizarre difficulties as to appear the stuff of magic realism rather than documentary. For the Peruvian critic Reynaldo Ledgard (1984: 81) among others, the filming of Werner Herzog's *Fitzcarraldo* (1982) is ultimately of more consequence than the cinematic result and the film 'becomes a metaphor of its own creation'.

For more than one commentator, Blank's film compares favourably to the project it chronicles. What is particularly interesting about *Burden of Dreams* is its exploration of the parallel between Herzog himself and the historical figure with whom he has become obsessed (the Irish entrepreneur and opera lover Brian Sweeney Fitzgerald). As with his previous Peruvian project, *Aguirre, Wrath of God* (*Aguirre, Der Zorn Gottes*, 1972), Herzog's fascination with a megalomaniac obsessive betrays a desire to emulate, or even surpass, his protagonist's ambition. Hence the famous scene of an entire steamship dragged over an isthmus (rather than the pragmatic solution of dismantling the ship, used by Fitzgerald himself) or the insistence upon filming in near-inaccessible reaches of the Amazon, raising production costs and creating severe logistical problems, in order to lend authenticity to the film. Significantly, Blank was invited by Herzog to record the production, in case *Fitzcarraldo* was never finished. It is an instance of what Jan-Christopher Horak (1986) sees as a careful cultivation of public image on the part of a filmmaker who places himself at the centre of his own mythology. Herzog had long before achieved identification with his own films to the extent that he claimed they are one and the same. Horak argues that Herzog's public persona has been consciously shaped through numerous extravagant gestures as well as by clear parallels with his own characters. Like Fitzcarraldo (and unlike Pasolini and Hopper), Herzog does enter into a relationship with the native peoples he is filming. However this is fraught with ambiguity; production entailed the movement of local people to other areas and their confinement in camps, resulting in tribal conflicts, disease and other problems. The consequent spate of deaths and injuries apparently contradict Herzog's professed concern for the Indians and their cultural survival. His anti-civilisation stance is also reminiscent of Pasolini, but there are crucial differences. Herzog offers no civilising balm of education or reason to tame this unknown other, but simply presents the wilderness as synonymous with the indigenous. The possible loss of both is a central human dilemma that must be explored even at the risk of furthering the destruction. Herzog is entirely aware of the absurdities and contradictions of his enterprise; having earlier declared that after *Fitzcarraldo* he might go to an asylum, he speaks of loving the jungle 'against my better judgement' but laments that it is 'unfinished' and 'prehistorical' [*sic*]. This is a contrast between the primeval and the mediocre: 'In comparison to the articulate vileness and baseness and obscenity of all this jungle ... we only sound and look like badly pronounced sentences out of a stupid suburban novel.' However the Machiguenga, whose territory this is, are accorded a nobility and integrity lacking in their environment. The erosion of their culture is 'a catastrophe and a tragedy': 'I don't want to live in a world in which there are no lions any more or where there are no people like lions, and they are lions.' Herzog is anxious to prevent cultural contamination of the Machiguenga during shooting, having nevertheless exposed them to filmmaking in the first place. His is the classic dilemma faced by anthropologists and cultural conservationists, though in this case inevitably amplified by publicity and the sheer scale of the enterprise.

As with the films of Pasolini and Hopper, the 'real life' filmmaker is the central feature of *Burden of Dreams* (and, effectively, of *Fitzcarraldo*). Blank's film renders Herzog's largely redundant, since it uses much the same elemental imagery and, in so far as either film is concerned with narrative, tells a similar tale of individual will reaching irrational objectives against enormous odds. Again, the difference with Herzog's project (as captured by Blank) is the involvement of the indigenous people. This is neither the naïve puppet-show required by Hopper nor the mute contemplation of the camera captured by Pasolini. Whatever the truth of allegations of ill-treatment by Herzog, the indigenous peoples are clearly willing collaborators, an active element both in the documentary and in the feature. The Aguaruna, having grabbed the opportunity to publicise their cause, criticise Herzog for presenting an antiquated view of them. The Machiguenga, as both Herzog and actor Klaus Kinski testify, are impressive actors, whilst the Campa are another creative presence on the set. *Burden of Dreams* warns against both underestimating the Amazonians' grasp of the potential of audio-visual media, and misrepresenting Herzog's intentions. The German's parable of doomed but inexorable passion, rather than exalting Fitzgerald's individualism, treats it with the same dispassionate scrutiny with which he himself is treated by Blank.

Numerous observations remain to be made and questions posed regarding the representation of tribal cultures. These are suggested both by the films discussed above and by various developments since the early 1980s and the making of *Fitzcarraldo*. Whilst there is not necessarily a steady chronological evolution in tackling this problem, Herzog displays a sympathy and curiosity towards his 'other' signally absent in both Pasolini and Hopper. The last two decades have seen events such as the quincentenary of Columbus' voyages in 1492, provoking a re-evaluation of views of the indigenous in the Latin American context at least. Filmmakers in Mexico, Brazil and the Andean countries began to follow the example of Sanjinés and other directors in looking seriously at filmic images of the '*indio*' and what these reflect upon the modern nation. Many tribal cultures have, of course, also changed during this time, becoming far more exposed to television and mass media but also learning how to manipulate these same elements. The alarm over Amazon deforestation in the 1980s, which conditioned both *Fitzcarraldo* and *Burden of Dreams* among other films, spawned the image of the Indian as capable of self-representation with Amazonian and other indigenous peoples engaged in projects to film and record their own realities in articles such as that by Patricia Aufderheide (1995). Corresponding issues of cultural survival are among the themes taken up by filmmakers in Burkina Faso, Senegal and elsewhere who, since the 1980s, have raised the profile of African cinema. Perhaps the kind of spurious adventurism undertaken by some metropolitan filmmakers will yet contribute to a tendency towards balanced self-representation on the part of marginalised peoples in a coherent new 'Third World' cinema.

## Works cited

Aufderheide, P. (1995) 'The Video in the Villages Project: Videomaking with and by Brazilian Indians', *Visual Anthropology Review*, 11, 2, 83–93.

Blank, L. and J. Bogan (eds) (1984) *Burden of Dreams: Screenplay, Journals, Reviews, Photographs*. Berkeley: North Atlantic Books.

Bolus-Reichert, C. (1998) 'Imaginary Geographies: The Colonial Subject in Contemporary French Cinema', in Cristina Degli-Esposti (ed.) *Postmodernism in the Cinema*. Oxford: Berghahn, 167–85.

Bordwell, D. and N. Carroll (eds) (1996) *Post Theory: Reconstructing Film Studies*. Madison: University of Wisconsin Press.

Burns, D. (1979) 'Dennis Hopper's *The Last Movie*: Beginning of the End', *Literature/Film Quarterly*, 7, 2, 137–47.

Coco, A. (1995) 'Un cinema utopico', *Segnocinema*, 15, 73, 18–21.

Combs, R. (1982) Review of *The Last Movie*, *Monthly Film Bulletin*, 49, 585, 219–22.

Dayan, D. (1999) 'The Tutor-Code of Classical Cinema', in L. Braudy and M. Cohen (eds) *Film Theory and Criticism: Introductory Readings*. Oxford: Oxford University Press, 118–29.

Fanon, F. (1986 [1952]) *Black Skin, White Masks*. London: Pluto Press.

Hall, E. (1991) *Inventing the Barbarian: Greek Self-definition Through Tragedy*. Oxford: Clarendon.

Hart, S. (2002) 'The Art of Invasion in Jorge Sanjinés' *Para recibir el canto de los pájaros* (1995)', *Hispanic Research Journal*, 3, 1, 71–81.

Horak, J-C. (1986) 'W. H. or the Mysteries of Walking in Ice', in T. Corrigan (ed.) *The Films of Werner Herzog*. New York: Methuen, 23–42.

Ledgard, R. (1984) Review of *Fitzcarraldo* and *Burden of Dreams*, *Hablemos de cine* (Lima) 77, 81.

López, A. (2000) 'Crossing Nations and Genres', in Chon Noriega (ed.) *Visible Nations: Latin American Cinema and Video*. London: Minnesota University Press, 33–50.

Pasolini, P. P. (1990 [1960]) *L'odore dell'India*. Parma: Ugo Guanda.

Podalsky, L. (1993) 'Patterns of the Primitive: Sergei Eisenstein's ¡*Que Viva México!*', in Manuel Alvarado, John King and Ana López (eds) *Mediating Two Worlds: Cinematic Encounters in the Americas*. London: British Film Institute, 25–39.

Rohdie, S. (1995) *The Passion of Pier Paolo Pasolini*. London: British Film Institute.

Shohat, E. and R. Stam (1994) *Unthinking Eurocentrism: Multiculturalism and the Media*. London and New York: Routledge.

Stam, R. (1989) *Subversive Pleasures: Bakhtin, Cultural Criticism, and Film*. Baltimore: Johns Hopkins.

____ (1992) *Reflexivity in Film and Literature*. New York: Columbia University Press.

____ (2000) *Film Theory – an Introduction*. London: Blackwell.

Viano, M. (1993) *A Certain Realism. Making Use of Pasolini's Film Theory and Practice*. Berkeley: University of California Press.

Wood, M. (1993) 'Buñuel in Mexico', in Manuel Alvarado, John King and Ana López (eds) *Mediating Two Worlds: Cinematic Encounters in the Americas*. London: British Film Institute, 40–51.

Young, R. (1990) *White Mythologies: Writing History and the West*. London and New York: Routledge.

# CHAPTER FIVE

# Mother lands, sister nations: the epic, poetic, propaganda films of Cuba and the Basque Country
Rob Stone

During the spring of 1968 graffiti appeared all over the Basque Country declaring *Euskadi, Cuba de Europa*: The Basque Country, Europe's Cuba (Antolín 2002: 176). Clearly the sense of isolation and embattled nationhood found empowerment in association. In political and commercial terms there have always been links between the two nations. Many early fortunes made by Basque businessmen at the turn of the twentieth century came from importing Cuban sugar, members of the Basque terrorist group ETA[1] have been given refuge and possibly training in Cuba, while the Basque-language television company Euskal Telebista has co-produced a number of films and television series with its Cuban counterpart, including the popular film *Maité* (Eneko Olasagasti and Carlos Zabala, 1995) and its spin-off television series.[2] It is the connection between film and the political and ideological struggle of the Cubans and the Basques that shall be explored in this comparative analysis of two propagandist films of the 1960s.

During the 1950s both the Cuban revolutionaries and the Basque separatist group EKIN (meaning 'to act'), whose military wing was ETA, drew their ideals and methods from Marxist theory in order to combat the dictatorships of their respective countries: Batista in Cuba and Franco in Spain. Accordingly, committed filmmakers in Cuba and the Basque Country rejected the genres of capitalist Hollywood and the home-grown plethora of jingoistic musicals that had flattered the regimes of Batista and Franco, and they turned instead to the theories and aesthetics of Soviet cinema. Pre-revolutionary Cuba had only a small, colonial film industry that depended upon co-productions with Mexico, while, prior to the Spanish Civil War, Basque filmmakers had made little more than propagandist travelogues by putting their cameras on the fronts of trams and trains. Short documentaries such as *San Sebastián en tranvía* (*San Sebastian by Tram*, 1912), *Paseo en tranvía por Bilbao* (*Bilbao by Tram*, 1912) and *Viaje de San Sebastián a Bilbao* (*Voyage from San Sebastian to Bilbao*, 1912), all produced by Pathé, were made to promote an idea of the Basque Country as a devout, hardworking nation that was proud of its unique culture and traditions, and these documentaries inspired an awareness that Basque cinema could serve as a medium for political ideology in the causes of Basque nationalism and the associated Socialist movement.

However, following the Francoist dictatorship's clampdown on any dissident expression, which included the outlawed Basque language, Basque filmmakers regrouped into semi-secret film clubs and collaborated on developing a cinematic language that would allow them to circumvent the censor. Thus, the rapid montage and dramatically-angled shots of their short, Soviet-styled documentaries on farming, fishing and popular Basque sports were exaggerated so as to symbolise the sharp sounds and erratic rhythm of Euskera, their otherwise forbidden language. A tentative example of this is Néstor Basteretxea and Fernando Larruquert's short film *Pelotari* (1964). The film exhibits staccato jump cuts and repetitive takes of the players of *pelota vasca* (Basque ball) mixed with slow-motion and abrupt fades to black. The clatter of consonants and jagged rhythms of the language were therefore symbolised in this visual metaphor of a montage that replaced the grammar of conventional filmmaking with the grammar of Euskera. Basterretxea and Larruquert, a sculptor and a musician respectively, made other short documentary films on the industry of Huarte and the Holy Week festivities in Alquezar as a way of building up to *Ama Lur* (*Mother Earth*, 1968).[3]

Meanwhile, following the establishment of ICAIC (Instituto cubano del arte e industria cinematográficos/Cuban Institute of Cinematographic Art and Industry) in March 1959, Cuban revolutionary documentarists had similarly begun to construct their documentary features in accordance with the theories of Soviet filmmakers such as Sergei Eisenstein, whose theory of intellectual montage is based upon the effects of juxtaposition, and Lev Kuleshov, whose narrative strategies were based upon ellipses and the gap-filling exercise of the audience. In a documentary genre called *Cine Rebelde* (Rebel Cinema) that was commissioned by Fidel Castro's administration to educate the Cubans in subjects that ranged from the use of machinery to the increasingly mythic exploits of Che Guevara, Cuban filmmakers copied the aesthetics and techniques of films such as Eisenstein's *Battleship Potemkin* (1925) and *October* (1927). Their films served to align Castro's revolution with that of his Soviet predecessors, just as the Basque films were made by dissidents who exalted a similarly Marxist revolution in the Basque Country. Thus, in both post-revolution Cuba and the Basque Country during the Francoist dictatorship, film was at the forefront of the cultural, political and artistic cause of reclaiming and protecting each nation's identity. Both Castro and the dissident Basques understood that film could be the primary exponent of their beliefs and causes because it was a populist medium that enjoyed an immediate, emotional connection with its captive audience.

The Basque film clubs devoured Soviet film theory, while the Cuban film industry benefited from the influx of Russian money, equipment and filmmakers, who came to train and to make their own films on how the Soviet model was being copied elsewhere. Castro was a film fan who understood the power of the medium and made its development a priority, passing a law that demanded re-education through the revolutionary inspiration of culture, entertainment and information. And, if the Basque and Cuban films had remained mere copies of the Soviet model there would not be much more to tell; but, as filmmakers in both nations studied and experimented, their films actually moved away from didactics and ever closer to the cinema of the avant-garde, with extravagant use of symbolism, metaphor and abstraction. In the case of historical representation or reconstruction, the first thing to go was the distinction between fiction and documentary. Filmmakers began to construct expressionist collages of freely-associated images that offered increasingly surreal perspectives on the Cuban and Basque situations, and a few of these films came to resemble epic, poetic meditations on the nature of nationhood that, nonetheless, obeyed the internal logic of their revolutionary causes. Two prime examples are the Cuban-Soviet film *Soy Cuba* (*I Am Cuba*), made in 1963 by Mikhail Kalatosov and Basterretxea, and Larruquert's *Ama Lur*.

Kalatosov was born in Georgia in 1903. His first film was the poetic documentary *Jim Shvante (marili svanets)* (*Salt for Svanetia*, 1930), which portrayed the benefits brought by Soviet power and the construction of a new road to an isolated part of the Caucasian mountains. Between 1945 and 1948 he was in overall charge of Soviet feature film production, and he is probably best known for the film *Letyat zhuravli* (*The Cranes are Flying*), which won the Cannes Palme d'Or in 1958. Shortly after, he led the Soviet mission to encourage film production in Cuba that had as its banner Stalin's remit to promote and legitimise the communist message to Cuba and the rest of the world. *Soy Cuba* was a co-production between Mosfilm and ICAIC, co-written by a Cuban, Pineda Barnet, and a Russian, Yevgeny Yevtushenko. It reconstructs the period leading up to the Cuban revolution as a grand opera, full of absurdly melodramatic gestures and an overwhelming, expressionist aesthetic that aims for an emotional response, believing that ideological reason will follow. It pummels its audience with dizzying camera movements and a chaotic, even bullying, visual rhythm. As Leif Furhammar and Folke Isaksson state, '*Soy Cuba* is more emotional in form than any other revolutionary film' (1971: 164).

*Soy Cuba* is structured in four episodes that show different aspects of life in pre-revolution Cuba. The narrative links are provided by a female voiceover credited as 'La voz de Cuba' ('The Voice of Cuba')[4] and, as Cecelia Lawless describes, 'this "Mother Cuba" becomes a poetic, ethnic personification of place [rather than] a serious placing of Cuba' (1998). The first episode is of a young girl forced into prostitution; the second shows a peasant evicted from his home by a landowner who has sold the land to an American company; the third is of a student revolutionary; and the last episode shows the guerrillas in the Sierra Maestra in the last days of the Batista regime. In each episode the politicised recreation of events is overwhelmed by a strident use of expressionist techniques that render the events as spectacle. *Soy Cuba* is constructed on endless, incredibly intricate handheld single takes, including one around a hotel full of Mafiosi that ends with the camera going into a swimming-pool and filming under-water.[5] The film becomes a *tableaux vivant* of pre-revolutionary Cuba that was never seen outside Cuba or the Soviet Union until 1998.[6] The film is packed full of revisionist sequences that verge on grim parody, such as the group of American sailors singing Frank Sinatra's 'Anchors Aweigh' (from George Sidney's 1945 film of the same name) along the streets of Havana before attempting to gang-rape a Cuban girl. A re-enactment of the student revolt on the steps of the Havana university is self-consciously modelled on the Odessa steps sequence from Eisenstein's *Battleship Potemkin*, while another sequence has the rebels standing up to be counted, stating 'Soy Castro' ('I am Castro') one after another, just like in Stanley Kubrick's *Spartacus* (1960). *Soy Cuba* even plays with film form in a subversive way: halfway through, at the tragic end of the sequence with the peasant, the female voiceover offers the rhetorical 'Who is to blame for so much blood and tears?' and the expressionist flow of images is interrupted by shots of Batista, just as if there were an abrupt interval for newsreel in the cinema, but the camera pulls back and we find ourselves in a drive-in cinema with student protestors throwing molotov cocktails at the screen. The apparent break in the main feature for propagandist newsreel is thus revealed to be a structural ploy by Kalatasov, who subsumes the form and content of pre-revolutionary Cuban cinema into his post-revolutionary, postmodern narrative in which the form is destroyed by new narrative strategies as the content is consumed by the flames onscreen.

Apart from the voiceover, *Soy Cuba*, like the Basque documentaries, does not rely on spoken rhetoric but has its own visual equivalent: stark angles and distorting lenses that turn its protagonists into mythic characters. However, the propagandist remit of 'grab their hearts and their minds will follow' is denied because the cold, formal complexities of the film are not conducive to any emotional involvement. As Lawless states, 'the cinematic Cuba here has become so overwhelmed by impressive technique and a radical dream-like style that the cinema has overshadowed and eventually displaced Cuba to replace it with a make-believe Cuba' (1998). Tolstoy claimed the degree of influence is the only measure of the value of art, but the Cubans responded to this film with great scepticism. 'No Soy Cuba' ('I Am Not Cuba') was the title of a scathing review in a Cuban film journal (Lawless 1998).

The acrobatic camerawork and striking montage employed in Kalatosov's reconstruction simply jarred with the experience of his audience, while the events of the film were too severe in their direction of emotional response. The aforementioned human characters are metaphors for Cuba, which are, sequentially, prostituted, evicted, raped, water-cannoned, bombed and shot, before joining the Rebel Forces in a kind of ecstatic union with the cause that is blessed by a brief, ethereal glimpse of Fidel Castro. *Soy Cuba* is not subtle, partly because the principle of selection that governed its montage eradicated complexity. Cuban filmmakers subsequently rejected the strident aesthetic of the Soviet model and in the films of Tomás Gutiérrez Alea, for example, moved more towards a social realist aesthetic. The lasting irony is that propaganda, even socialist propaganda like *Soy Cuba*, cannot afford to be democratic. It becomes, instead, a totalitarian film form that preaches to the converted. A film such as *Soy Cuba* is an emotional construction in which, to borrow Laura Mulvey's (1975) theory of visual pleasure and narrative, the viewer is obliged to identify either with the revolutionary point of view, or with the object of the revolutionary's desire.

Nevertheless, it is possible that Kalatosov's 'make-believe Cuba' might have been the point. As propaganda, *Soy Cuba* is certainly over-zealous and absurdly bombastic at times; but as an expressionist, poetic, even surreal evocation of the spirit of revolution, the film is almost unique – and I say 'almost' because the Basques were making something similar. Like *Soy Cuba*, *Ama Lur* is a construct of poetic logic that, though it can be deconstructed as a propagandist spin on reality, is actually more of a rhapsodic representation of a Basque utopia. The makers of *Ama Lur*, Nestor Basterretxea and Fernando Larruquert, had developed their technique on short films, but *Ama Lur* was a full-length documentary and, indeed, the first full-length film to have been made in the Basque Country since the Civil War.

Basterretxea and Larruquert began a project called *Euskalherria* (Land of the Basque Speakers) that was to be a compilation of documentary shorts, but could not raise the estimated 4 million pesetas budget. Their producer Frontera Films wrote to

4,000 people requesting donations and received 45 replies amounting to 125,000 pesetas. The project was reorganised into a limited company – Ama Lur, S.A. – that offered shares at 100 pesetas each in 'a film of the people, made by the people' (Gutiérrez, Jáuregui & Maraña 1993: 72); 2,200 shareholders soon provided 4,900,000 pesetas. *Ama Lur* was made without a script, but in order to get a shooting permit its makers had to submit 51 pages of text describing 72 of the possible sequences. It took two years to film and the first rough cut was 11 hours long. It premiered at the 1968 San Sebastian Film Festival but only after much meddling from the censor who demanded, for example, that the word 'España' should be heard three times during the film and that the image of Picasso's painting *Guernica*, which commemorated the bombing of the Basque town, be cut. The censor also ordered that the makers film again a wintry image of the emblematic Tree of Guernica, where Basque leaders traditionally swore their allegiance to ancient Basque laws called *los fueros*, so that the political connotations initially suggested by the tree's bleak bareness would be reversed by a new shot of it in full bloom on a sunny, spring day. Amazingly, the film was allowed to retain its incidental commentary in both Spanish and Euskera, perhaps for the same reason that Santiago de Pablo surmises *Ama Lur* was awarded a top prize in the festival (1995: 68), because of an attempt by Francoism to subsume the film into Spanishness and thereafter refer foreign nations seeking reassurance of human rights to the incident as evidence of a tolerance of pluralism that was truthfully inexistent.

Basterretxea and Larruquert filmed and edited *Ama Lur* themselves, though for union reasons, the cinematography is credited to Luis Cuadrado, director of photography on Carlos Saura's *La Caza* (*The Hunt*, 1965) and Víctor Erice's *El espíritu de la colmena* (*The Spirit of the Beehive*, 1973) who shot only one week out of the 24 months. The same was decreed of the editing, by which an uncredited Basterretxea and Larruquert purposefully imitated the *bertsolari* (the traditional, improvising Basque poet) in their free association of images. This two-hour flow of Basque motifs, traditions and rituals appears experimental, but it obeys an internal logic of national pride, and its accumulating images express a defiant display of Basqueness. In effect, the language of this film is similar to the language of memory. That is to say, the film is a mnemonic, something like a verse to aid memory; a memory of what the Basque Country was like before Franco, and an idea of what it might be again.

Thus, the images flow from a pagan harvest festival in which an idol is burnt to woodsmen lighting torches, to a religious procession, to a play in which the devil appears as a goat, to a flock of sheep, to a montage of photos of Basque shepherds, to a competition between herdsmen whose cows pull blocks of stone, to battling rams, to battling *aizkolari* (the Basque log-choppers familiar from Julio Medem's 1992 film *Vacas*), to weightlifters, to a *pelotari* match, and so on. The film aspires to what its makers described as 'the recuperation of the *bertsolari* that exists in each one of us' (Roldán Larreta 1997: 22) and its poetic vision of the ordinary and commonplace became a poignant source of pride and anger as well as a recurring aesthetic in films by Basque directors such as Víctor Erice and Montxo Armendáriz.[7] Unlike the cold response afforded *Soy Cuba*, *Ama Lur* was a sensation in the Basque Country and inspired many, both politically and artistically.[8]

Why the difference in reception afforded these films? Probably the key difference is their context: *Soy Cuba* is a post-dictatorship film about expressive possibility, while *Ama Lur* was made during a dictatorship and is about the lack of expressive possibility. *Soy Cuba* tells the stories of four individuals, with Kalatosov deliberately choosing non-professional actors for each role, believing that the spectators would, in the third sequence about Pedro the peasant for example, respond to 'a man who carries all the signs of a struggle with the earth and the elements ... a symbol of all the Cuban peasants with their difficult and exploited lives ... a synthetic image of the Cuban peasant [who] has many characteristics of peasants from all countries' (García Borrero 1999: 328). Alternatively, there are no individuals in *Ama Lur*; there is only a collective, a Basque people that is symbolic of nothing but itself. Both films clash with the ethical problem of reconstruction, what Brian Winston derides as 'a tendency to seek the picturesque' (1995: 38), but, where *Ama Lur* is deliberately and uniquely Basque, Pedro the composite peasant is no longer just Cuban but obliged to become a symbol of all the peasants in every socialist country. And, therefore, when compared to *Ama Lur*'s sombre, poetic meditation on a unique ethnography, *Soy Cuba*'s symbolic discourse resembles at best a myth, and at worst a pantomime of a Marxist revolution.

What place art, poetry and film in a revolution? As far back as 1930, Aleksandr Dovshenko challenged the formalism of Eisenstein and Vsevolod Pudovkin with his film *Zemlyn* (*Earth*), which mixed folklore and mysticism with political fervour and achieved a poetic sense of revolution that linked, for example, hard work, rain, Socialism and apples. The challenge pointed out the tension between a poetic perspective and a propagandist one. How to reconcile the two? When Marxist rhetoric is imposed on the filming (as with *Soy Cuba*), the film's 'reality' becomes the product of a single point of view and anyone who disagrees with that reality becomes an enemy of the revolution. That is to say, although rhetoric provides a forum for the argument of social and political issues, it is a forum constructed upon a historically and culturally defining view of the world that protects the centrality of that position and presumes an audience of like-minded individuals. As Aristotle states, 'the political or deliberative orators aim is utility: deliberation seeks to determine not ends but the means to ends' (1990: 158). In other words, rhetoric presumes an end that it functions to serve, just as *Soy Cuba* obliges like-minded individuals to apply Marxist thought to its Marxist puzzles because that is the only way the film can be understood. On the other hand, if the connections between images and events are dependent not on dogma but on the perception and emotion of each individual spectator (as with *Ama Lur*), then the immobile, Marxist concept of reality and its revolutionary promise is just one of many possible perspectives because each and every individual spectator is free to construct his or her own meaning from an abstract flow of imagery. Unlike *Soy Cuba*'s rigid, unrecognisable representation of Cuba and the Cuban Revolution, *Ama Lur* simply presented all the signs and signifiers necessary to render the Basque Country as retellable myth, as a still-possible utopia. Thus, although *Soy Cuba* was made post-dictatorship and *Ama Lur* was made in the middle of one, the irony is that the beleaguered Basque audience was actually freer to construct their film's meaning. And freedom is, after all, the true aim of revolution.

# Notes

1 Euskadi Ta Askatasuna (ETA)/Basque Homeland and Freedom.
2 Eneko Olasagasti and Carlos Zabala co-wrote the script with Senel Paz, who had written the script for Tomás Gutiérrez Alea and Juan Carlos Tabío's classic Cuban film *Fresa y chocolate* (*Strawberry and Chocolate*, 1994). The television series was produced by Euskal Telebista in 1998 and directed by Olasagasti and Zabala.
3 Excerpts from both *Pelotari* and *Ama Lur* appear in Julio Medem's *La pelota vasca: la piel contra la piedra* (*Basque Ball: The Skin Against The Stone*, 2003).
4 The voiceover is credited to Raquel Revuelta.
5 Seen now, this scene recalls a mixture of similar scenes in Martin Scorsese's *GoodFellas* (1990) and Paul Thomas Anderson's *Boogie Nights* (1997), though, of course, *Soy Cuba* was made long before either.
6 Martin Scorsese sponsored the screening of *Soy Cuba* in the US in 1998. *Ama Lur* was finally screened to a public audience in the UK in May 2004 as part of a season of Basque cinema at the National Film Theatre in London that was curated and presented by the author, Rob Stone.
7 As well as *The Spirit of the Beehive* Víctor Erice is the director of *El sur* (*The South*, 1983). Montxo Armendáriz is the director of *Tasio* (1984) and *Secretos del corazón* (*Secrets of the Heart*, 1997).
8 Franco had closed universities in fractious provinces of Spain; Basques and those with an urge to make their own short films and documentaries were obliged to move to Madrid to study at the Official Film School, including Víctor Erice, Imanol Uribe, Iván Zulueta, Eloy de la Iglesia, Antonio Mercero and Pedro Olea.

## Works cited

Antolín, M. (2002) *Mujeres de ETA: piel de serpiente*. Madrid: Temas de Hoy.
Aristotle (1990) 'From Rhetoric', in P. Bizzell and B. Herzberg (eds) *The Rhetorical Tradition: Readings From Classical Times to the Present*. Boston: Bedford, 151–94.
de Pablo, S. (1998) 'País Vasco', in J. M. Caparrós Lara (ed.) *Cine Español: Una historia por autonomias Volumen II*. Barcelona: Promociones y Publicaciones Universitarias, SA, 195–235.
_____ (1995) *Cien años de cine en el País Vasco (1896–1995)*. Vitoria-Gasteiz: Diputación Foral de Alava.
Furhammar, L. and F. Isaksson (1971) *Politics and Film*. London: Studio Vista.
García Borrero, J. A. (1999) *Guía Crítica del Cine Cubano de Ficción*. Cuba: Editorial Arte y Literatura.
Gutiérrez, J. M, G. Jáuregui and F. Maraña (1993) *Haritzaren Negua: 'Ama Lur' y el País Vasco de los años 60*. San Sebastian: Euskadiko Filmategia/Filmoteca Vasca.
Lawless, C. (1998) 'Dispalced Location: Where is Cuba in "Yo Soy Cuba"?', unpublished conference paper, Ithaca College, Cornell University.
Mulvey, L. (1975) 'Visual Pleasure and Narrative Cinema', *Screen*, 16, 3, 6–18.
Roldán Larreta, C. (1999) *El cine del País Vasco: De Ama Lur (1968) a Airbag (1997)*. Don-

osti/San Sebastian: Eusko Ikaskuntza/Sociedad de Estudios Vascos.

Winston, B. (1995) *Claiming the Real: The Documentary Film Revisited*. London: British Film Institute.

# CHAPTER SIX

## The dialectics of transnational identity and female desire in four films of Claire Denis

Rosanna Maule

'It's a bit romantic. I feel like a bit of a foreigner, but I know I'm French. When I was very young I regretted this, I wanted to be anything but French.'

– Claire Denis[1]

French filmmaker Claire Denis' *Chocolat* (1988), *S'en fout la mort* (*No Fear, No Die*, 1990), *J'ai pas sommeil* (*I Can't Sleep*, 1994) and *Beau travail* (1999) examine the troubled intersection of gender, class, ethnicity and cultural identity in colonial and postcolonial society. *Chocolat*, Denis' debut film, investigates class and interracial relations in colonial and postcolonial Cameroon. *S'en fout la mort* and *J'ai pas sommeil* continue this inquiry in 1990s France, dealing with the problems of multicultural integration in Paris. *Beau travail*, the film that marks Denis' return to an African setting, focuses on power relations and masculinity in the French Foreign Legion, via a narrative loosely inspired by Herman Melville's novella *Billy Budd, Sailor*.[2]

My discussion of these four films is premised on a postcolonial and feminist framework, particularly suitable to their focus on Western and non-Western characters' alienation in colonial and postcolonial Africa and France. As a child, Denis lived in several West African countries, including Somalia, Djibouti and Burkina Faso, where her father worked for the French colonial administration. Her representation of cultural identity is predicated upon the critique of the Western concept of Otherness, a position consolidated through her personal experience as a 'child of Africa' who received an anti-racist education, as well as through the reading of French psychiatrist and theorist Frantz Fanon.[3] My purpose here is to demonstrate how *Chocolat*, *S'en fout la mort*, *J'ai pas sommeil* and *Beau travail* propose a critique of the master/servant dialectics lying beneath cultural and gender relations in contemporary Western society.[4]

### The Western woman, the native, and otherness: *Chocolat*, *S'en fout la mort* and (post)colonial identity

To survive, 'Third World' must necessarily have negative *and* positive connotations: negative when viewed in a vertical ranking system – 'underdeveloped' compared to over-industrialised, 'underprivileged' within the already Second sex – and positive when understood sociopolitically as a subversive, 'non-aligned' force. Whether 'Third World' sounds negative or positive also depends on *who* uses it. Coming from you Westerners, the word can hardly mean the same when it comes from us members of the Third World. Quite predictably, you/we who condemn it most are both we who buy in and they who deny any participation in the bourgeois mentality of the West. For it was in the context of such mentality that 'Third World' stood out as a new semantic finding to designate what was known as 'the savages' before the Independences. (Minh-Ha 1989: 97–8)

Denis considers *Chocolat*, *S'en fout la mort* and *J'ai pas sommeil* as a trilogy on post-colonial issues inspired by Fanon's writings (Reid 1996: 69). Indeed, these films seem almost an illustration of Fanon's warning about the complexity involved in the de-colonising process, the deep-rooted violence in the social relationships implied by the colonial system, and the colonising perspective of Western modern culture. Denis' self-conscious rejection of any conciliatory representation of the problems and con-tradictions of colonial and postcolonial society has given her a unique place within a group of filmmakers affected by what Dina Sherzner has labeled the 'colonial syn-drome' of recent French cinema.⁵ Catherine Portuges places Denis among a group of French women filmmakers who in the past twenty years have addressed France's colonial past within 'a cinema of memory, a kind of "colonial féminin" in which border crossings translate into a *mise-en-scène* that destabilises hegemonic ideas of national-ity, sexuality and the family' (1996: 81).⁶ According to Portuges, these films offer more than merely self-promoting exercises in melancholic nostalgia or innocent complicity, for they reinscribe French colonial history within a visual space that – implicitly, if not explicitly – critiques prior erasures of women's subjectivity from the horizon of colonial stories (ibid.).

In *Chocolat*, Denis' effort to depict Africa while staying away from nostalgic or Western-centred biases is parlayed via a French woman emblematically named France, who returns to Cameroon, the country where she had lived with her parents when she was a child.⁷ The trip brings her memories to life, in a long flashback that also consti-tutes the core of the film's narrative. The flashback depicts France's childhood in 1950s Cameroon and the power relations involved in the colonial environment where she lived. The narrative is centred on the dialectic of desire established between Aimée, France's mother, and her 'boy', Protée, paralleled by young France's close relationship with him, equally punctuated by perverse power games, although without sexual un-dertones. The situation, complicated by the interaction with some guests arriving at the farm, is finally disrupted by two interrelated incidents, which also put an end to the flashback and to France's childhood memories. The first episode concerns Aimée's sexual advance to Protée, who proudly turns it down, and is then confined to work outside the house. Soon afterwards, Protée breaks his loyalty to France by letting the girl burn her hand on the hot tube of the generator after having put his hand on its surface to reassure her.

For Portuges, *Chocolat* represents Denis' coming to terms with history through the reconstruction of a childhood trauma, and an index of the filmmaker's 'hybridised positionality' (1996: 83). As Alison Butler notes, quoting Caren Kaplan, in *Chocolat* 'both the colonised and the women colonisers become subjectivities-in-between, both irrevocably changed by their interaction in the new space within which they live and work because of imperialism' (2002: 108).⁸

From this perspective, Protée is a reminder of Fanon's figure of the black colonised body as a humiliated identity objectified by the Western gaze, and France is a symbol of the impossible reconciliation of Western people with their colonial past. The impossibility of such reconciliation is restated in contemporary Cameroon, where the adult France feels a stranger and William J. Park, the African-American man who has migrated to Africa to find his origins, finds himself treated as a foreigner.

Denis' commitment to a transnational and multicultural discourse highlights an important paradox in the representation of non-Western cultures from Western-based theoretical foundations that remain essentially Western-centred in their attempts to disengage themselves from totalising subject positions. This dilemma is the object of Ella Shohat and Robert Stam's critique of Eurocentrism, which they describe as 'the procrustean forcing of cultural heterogeneity into a single paradigm in which Europe is seen as the unique source of meaning, as the world's centre of gravity, as ontological "reality" to the rest of the world's shadow' (1994: 3).

Shohat and Stam argue that cinema has contributed greatly to the construction of the Eurocentric imperial imaginary, due to its consolidation as the apparatus of bourgeois society, predicated upon the production of master narratives (1994: 101–3). In their opinion, cinema's imperialist mandate has continued also after the end of colonialism, hidden in submerged elements of the narrative or manifest in the 1980s and 1990s European cinema's revival of imperialist epics and dramas (1994: 123). In this respect, *Chocolat* is for Shohat and Stam an example of one of the 'few critical "nostalgia" films' on the colonial period, which 'shift their focus from male aggressivity to female domesticity, and to the glimmerings of anticolonial consciousness provoked by transgression of the taboo on interracial desire' (ibid.).[9] This reading seems a little reductive. As Butler has demonstrated, *Chocolat*'s portrayal of colonial Africa does more than offer interracial desire as an easy way to reconcile Western and colonial identities (2002: 107). *Chocolat* rejects essentialist views of 'European' versus 'non-European' subjectivities and presents a view of social relations that is headed in Shohat and Stam's direction: 'historically configured relations of power' in which 'Eurocentrism is an implicit positioning rather than a conscious political stance' (1994: 4).

Many theoretical discussions developed in the context of postcolonial discourse acknowledge the danger that, as Western epistemology theories are wedded to modernist categories and agendas, they will remain decidedly Eurocentric. Such cultural snafus occur most often in the objectification of so-called Third World Women as privileged signifiers of difference. Gayatri Chakravorty Spivak, one of the most eminent examples of a feminist scholar whose postcolonial identity allows her an analytical mobility, acknowledges the risk of postcolonial approaches assuming 'native' points of view, which is likely to produce an ethnocentrism wherein the Western scholar patronises the other and transforms the Third World into a 'convenient signifier' (Young 1990: 168).[10] Inderpal Grewal and Caren Kaplan perceive some contradictions in feminist approaches to postcolonialism that 'use the colonial discourse in order to equate the "colonised" with "woman," creating essentialist and monolithic categories that suppress issues of diversity, conflict and multiplicity within these categories' (1994: 3). When resting on modern epistemology, postcolonial discourse is always at risk of becoming an inverted form of cultural ethnography.[11] Denis avoids this danger by assuming a postcolonial position set against the Western lock of fixed subjectivity and identity, as well as foregrounding her own postcolonial identity as a white, Western woman raised in a colonial society. As Butler reminds us,

> the question of white women directors' relationship with postcolonialism impinges on a number of difficult questions, concerning the extent and the nature of women's complicity and culpability in colonialism, the ways that white femininity signifies in racist ideology, and the meanings which white women have projected onto the colonised landscape and indigenous people. (2002: 105)

In *S'en fout la mort*, a film that further develops *Chocolat*'s quandary over 'the impossible desire for reconciliation between coloniser and colonised' (Butler 2002: 95), Denis relinquishes her subject position to focus on the condition of non-Western identities in postcolonial France. In *S'en fout la mort* the protagonists are Dah, an immigrant from Beni, who makes a living in Paris dealing fighting cocks for illegal gambling, and his associate Jocelyn, a cock trainer from the Caribbean.[12] Hired to organise an illegal gambling parlour, the two men are forced to live in a squalid basement underneath one of their employer's properties. Their boss is Ardenne, a restaurant and club owner who had lived for years in the Antilles and had been the lover of Jocelyn's mother.

Both victims of postcolonial racism and capitalist exploitation, Dah and Jocelyn's reactions are quite different. Jocelyn, a quiet, withdrawn man attached to his traditions and principles, is shattered by the environment in which he is caught.[13] Suffering under Ardenne's increasingly patronising attitude (the man at times insinuates the possibility of being his father) and his secret infatuation with Ardenne's lover, Toni, he begins drinking heavily and in the end is stabbed to death by Ardenne's son. This dramatic scene occurs at the cockpit, where Jocelyn arrives during a fight completely drunk and starts hallucinating and abusing the cockfight's patrons in Creole. Jocelyn's gradual descent into madness is concomitant with the re-enactment of a coloniser/colonised relationship that Fanon (1961) lucidly describes as a reaction of self-abasement.

In contradistinction, Dah (a character portrayed by Isaach de Bankolé, the actor who plays Protée in *Chocolat*) is proud and uncompromising. He reacts to Ardenne's attempts to take economic advantage of him and remains untouched by his harsh treatment. Throughout the film, Denis gives Dah narrative perspective, inserting his voiceover as a narrative justification and commentary – and as a resistant point of view. In the opening scene, Dah is filmed from the back, sitting in a van at night. His first words repeat the film's opening text, a quotation from Chester Himes: 'Every human being, whatever his race, nationality, religion or politics, is capable of anything and everything.'[14] In the final scene, after attending a funerary ceremony for his dead friend, in which Dah tells him of a future reconciliation with his mother in the Antilles, Dah leaves Paris behind, taking with him the money gained with the last fight organised.

When she presented *S'en fout la mort* in New York, Denis recalls having been criticised by a group of young African-Americans for having portrayed a negative and tragic image of Jocelyn. Commenting on her unsuccessful attempt to explain to these young men, via Fanon, the political meaning of having a black man die at the end of her film, Denis says: 'Maybe I have gotten old and my thoughts [are] out of touch with the new generation. But I still don't think that serious social inequities can be solved by nonviolent means. I really believe this' (quoted in Reid 1996: 73).

Denis' non-compromising postcolonial discourse in *S'en fout la mort* refuses both essentialist revisionism and politically correct visions. In interviews, Denis frequently addresses the problems and controversies that her particular outlook on racial representation poses, both for conservative and progressive viewpoints.[15]

For Denis, re-acquainting oneself with one's colonial past or facing the reality of today's racial biases involves cultural shock and emotional disillusionment. In this respect, *Chocolat* and *S'en fout la mort* are powerful illustrations of what Fanon says about de-colonisation:

> De-colonisation is the encounter of two forces congenitally antagonistic, which derive their originality precisely from this sort of substantiation, which secretes and aliments the colonial situation. Their first confrontation unfolded under the sign of violence and their co-habitation – more precisely, the exploitation of the colonised by the coloniser – was pursued by the reinforcement of bayonets and cannons. The coloniser and the colonised are old acquaintances. And, actually, when the coloniser says: he knows 'them', the colonised, he's right. It is the coloniser who *made* and who *continues to make* the colonised. From the colonial system, the coloniser gets his truth, that is, his possessions. (1961: 29–30)[16]

## Bodies that matter: *J'ai pas sommeil, Beau travail* and the recontextualisation of the postcolonial body

In the 1993 anthology *Construction of Race, Place, and Nation*, Peter Jackson and Jan Penrose underscore the necessity of going beyond essentialist assumptions of race and gender through a diachronic and dynamic scrutiny of how these terms form a transnational and class-specific position, from which race, place and nation are constructed and multifaceted entities, variously manifested in different geocultural contexts (1993: 19). Cross-cultural analyses that position themselves within diasporas share a similar problem. Caught between critiques of modernity and assertions of authentic identities, some theorists cannot see postmodern methodologies as a viable feminist practice (Grewal & Kaplan 1994: 21).

Using a frequent strategy of feminist postcolonial discourse, that of situating subjectivity and political agency at the conjunction of body and place, Radhika Mohanram proposes a 'cartography of bodies' in which 'a postmodern understanding of identity is based on a comprehension of nation and race as arbitrary or as a political construct' (1999: xii). Her central argument is that 'not only does a sense of place participate in the construction of a perception of physical identity, it is also central to the formation of racial identity' (ibid.). In her book, Mohanram examines the connections between pre-modernist, modernist and post-modernist notions of subjectivity in relation to race. Integral to her discussion is the argument that Western-centred theories of subjectivity have kept the body and the 'submerged concept of place/landscape' in a subaltern relation to notions of spirit, rationality and civilisation. Mohanram's historiographical and methodological purpose is

> to show the connections among the various strands in postcolonial studies: the politics of place/displacement, the concept of diasporic identity vs. indigenous identity, the identity of woman in the nation and the spatial construction of femininity, the identity of the black body and its national relationship to knowledge. (1999: xv)

As Mohanram argues, Western ontology and epistemology traditionally identify whiteness with spirituality and blackness with corporeality. She quotes Fanon on this opposition:

> Yes, we are – we Negroes – backward, simple, free in our behaviour. This is because for us the body is not something opposed to what you call the mind. We are in the world ... Emotive sensitivity. Emotion is completely Negro as reason is Greek. (1999: 27)

*J'ai pas sommeil* and *Beau travail* are films in which Denis propounds a politically viable critique of Western subject positions. These films do not try to resolve the contradictions they highlight, but rather leave the contradictions unresolved or further problematise them via the representation of physical and social bodies that transgress predetermined definitions of cultural identity. *J'ai pas sommeil* is based on a true criminal case that had polarised France's public opinion in the 1980s – that of Thierry Paulin, a black gay man who, with the complicity of his lover, killed and robbed dozens of old ladies in Paris. When she started working on the film, Denis was well aware that she was playing with a hotly controversial subject. Throughout pre-production and production, she carefully bypassed the social and cultural clichés of both the Caribbean and gay communities, to the point of making changes to the representation of the real people and places, about whom she had gathered an impressive quantity of research. Not only did she change the name of the real serial killer (who in the film is called Camille) and omit the sensational aspects of the real criminal case, including Paulin's flamboyant personality and social life; she also inserted Camille's narrative within the framework of other characters' stories, thus providing a rounded image of his environment from a perspective that tries to understand his actions, although never to explain or justify them. In this respect, a characteristic of the film is its lack of social commentary. The representation of Camille's social and familiar entourage never becomes mere reportage on multicultural groups or ethnic minorities.

Denis also abstained from portraying Camille as a monster by inserting his story in a multiple narrative of people that, as Denis puts it, live a condition of social otherness, a community of people whose destinies accidentally intersect with each other in the multicultural Parisian district of the eighteenth arrondissement. In this multicultural human comedy, two groups of immigrants – one from Martinique, one from the former Soviet Union – cross paths with each other throughout a parallel montage that interweaves individual characters and events from each group without ever really making them encounter each other, even occasionally. The film's plural nature is foreshadowed by an opening sequence showing two policemen flying over Paris in a helicopter and suddenly bursting into laughter. This apparently unrelated scene stands as a frame to the film's narrative puzzle and foreshadows the film's non-linear treatment of the plot. *J'ai pas sommeil* does not seek narrative closure; its descriptive tone lingers on Parisian streets, interiors, captures moods and atmospheres, and presents each character as indefinite and ambiguous. The film's cinematic style also suggests a collective type of enunciation, using shot scale and editing direction so as to deflect or multiply the points of view.

Many critics have stressed Denis' ability to work with bodies and her obsession with bodily expression as a metaphor for power relations. Denis herself acknowledges the importance of this motif in her films. In 1994, when two critics of *Cahiers du cinéma* noted that, with the then just-released film *J'ai pas sommeil*, she had finally succeeded in doing the '*mise-en-scène des corps*' that she had only hinted at in *S'en fout la mort*, she replied: 'Maybe this has taken shape … At any rate, there are first of all bodies in this film. This is not humour, filming bodies is really the only thing that interests me. It's quite intimidating, especially when they are men's bodies' (Denis 1994: 25).[17]

This investigation on the male body as a progressive point of convergence in Denis' work reaches its climax with *Beau travail*. With this film, Denis returns to the exploration of the body as a site of and a metaphor for power relations. Although not as overtly political as the previous films examined here, *Beau travail* is undoubtedly linked to colonial or postcolonial motifs. The film, set in a former colony of West Africa, is centred on the neo-colonial situation established between the Foreign Legion and the local population and foregrounds a self-reflexive use of literary and cinematic references to imperial France. For the first time, in *Beau travail* Denis works with an almost exclusively male cast (the female roles being confined to the role of extras), as she explores class and race relations within the homosocial context of the military system.[18] About her new 'fascination with watching men fighting or working', Denis comments:

> I like writing stories about men not because I want to dominate them but because I like to observe and imagine them. A man is a different world and this masculinity interests me. French cinema is so full of talk – I couldn't care less about these people talking about their lives. Godard said that in cinema there are women and guns and I agree completely. That's to say, there's sex and violence. Cinema functions through these even if one is highly intellectual. (Darke 2000: 17)

Scott Heller points out that Denis' occupation with 'the worlds of the marginal, portraying immigrants and ethnic minorities' is accompanied by a distinctively female gaze, which is often fixed on 'the troubled nature of masculinity' (2000: 42). According to Heller, *Beau travail* is perhaps the epitome of Denis' progressive concentration on the body as a motif, following a gallery of 'troubled' male characters that include Protée, Dah and Jocelyn, and Camille and his brother Théo from the earlier films.

In her analysis of the film, Susan Hayward points to the relation between identity and place as a coloniser/colonised relationship as a key element of *Beau travail*, complicated by notions of dislocation, displacement, context and specificity. In Denis' work, Hayward asserts, postcolonial bodies cannot be encompassed or contained within a Western-oriented context of discourse. She also writes: 'In her films Denis shows in different ways the struggle, if not the impossibility, of reinscribing the self into the dislocated space and the impossibility of reinventing a narrative and myth (or reclaiming a memory)' (2001: 161).

In *Beau travail* the soldiers' secluded training in the beauty of the natural landscape is juxtaposed to their problematic relationships with the women living in the small city nearby, and particularly the women whom they meet at the local disco, extending the issue of power relations within the military homosocial context to that of a postcolonial, heterosexual one, too. For a film that contains long sequences of soldiers in training, Denis did not hire a military expert but a dance choreographer. As Heller notes, the legionnaires' exercises 'begin as calisthenics, morph into martial arts, and become a vigorous form of modern dance' (2000: 42).[19] Similarly, Stéphane Bouquet has noted that:

> For Claire Denis, putting in contact dance and the army is a way of interrogating the notion of the collective body. Dancer and soldier try to reach an ideal body, even if it is not exactly the same body. And to what point can one disappear into a super-body? To the point of becoming fused within the rhythm [the law] of another; and what pleasure is there to abolish oneself as a subject in order to participate in the beauty of the group, of the norm? (You are no longer an African, we hear, you are a legionnaire). (2000: 49)[20]

For Bouquet, choreography participates in the creation of 'an ideal of Beauty ideologically de-valorised (military, army) or sexually connoted (homosexual)' (ibid.). Denis herself has reckoned that the film forwards an explicitly homosexual subtext, which she finds present also in Melville's novella.[21] In *Beau travail*, the glances exchanged between the lieutenant Galloup, the captain Forrestier and the soldier Sentain are openly erotic, and the fascination with the male body plastically rendered by the framing and *mise-en-scène*. Yet throughout the film, Denis worked with the actors to put a distance between the camera and the male bodies, so as not to objectify them (Denis 2000: 52–3). Bouquet observes that 'the logic of the bodies differs' between the nervous Galloup and the 'slow, hieratic, fantomatic' legionnaires, compared to angels with a quote from Rainer Maria Rilke's *Elégie de Duino*: 'Angels (they say) often don't know if they pass through the living or the dead' (2000: 49). For Bouquet, Denis' fascination with the masculine body is ultimately a question of showing that 'the body takes hold of itself again, escapes from the dream of fusion, frees itself from the group' (ibid.). Once again, as in other films by Denis, this process of assuming one's subjectivity passes through the assumption of one's body and is done via the dialectic of desire and violence. In the interview with Chris Darke appropriately titled 'Desire is Violence' Denis formulates her work in terms of this dialectic: 'There must be violence for there to be desire, I think – and that's what's so beautiful about Oshima's films. I expect if I went into analysis I'd be found abnormal – I think sexuality isn't gentle. Desire is violence' (2000: 17).

## Conclusions

Denis' work has received relatively sparse attention by the circuits and components of international distribution. This omission is partly due to the particular subject matter of her films, partly to her visually challenging and narratively non-traditional style, partly to her commitment to a transnational and multicultural discourse that refuses easy compromises and postures, which instead asks questions from a polemical perspective. In the above-mentioned interview, Darke asked Denis whether her 'marginality has to do with the fact that [she is] a woman making films in France'. Denis replied in a manner that belies her conception of otherness as a political strategy:

> No. I don't think I make the sort of films which have the characteristic traits of French cinema, which is to say a lot of dialogue and a very social focus. Some suggest my marginality has to do with the fact that my films have a lot of marginal characters in them. But I don't think so. I think it's more that I don't express myself like mainstream French directors. But being marginalised is a way of being slightly protected – I'm doing my own thing with no one interfering and that suits me. (Darke 2000: 18)

Denis' films provide an alternative model of female desire as a subjective point of view, deploying the social and cultural contradictions in colonial and postcolonial society. Her assumption of a female gaze inserts the dialectic of sexual desire and violence within the context of cultural, ethnic and gender power relations, a gambit which brings into question her own identity and authorial position. Her films are an important alternative model of femininity as a subjective point of view, one that offers new possibilities of representing otherness through the articulation of gender and cultural specificity.

## Notes

1   This statement is taken from an interview with Chris Darke (2000: 17).
2   *Billy Budd, Sailor* is an unfinished work, rediscovered and published in 1924, 33 years after Melville's death. The novella is part of a group of short stories that Melville wrote after the publication of *Moby Dick* (1851). Melville gradually abandoned prose writing, discouraged by his readers' alienation from his increasingly difficult prose. He eventually took a job as a deputy inspector in the New York Custom House. Since 1857 he wrote poetry exclusively, which he published in small editions. Two of Melville's poems are cited in *Beau travail*, 'The Night March' and 'Gold in the Mountain'. The first praises the synchrony of a group of soldiers marching, the second refers to greedy men whose desire to find 'gold in the mountain' is bound to remain unsatisfied.

3    Born in Paris in 1948, Denis went to Cameroon with her parents when she was only two months old and lived there for thirteen years. She returned to France when she and her sister contracted polio and needed hospital treatment. When her sister became paralysed as a consequence of her illness, her mother refused to join her husband back in Africa and the family eventually relocated to France. Denis missed her life in Africa; at 17 years of age, she went to Senegal to attend high school, and lived for some time with friends of her parents (Reid 1996: 68). Denis first read Fanon in 1961, upon her reluctant return to France and difficult integration into French society.

4    As Susan Hayward has remarked, Denis' films propose a multiple model of post-colonial subjectivity that challenges the objectification of the colonised body as a 'single unity and subjectivity whose multiplicities were deliberately dissimulated under [the] Western [Law of the Father] rule' (2001: 160). Such multiplicity, Hayward notes, also encounters many problems in expressing itself, as many postcolonial characters in Denis' films demonstrate (ibid.).

5    Among the filmmakers that throughout the 1980s and 1990s amended the long silence on France's colonial period (which previously had only seen interspersed works that denounced the colonial system and its ideology), those who re-examined African colonialism include Bertrand Tavernier (*Coup de torchon*, 1981) and Alain Corneau (*Fort Saganne*, 1984). On this subject, see Sherzner 1996: 6–7.

6    The group includes, among others, Marie-France Pisier, who in 1990 directed *Le bal du Governeur*, and Brigitte Rouän, whose *Outremer* came out in the same year. Like Denis, Rouän was raised in Africa, in Algeria, in a Catholic family which adopted a highly critical view of colonialism. On these three films, see Strauss 1990.

7    Commenting on the preparation of the film, Denis has said that she used Fanon's *Peau noire, masques blancs* (*Black Skin, White Masks*, 1952) to create a supplementary filter to the ones assured by the recourse to fiction and the collaboration with the playwright Jean-Pol Fargeau (Reid 1996: 68). These filters allowed her to 'se débarrasser d'une gigantesque idée reçue qui s'appelle Afrique' ('get rid of a giant prejudice that is called Africa') (quoted in Gili 1988: 15). Since this first experience, Fargeau has co-written all of Denis' films, with the exception of *Vendredi soir* (2002), which Denis co-wrote with Emmanuèle Bernheim, the writer of the novel from which the film is adapted.

8    The Kaplan article here quoted is titled 'The Politics of Location as Transnational Feminist Practice' and appears in Grewal and Kaplan 1994: 137–52. In her book, Butler makes a comparative analysis of Denis' *Chocolat* and Jane Campion's *The Piano* (1993) as two opposite examples of white female filmmakers' takes on postcolonialism. In Butler's opinion, whereas *The Piano* still presents the colonised as a radical Other (in this case, the Maori population of New Zealand, Campion's native country) and reduces power relations in sexual difference and cultural difference to metaphors for each other, *Chocolat* 'explores colonial relationships in their raw immediacy and finds no easy possibility of reconciliation' (2002: 108).

9    Besides *Chocolat*, Shohat and Stam also mention *Le bal du Gouverneur* and *Outremer*.

10   Spivak adopts continuously shifting strategies, discursive re-inflection of subject positions, including her own, particularly with respect to the formulation of feminist discourse on Third World women. As Robert Young stresses, 'Spivak is only too well

aware of the way in which radical criticism, such as certain forms of feminism, even as it takes an interest in women of the Third World and Third World literature, unconsciously reproduces imperialist assumptions – such as the unquestioned promotion of feminist individualism as the greatest good, 'as feminism as such' outside of any historical determination' (1990: 162). Yet, Young also argues, Spivak falls into essentialist positions when she tries to combine deconstruction with Marxist theory and maintain heterogeneous discontinuity and differences within a 'syncretic frame' (1990: 173).

11 Grewal and Kaplan propose postmodernism as an analytic position that 'gives us an opportunity to analyse the way that a culture of modernity is produced in diverse locations and how these cultural productions are circulated, distributed, received and even commodified' (1994: 5).

12 The titles of the two films both present a double meaning. As Kathleen Murphy notes, both films deal with the notion of betrayal. *Chocolat* refers to the colonial jargon for black people and also signifies 'to be cheated' (1992: 63). In *Chocolat*, Aimée asks her husband to confine Protée outside of the house after he has refused her sexual pass and Protée, in turn, breaks his close relationship with France by purposely letting her burn her hand. *S'en fout la mort* is the name of Jocelyn's champion cock, whose final death anticipates that of its trainer, whose suicidal trajectory emblematically ends in the cockpit. The expression 's'en fout la mort' refers to a phrase that in Africa or the Antilles would mean 'a fetish against coming apart, death' (ibid.).

13 Jocelyn is played by Alex Descas, who also features in two other films by Denis, *J'ai pas sommeil* and *Trouble Every Day* (2001).

14 The quote appears in François Audé's article on the film (1990: 71) and in Tarr and Rollet 2001: 221.

15 About the difficulties she encountered casting black actors in leading roles Denis says: 'Film producers react negatively to how I dramatise a topic in my films. They don't understand how I want to cast blacks; producers regularly suggest that if I cast black actors, they should be erotic "objects". In my films, black people are never objects. They are subjects who actively choose what they want. Producers usually have a very exotic idea about what black actors should do and where they should be seen. Producers' scripts would liken black characters to lions and elephants. In contrast, I think blacks featured in my films are "noir" ("black")' (quoted in Reid 1996: 69). Parenthetically, film journals also manifest problematic attitudes vis-à-vis black actors, especially when it comes to identifying them. In the articles on *S'en fout la mort* here cited, the captions of the photos relative to the two main actors, Alex Descas and Isaach de Bankolé, swap the two men's identities. So in *Positif* De Bankolé becomes Descas (Audé 1990: 71) and in *Film Comment* Descas is presented as 'Isaach de Bankholé' (Murphy 1992: 62).

16 My translation. The paragraph, selected from the opening pages of Fanon's *Les damnés de la terre* (*The Wretched of the Earth*, 1961), begins as follows: 'De-colonisation that aims to change the world order is, we can see, a program of absolute disorder. But it cannot be the result of a magic operation, of a natural upheaval, or of a friendly agreement. De-colonisation, we know this, is a historical process: that is, it can only be understood that it may find its intelligibility; it becomes translucent to itself only insofar as we identify the historicising movement that gives it its form and content' (1961:

126–7, my translation).

17  My translation. The pun with the word body – *Peut-être que ça a pris corps advantage* – is untranslatable in English.

18  *Beau travail* is an ironic title that translates as ' job well-done', the praise given to the soldier's correct execution of his duty. The film's title is also a reference (as Denis has acknowledged) to the Hollywood classic *Beau Geste*, particularly its 1939 version directed by William Wellman and starring Gary Cooper.

19  Denis accompanies the soldiers' elaborate choreographies with Benjamin Britten's *Billy Budd*.

20  My translation.

21  The film presents substantial differences with the Melville novella. Besides having changed the narrative's time and setting from eighteenth-century Great Britain to contemporary Africa, Denis' film also changes plot development and characters' names and fates. In *Billy Budd, Sailor* the master of Claggart the master-of-arms (the lieutenant Gallupp in the film), is accidentally killed by the handsome sailor Billy Budd while the three are gathered in the captain's cabin. Hearing that the evil and envious master-of-arts is unjustly accusing him of insubordination in front of the captain, Billy Budd punches him in an outburst of rage, making him fatally hit his head. Although siding with the sailor and understanding his position, the captain is obliged to sentence him to death, to avoid possibilities of mutiny. After a private conversation with the captain, Billy Budd dies heroically, blessing the captain in his last words. What remains intact in *Beau travail* is the palpably homoerotic atmosphere of the novella (especially manifest in the captain and the entire crew's infatuation with the handsome sailor), as well as some traits of Claggart's twisted psychology. On this subject, see Grant 2002.

## Works cited

Audé, F. (1990) 'S'en fout la vie (*S'en fout la mort*)', *Positif*, 356, 70–2.

Bouquet, S. (2000) 'La hiérarchie des anges', *Cahiers du cinéma*, 545, 48–9.

Butler, A. (2002) *Women's Cinema: The Contested Screen*. London: Wallflower Press.

Darke, C. (2000) 'Desire is Violence', *Sight and Sound*, 10, 7, 16–18.

Denis, C. (1994) '*J'ai pas sommeil*. Entretien aven Claire Denis', interview with Thierry Jousse and Frédéric Strauss, *Cahiers du cinéma*, 479/80, 25–30.

_____ (2000) 'Je me reconnais dans le cinéma qui fait confiance à la narration plastique: Entretien avec Claire Denis', interview with Jean-Marc Lalanne and Jérôme Larcher, *Cahiers du cinéma*, 545, 50–3.

Fanon, F. (1961) *Les damnés de la terre*. Paris: François Maspero.

Gili, J. A. (1988) 'Entretien avec Claire Denis sur *Chocolat*', *Positif*, 328, 14–16.

Grant, C. (2002) 'Recognising Billy Budd in *Beau travail*: Epistemology and Hermeneutics of an Auteurist "Free" Adaptation', *Screen*, 43, 1, 57–73.

Grewal, I. and C. Kaplan (eds) (1994) *Scattered Hegemonies: Postmodernity and Transnational Feminism*. Minneapolis: University of Minnesota Press.

Hayward, S. (2001) 'Claire Denis' Films and the Post-colonial Body – with special reference to *Beau travail* (1999)', *Studies in French Cinema*, 1, 3, 159–65.

Heller, S. (2000) 'Playing Soldier', *American Prospect*, 7, 14, 42–3.

Jackson, P. and J. Penrose (eds) (1993) *Construction of Race, Place, and Nation: Postmodernity and Transnational Feminist Practices*. Minneapolis: University of Minnesota Press.

Minh-Ha, T. T. (1989) *Woman, Native, Other: Writing Postcoloniality and Feminism*. Bloomington and Indianapolis: Indiana University Press.

Mohanram R. (1999) *Black Body: Women, Colonialism, and Space*. Minneapolis: University of Minnesota Press.

Murphy, K. (1992) 'The Color of Home', *Film Comment*, 28, 62–3.

Portuges, C. (1996) 'Le Colonial Féminin: Women Directors Interrogate French Cinema', in D. Sherzner (ed.) *Cinema, Colonialism, Postcolonialism: Perspectives from the French and Francophone World*. Austin: University of Texas Press, 30–102.

Reid, M. (1996) 'Colonial Observation: Interview with Claire Denis', *Jump Cut*, 40, 67–73.

Sherzner, D. (ed.) (1996) *Cinema, Colonialism, Postcolonialism: Perspectives from the French and Francophone World*. Austin: University of Texas Press.

Shohat, E. and R. Stam (1994) *Unthinking Eurocentrism: Multiculturalism and the Media*. London and New York: Routledge.

Strauss, F. (1990) 'Mémoires d'exil: Féminin colonial', *Cahiers du cinéma*, 434, 28–33.

Tarr, C. and B. Rollet (2001) *Cinema and the Second Sex: Women's Filmmaking in France in the 1980s and 1990s*. New York and London: Continuum.

Young, R. (1990) *White Mythologies: Writing History and the West*. London and New York: Routledge.

# PART THREE

# Carnival and Transgression

# CHAPTER SEVEN

# Carnivalesque meets modernity in the films of Karl Valentin and Charlie Chaplin
David Robb

In the films of Charlie Chaplin and Karl Valentin techniques from the carnivalesque tradition of theatre are used to express social conflicts within modernity. This chapter will argue, particularly in relation to Chaplin's *The Great Dictator* (1940), that precisely because of its ambivalent stance the carnivalesque does not sit comfortably as a tool in the hands of political ideology. Nonetheless, it does contain a moment of subversion which lends itself well to express an outsider's comic struggle against dominant discourses of modernity, be they social, ideological, linguistic or racial. Furthermore, particularly in the illogical, upside-down world of Valentin, one notices an overlapping between the carnivalesque and artistic trends in modernism such as dadaesque absurdity and temporal and spatial dislocation.

Although Karl Valentin never made a name for himself outside of Germany, contemporaries such as Kurt Tucholsky, Bertolt Brecht and Lion Feuchtwanger believed him to have a genius akin to Chaplin.[1] Roland Keller writes: 'no other German comedian … has portrayed the inadequacy of our existence … better than Valentin' (1996: 7). At the same time Valentin cannot be seen merely as a German Chaplin. The nearest likeness is in the slapstick of his silent films between 1912–30. Particularly in his films of the 1930s the added dimension of language– the play on words, the inversions of all linguistic and semantic logic – enabled Valentin to display the true uniqueness of his art.

Like Chaplin, Valentin was a popular clown figure who also enjoyed the acclaim of the artistic avant-garde. For Brecht, he was an example of a Hanswurst[2] figure from the tradition of German and Austrian plebeian popular comedy (*Volksstück*) which he and other modern dramatists such as Horváth, were trying to revive in a twentieth-century context (Hein 1987: 86). Indeed the uniqueness of Valentin's art form lay in its straddling of the high and the low: avant-garde theatre and traditional German *Volkssänger* (Pemsel 1982: 57). On one hand, his shows (and their adaptations for film) were orientated towards the form and structure of the *Volkssänger* genre. This was evident in the songs, solo numbers, one-act comedies and the traditional stage requisites and techniques associated with it, which included the backdrops, musical instruments and masked role-play (Pemsel 1982: 59–60). Simultaneously Valentin pushed the form beyond its conventional limits, applying to it what Kurt Tucholsky described as 'Linksdenkerei' – a dadaesque, illogical train of thought (see Keller 1996: 96). While this brought a more biting irony in his depiction of social types and behaviour, Valentin's art cannot be seen as a political protest. It is rather a comical portrayal of human inadequacy, an obstinate picking apart of the systems of logic which people construct in order to survive. A major object of caricature is 'the literal adherence to all rules' (Gürster 1982: 13). His petit-bourgeois audiences, however, whose milieu and legendary stubborn characteristics provided the inspiration for Valentin's parodies, were not offended. His natural instinct for defamiliarisation discouraged emotional identification and allowed the audience rather to laugh at *him* and the lack of sense in the world he portrayed.[3] At the same time, it was precisely this deeper philosophical aspect to Valentin's comedy which endeared him to the Berlin avant-garde including Tucholsky, who described his performance art as 'an infernal dance of reason around both poles of madness' (quoted in Keller 1996: 99).[4]

The routines of both Valentin and Chaplin thus had their roots in popular theatrical forms: Valentin in the *Volkssänger* milieu, Chaplin in the Variety Halls of London. Both of them could trace their artistic lineage back to traditional marketplace theatre, which had increasingly been subsumed by the circuses in the nineteenth century. By the early twentieth century these mime artists, acrobats, dancers and singers had also found their way into the Varieties or Vaudevilles in Britain, whose German counterparts (although distinct in themselves) were the *Volkssänger* and *Tingel Tangel* cabarets. The comic routines of these entertainment forms contained remnants of a carnivalesque folk culture as represented by the Italian *commedia dell'arte*, which Mikhail Bakhtin describes in *Rabelais and his World* (1984). In the Middle Ages and the Renaissance the carnival festivities represented a temporary time-out from the constraints of the 'official' world and the dictates of the church. The carnival celebrated the idea of metamorphosis, as seen in its emphasis on masks and disguises. It offered the ritual enactment of an upside-down world. With its suspension of all hierarchical rank, it symbolised a utopian realm of community, equality and freedom. The Italian masked theatre *commedia dell'arte* developed out of this culture of carnival festivities. Its techniques and motifs were laden with carnivalesque symbolism. Typical traits of *commedia* characters were images of the grotesque body: elongated noses, exaggerated lips and the emphasis on the lower-bodily functions, particularly in the robustly physical interactions between characters. In their sexual allusions these motifs were symbolic of changes of state: renewal and the eternal cycle of life. The slapstick which developed out of this in circus clown acts contained a similar symbolism. For example, when clowns clambered over one another ending up in upside-down positions – 'the buttocks persistently trying to take the place of the head and the head that of the buttocks' – this suggested 'the rotation of earth and sky' (Bakhtin 1984: 353). Such motifs (including comic transformations, mistaken identities and dual character configurations) symbolised this ambivalent 'two-world condition' of carnival. The significance of these comic motifs in the work of Chaplin and Valentin will form the focus of this chapter. The carnivalesque clashing of worlds which takes place – between order and anarchy, reason and absurdity – will be seen to reflect the struggle of the individual in the face of opaque, overpowering structures of modernity.

From the temporary subversion of structure in carnival there emerges a particular perspective on time and space: what Bakhtin calls a 'time-space negation' (1984: 411). This can be seen in the comic inversions and the illogicalities which constitute Chaplin's and Valentin's work. Temporal negation is evident in Chaplin and particularly Valentin's disregard for the authority of time and clocks. Here we see a parallel with artistic developments in art of the modernist era in general. The calamity of World War One had shattered the ideals of progress and logic which had dominated since the Age of Enlightenment. The montage aesthetic of the Berlin Dadaists, for example, entailed the juxtaposition of random phenomena, reflecting the fragmentation of modern city life devoid of sense or purpose (see Robb 2001). This displays a dislocated relationship to time: a sense of temporal fragmentation, which was also perceived by contemporary writers. In James Joyce and D. H. Lawrence, for example, Randall Stevenson notes 'a hostility to clocks and clockwork' (1992: 86). Marcel Proust and Virginia Woolf abandon chronological form, and their narratives move between dream, memory and sleep. For a generation of writers also influenced by the theories of Freud and Einstein, a 'time in the mind' emerges which is 'quite separate from what is happening in external reality' (1992: 89). While this reflects a general unease with the sense of time itself, it is also a reaction to increasing technological control over the time and life of the individual (1992: 123). A classic reflection of this is in Chaplin's *Modern Times* (1936) in which the workers are depicted as slaves of the clock, who even have to clock-in and clock-out to go to the toilet. The reaction of Charlie, the anarchic clown, is to disrupt the clockwork efficiency of the factory. In this way the world, as in carnival, is knocked out of its 'consecrated furrows' (Bakhtin 1984: 89).

According to Stevenson, the reaction of modernist writers to such technological control by creating a 'time in the mind' must be seen in the context of the Greenwich Mean Time Conference in 1884, when local times had been synchronised with na-

Charlie Chaplin in *Modern Times* (1936)

tional standards in conjunction with national train networking. In view of Stevenson's observation that such events must have had a dramatic effect on the temporal awareness of artists growing up in that time (1992: 119), it is significant to note that Valentin shares his year of birth, 1882, with Joyce, Woolf and Franz Kafka. He, too, continually attempts to assert his own flow of time, his temporal autonomy against standard time. However, the clown Valentin's reaction to the clock is quite different to that of, for example, Kafka. In the latter's short story 'Give it Up', the narrator, on his way to the station, looks up and discovers that the tower clock shows a later time than that shown on his own watch. The narrator bows to the authority of this clock, just as he subordinates himself to the policeman when, in his uncertainty, he asks him for 'the way'. This question is met with disdain by the policeman and becomes a metaphor for the disorientated subject's self-subjugation before authority (Kafka 1970: 358). In direct contrast to this, Valentin shows complete disregard for the town hall clock in the one-act play 'Collar Button and Hands of the Clock'.[5] Every morning he looks up at the clock, notes this time for the rest of the day, and simply discards his watch in order, as he claims, not to use it up (Valentin 1978: 77). With Kafka and Valentin we therefore see opposite reactions to one and the same phenomenon: the structure imposed by clock time subjugates the respectful citizen, but is simply ignored by the clown. For Valentin, his own *sense* of time is all that counts. Time is *his* servant and not the other way round. Called on to fix a spotlight in *Der verhexte Scheinwerfer* (*The Bewitched Spotlight*, 1934) Valentin, the foreman, estimates it will take him between two and ten-and-a-half days! When he drops his work tools onto someone's table, the guest says: 'Be careful', to which Valentin retorts: 'What do I need to be careful for, I've dropped it already' (see also Robb 2001: 80). The time in his mind has already moved on to a new reality. This is reminiscent of Bakhtin's comments on the 'time-space negation' in the topsy-turvy world of carnival. It 'considers the phenomenon in its becoming ... It does not deal with an abstract concept (for this is no logical negation), it actually offers a description of the world's metamorphosis, its remodelling, its transfer from the old to the new' (1984: 411–12). Another example of such time-space negations in the work of Chaplin and Valentin which will later be discussed is their 'wrong' utilisation of objects, contrary to their common use.

But, like Chaplin in *Modern Times*, Valentin's sense of time is invariably defeated by external reality. In the 'Train Station' scene, for example, Valentin's stage and film partner Liesl Karlstadt attempts to turn the clock back in order that she may catch her already departed train:

*Porter*:   If you'd come three minutes earlier, you would have caught it.
*Woman*:   Okay, I'll just go home and come back again three minutes earlier.
*Porter*:   But then you'd arrive even later. (Valentin 1978: 484)

Despite all contortions of logic, the real world prevails. In the end Valentin and Karlstadt remain the defeated clowns.

The fragmented relationship to linear time typical of modernist art thus had certain parallels with the comic time-space negation of carnival. Modernity and the carnivalesque, despite their differing origins and motivations, meet up in twentieth-century artists such as Chaplin, Valentin and Brecht. Here it is again useful to look at time perception. The carnival of the Middle Ages celebrated the cyclical nature of life, recurring events such as seasons, births and deaths on days in which the normally fixed social hierarchies were suspended, and time was temporarily frozen in its tracks. In this, the carnivalesque perspective was at odds with the idea of temporal continuity championed by the oncoming Age of Enlightenment. From this period right up to the modern day, the relative timelessness of the clown's grotesque world, with its roots in pre-modern folk culture and mythology, would clash with the logical structures and hierarchical constraints of the new bourgeois society. The clown became a marginalised and even censored figure, comic theatre increasingly lost its aspect of the grotesque. By the twentieth century, however, a context emerged in which the carnivalesque had a role to play. Writers who had little if anything to do with folk culture were reacting, as we have seen, against the rigid time structures of modernity. The goal of writers such as Thomas Mann and Kafka, as Ricardo Quinones observes, was 'to break up the continuities of history, to disrupt the linear, to shed routine, and that goal was to look at experience with the vision of the timeless, or mythic' (1985: 29). This echoes Walter Benjamin's opposition to the idea of history as a linear continuum. In his 'Theses on the Philosophy of History' he states that history 'is the subject of a structure whose site is not homogeneous, empty time, but time filled by the presence of the now' (1992: 252–3). Particularly in periods of revolution, history reacts explosively with the present creating this '*Jetztzeit*' in which time stands still (see Mitchell 1973: xvi–xvii). For Benjamin: 'The [new] calendars do not measure time like clocks do; they are monuments of a historical consciousness of which not the slightest trace has been apparent in Europe in the past hundred years' (1992: 253). This approach to the concept of time was reflected in the time-leaps and flashbacks of Brecht's Epic Theatre. As this was an artificial construct, time could be manipulated and defamiliarised to demonstrate a particular argument. The logical continuities of Naturalism were no longer important. In this respect Brecht's Epic Theatre showed formal overlappings with the time-leaps, improbable disguises, masks and the stylised acting of the traditional *commedia dell'arte*. Karl Valentin was also highly influenced by this tradition. Indeed Benjamin himself documents how Brecht credited Valentin with giving him the original idea of epic defamiliarisation. In the rehearsals for *Edward II* a comment of Valentin's inspired the artificial portrayal of the soldiers whereby their fear was accentuated by the chalking of their faces (Benjamin 1973: 115). Around this time Brecht collaborated with Valentin on a silent film from 1923 called *Mysterien eines Friseursalons* (*Mysteries of a Barbers Shop*). Here, dadaesque absurdity combines with clownesque slapstick. In one scene Valentin, a barber with an elongated nose, is shaving a customer with an absurdly large butcher's knife. When distracted by a noise, he mistakenly decapitates the customer. This displays a strong element of grotesque which would later influence the limb-severing clowns' number of Brecht's *Baden Lesson on Consent* (1929). In this, as in *Man Equals Man* (1926), Brecht appropriated the grotesque violence of clownesque slapstick to make aesthetic abstractions of violent struggles and oppositions in modern capitalist society (Schechter 1994: 76).

Despite having influenced Brecht formally, Valentin's films were never overtly political themselves. However, they are frequently grotesque reflections of social phenomena and relationships. They often reflect a conflict with social structure, one that invariably ends in chaos. The importance of language, in its register, tone and dialect, is paramount. For this reason, his talkies from the early 1930s onwards were able to convey the essence of his stage productions more effectively than the earlier silent films.[6] There is a dialogic interplay between his provincial, often stuttering Munich dialect and the official High German of professional life. In this respect Valentin appears as the insecure petit-bourgeois, comically out of his depth in the social hierarchy and an alien world of technology. In the classic one-act play *Bookbinder Wanninger*,[7] for example, he is unable to fathom a company's telephone extension system. Technology forces the bookbinder into a particular social role-play which he cannot master. He gives an excruciatingly long explanation of his query with each person he is connected to, his sense of individuality disintegrating with the failure of each communication attempt. This is also reflected in the collapse of his language as his sentences degenerate into a confused jumble. The inappropriateness of his dialect in this public professional context only exacerbates his loss of confidence. It is only after he hangs up in despair and humiliation that he recovers his sense of individuality and curses the faceless switchboard operators: 'Hoodlums, filth!' (Valentin 1978: 254). Here Valentin's alienation reflects what has been called a 'soul torn in two between dialect and High German' (Kuh 1982: 18).

Such alienation of clown figures of industrial modernity has been described as an expression of eternal 'public loneliness' akin to the Harlequin and Pierrot figures of *commedia dell'arte* and *commedie francaise* (von Berloewen 1984: 143). The clown (representing the individual) of earlier medieval times had enjoyed the security which a fixed position in the cosmic order provided (1984: 154). The world was fixed, the sun rotated round it, and everyone had their strict place in a vertical hierarchy that stretched down from God in Heaven down to the lowest peasant on the ground. With the new open-ended mindset of the Renaissance the world was no longer perceived as a ready-made, vertical structure; the individual was abandoned to a secular void. Caught up in the transition from feudal to bourgeois society in the seventeenth and eighteenth centuries, the Harlequin and his Western European variations were comically at odds with new etiquette and rules. Rudolf Münz writes of the harlequinesque Kurz-Bernadon figure of that period in Austria: 'It was about ... the artistic, admittedly fantastic expression of certain sides of the relationship between the individual and society – a relationship that was ... in contrast to the claims of bourgeois ideology, disturbed ... because the individual seemed exceptionally endangered, not the subject, but rather the object of happenings' (1979: 148). The Harlequin, like his descendants Valentin and Chaplin, typically reacts to such alienation with mischief and laughter. In carnival, laughter had the function of allowing the small man to come to terms with his fear of the 'mystic terror of God' and the authoritarianism of the church: 'All that was terrifying becomes grotesque' (Bakhtin 1984: 90–1). In the twentieth century the grotesque slapstick of Chaplin and Valentin similarly attempts to demystify the authority of the modern industrial era, often expressed in the form of technological control. Viewed in this light, these are Harlequins of the twentieth century, two clowns who embody the aforementioned state of abandonment in a world bereft of rhyme or reason; a world in transition and upheaval. This is particularly so in view of the devastation of cultural certainties in the wake of World War One, the social and political turmoil of the Weimar Republic and the not-unrelated Wall Street Crash of 1929.

In the case of Chaplin's *Modern Times*, the worker is reduced to a mere object, a cog in the wheel of the factory machinery. The absurdity of such dehumanisation is portrayed by a series of inversions including objects being used in ways contrary to their common use. This recalls the carnivalesque time-space negation where objects are 'turned inside out, utilised in the wrong way ... Household objects are turned into arms, kitchen utensils and dishes become musical instruments' (Bakhtin: 1984: 411). In one scene of *Modern Times* Charlie files his nails with a chisel. In another, he uses an oil funnel or chicken carcass to pour coffee down the throat of a worker whose head is caught in the machinery. There are further expressions of the carnivalesque in the feeding machine in *Modern Times*, which turns into an instrument of torture, or in the flag which mutates into a banner of industrial protest. Charlie picks it up when it falls off a truck, only to find himself arrested as a workers' ring leader. With Valentin such comical defamiliarisation is expressed by the telephone in *Beim Rechtsanwalt* (*At the Lawyers*, 1936), which actually hinders communication (Keller 1996: 94–5). We also see it in the absurd objects of his ill-fated Pantoptikum museum such as the nose-picking machine for children (see Köhl 1984: 13) or the clock that always tells yesterday's time.[8]

The upside-down world is further evident in the wilful subversions of hierarchy. When Charlie is swallowed up by the machine in *Modern Times*, in a parodic celebration of beauty and cold perfection he is portrayed as being in perfect unison with technology. But this poetic tribute flips over and becomes a dance of destruction as Charlie brings the factory to a standstill. Similarly in Valentin's film *Der Antennendraht* (*The Arial Wire*, 1937) the protagonist obstructs the smooth running of the machine. He wanders into a radio studio looking for wire to fix his own radio set. With a live transmission imminent, the layman Valentin is engaged to do the sound effects for the show. Chaos ensues. If the studio is a symbol of modern power relations in which the small man has no part to play, Valentin gets his own back by sabotaging the broadcast (Keller 1996: 149).

Valentin's various types of confrontation with convention – linguistic or philosophical – recall the dialogism embodied in the 'two-world condition' (Bakhtin 1984: 6) of the carnival: the constant apposition of the sacred and the profane, the high and the low, the official and the 'other' reality. In carnivalesque literature and theatre, dialogism was evident in the dual configurations (for example, Don Quixote and Sancho Pansa) and the comic transformations of characters themselves. The Harlequin figure of *commedia*, for example, was not a constant character, but rather the incarnation of change and otherness. His carnivalesque ambivalence was a foil for the social straightjacketing and convention which stamped society of the newly emerging Enlightenment. As Rudolf Münz writes, variations of Harlequin all seem to have in common the symbolic reference to the 'other' world. The clown's mask, in its infinite transformability, hit one of the most sensitive nerves of the Age of Reason: it revealed the inconsistency of the individual (1979: 82). In this he posed a threat to order. In Germany this culminated in a campaign in 1727 led by the moralist Johann Christoph Gottsched against Hans Wurst, the profane harlequinesque figure from *Volkstheater* and a forefather of Valentin. Ten years later Hans Wurst was banned in Leipzig (Berthold 1988: 25).

Dialogue with the 'other' was also often achieved by means of doubles, disguises or mistaken identities – motifs from popular comedy which, of course, were appropriated by Shakespeare in plays such as *Twelfth Night*. The donning of the fool's cap illustrates this dialogic process. The mask has a liberating function. By virtue of the mask, as Bakhtin writes, the fool is invested with 'the right to be "other" in this world, the right not to make common cause with any single [concern]' (1981: 162). Through his or her disguise, the masked character can reveal what is otherwise obscured from view. This is an aspect of defamiliarisation in clowns theatre which so interested Brecht. Valentin's film *Im Schallplattenladen* (*In the Record Shop*, 1934), for example, portrays this property of the fool. The customer, Valentin, taxes the patience of the pompous sales assistant with his endless and gratuitous requests to hear records. Similarly to *The Arial Wire*, he ultimately wreaks havoc in the shop, scratching and smashing the records and scaring away other customers. Here, the mask of the fool has the effect of *unmasking* the forces which encourage random consumerism, where the alienated small man is simply out of his depth, faced with a choice of wares between which he is unable to differentiate. This recalls the dialogic function ascribed by Bakhtin to the fool's trait of stupidity. This tears away the mask of 'a lofty pseudo intelligence … At its heart lies a polemical failure to understand … someone else's pathos-charged lie that has appropriated the world and aspires to conceptualise it' (1984: 403).

This dialogic essence of the carnivalesque is evident in the dual configuration of Valentin and Liesl Karlstadt. This is the traditional motif of opposite pairs which in comic history have included, for example, the crafty Arlecchino and the clumsy Brighella, the idealistic Don Quixote and the down-to-earth Sancho Pansa, and the thin Stan Laurel and the fat Oliver Hardy. Bakhtin traces the emergence of such comic opposite pairs in the early Renaissance. At that time the dual tone of popular speech and the dual image of the body (as known in medieval carnival culture) was under threat from 'stabilising tendencies of the official monotone' in the newly emerging epoch. Bakhtin writes: 'As the ancient [dual] image disintegrated, an interesting phenomenon in the history of literature and spectacle took place: the formation of images in pairs, which represent top and bottom, front and back, life and death. The classic example of such pairs is Don Quixote and Sancho … These debates are an organic part of the system of popular-festive norms, related to change and renewal' (1984: 433–4).

Valentin and his partner Liesl Karlstadt reflected this continuing dialogic tradition in twentieth-century clowning. The one represented reason and order, the other madness and anarchy. In such pairings there is a reciprocal need whereby the one needs the other to survive. It is also evident in tragedy, for example, in the relationship between King Lear and his fool, where Lear needs the fool's madness, and the fool needs the King's grace. In these instances the boundary between the two opposites can become blurred and roles reversed. Take, for example, Chaplin and Jackie Coogan in *The Kid* (1921): it is the child who cooks breakfast, and who has to order Charlie, the eternal child, out of bed in the morning (Robinson 1989: 303). Their roles are also reversed in the fight scene. When picked upon by an elder child, the streetwise kid proves able to look after himself whereas the helpless Charlie walks into danger at every turn. By the same token, it is Charlie's child-like sense of fun which frequently saves him.

An extension of the motif of opposite pairs is that of the double. If Chaplin had portrayed the kind-hearted altruist in *The Kid*, in his earlier films he was often the heartless rogue. In *An Evening in the Variety* from 1915 the motif of the double turns up for the first time; here a dubious singing group on stage is cruelly heckled by the noble Mr Pest played by Chaplin, who simultaneously plays a poor spectator in the balcony. In later films the motif of the double leads to comical mistaken identities. This technique enables Chaplin to portray the ambivalent split within people (the side by side existence of opposite characteristics, for example master/servant, bully/victim, strength/weakness). Maybe it reflected the split in his own person: on the one hand, the big man: the dictatorial film director and lover, and on the other hand, the small man: the pursued impoverished immigrant who left England for America.[9] It is executed with the most dramatic effect in *The Great Dictator*. In scrutinising the figure of Hitler in the Nazi *Wochenschau* propaganda films, Chaplin believed he could see the dual characteristics of tyrant and clown (the big man and the small man) (Tichy 1974: 100–3). The character Hynkel displays this comical ambivalence. At the height of his megalomania he still shows vulnerability, as in his dance with the globe, or when he pours water down his trousers during his speech to the masses. This ambiguity is expressed further via the main dualism in the film: Chaplin's double role as the evil dictator Hynkel and the persecuted Jewish hairdresser. Inevitably this leads to the mistaken identity whereby the hairdresser assumes the role of the dictator. In a carnivalesque inversion, he uses all of Hynkel's oratory skill and hypnotic charisma to deliver his own speech to the masses – not a hateful tirade against Jews, but a utopian vision for mankind.

However, this ironic use of typical Nazi techniques in propaganda films to whip up emotion (including the use of emotive Wagner music) incensed left-wing critics such as Theodor Adorno (Tichy 1974: 104). They thought he was playing down the evil in Hitler. One can see where they were coming from. There is an open-ended moment in carnivalesque humour which precludes it from being appropriated by politics or ideology. Unlike the superior humour of the satirist, the laughter of the market place embraces 'the wholeness of the world's comic aspect' (Bakhtin 1984: 12). It is directed at those laughing as well as at those being laughed at. Such ambivalence was not acceptable for the anti-fascist camp, who were neither prepared to portray Nazism as a laughing matter, nor to see their own ideals in a comical light. And there is just a hint in this speech that Chaplin's expressive speech is on the verge of flipping over to become a parody of itself, and therefore of anyone who broadcasts ideological dogma, be it from a humanist or fascistic stance. In the end the serious pathos appears to overshadow the comedy. This led to the aesthetic confusion for which the film was criticised and which Chaplin, the clown, in his first excursion into politics, was not able to resolve.

Valentin never followed Chaplin into the precarious world of politics. Unlike his contemporaries in the avant-garde, he never left Nazi Germany, but rather chose to remain and work in his native Munich. But like his Hanswurst forefather of the eighteenth century, he too was censored, in his case without even trying to provoke. His film *Die Erbschaft* (*The Inheritance*, 1936) was banned by the Nazis for depicting social misery (Korowski 1988: 106). He continued to produce films increasingly sporadically until 1941 when he was forced to retire due to lack of work opportunities. Here we see a further contradiction of the laughter of the fool: on the one hand, it has eluded censorship more easily than satire, enjoying 'the freedom of the fool' due to its lack of directness;[10] on the other, this freedom cannot be taken for granted. In its undermining of fixed categories and the official discourse, it can also be perceived, as in the case of Valentin, as a threat.

In their films, Charlie Chaplin and Karl Valentin confronted the new power relationships of modernity with traditional carnivalesque techniques and dialogic devices. These were rooted in the trade they had learned in the concert halls and *Volkssänger* cabarets respectively. If the carnivalesque had traditionally been an aesthetic weapon of defence against the dogmas and social hierarchical constraints of previous eras, it was now a response to humiliations suffered at the hands of the new authority: modern technology. By ripping off its mask, Valentin and Chaplin exposed the fallibility of clockwork logic and machine-like certainty. This approach mostly did not have a political agenda. But where there was, it served to show the irreconcilable interests of the carnivalesque and ideological dogma.

## Notes

1   See Keller 1996: 7; see B. Brecht, quoted in Keller 1996: 79, and K. Tucholsky, quoted in Keller 1996: 97–9.
2   A German/Austrian equivalent of the Harlequin clown figure from *commedia dell'arte*.
3   Klaus Pemsel writes of how Valentin simultaneous parodied the *Volkssänger* genre and the customs of the petit-bourgeois class whose milieu was depicted (1982: 67).
4   Valentin had already been befriended by Brecht while the young playwright was still resident in Bavaria.
5   This scene was not filmed. All titles and quotations in German in this chapter are translated by David Robb.
6   Indeed Valentin allegedly saw films as having precisely this function, much to the frustration of his directors and technicians; see Keller 1996: 58.
7   This was never filmed but is available as a recording.
8   It displays the joke-caption: 'This clock shows yesterday's time exactly'; quoted in Wöhrle 1984: 49.
9   See C. J. Phillipe (1997) 'Charlie und sein Double', in *Ein Tramp im Rampenlicht. Charlie Chaplin*. Documentary TV film for ARTE.
10  Bakhtin writes about the differing respective fates of Rabelais and his friend Dolet: 'Rabelais' friend Dolet perished at the stake because of his statements, which although less damning had been seriously made' (1984: 268).

# Works cited

Bakhtin, M. (1981) *The Dialogic Imagination*. Austin: University of Texas Press.

\_\_\_\_ (1984) *Rabelais and his World*. Bloomington: Indiana University Press.

Benjamin, W. (1973) *Understanding Brecht*, trans. A. Bostock. London: New Left Books.

\_\_\_\_ (1992 [1950]) 'Theses on the Philosophy of History', in *Illuminations*. London: Fontane, 245–55.

von Berloewen, C. (1984) *Clown. Zur Phenomenologie des Stolperns*. Munich: Ullstein.

Berthold, M. (1988): 'Alterloses Theater: Commedia dell'arte. Gestern und heute', in W. Stock (ed.) *Gauckler, Clowns und Komödianten. Tragikomödie im Film. Von Chaplin bis Fellini*. Gerolzhofen: Landesarbeitsgemeinschaft für Jugendfilmarbeit und Medienerziehung, 11–27.

Brecht, B. (1997 [1929]) *The Baden-Baden Lesson on Consent*, in *Brecht Collected Plays* 3. London: Methuen, 21–44.

\_\_\_\_ (1994 [1926]) *Man Equals Man*, in *Brecht Collected Plays* 2. London: Methuen, 1–76.

Gürster, E. (1982) 'Der Stegreifspieler Karl Valentin', in W. Till (ed.) *Karl Valentin. Volkssänger? Dadaist?* Munich: Schirmer, 12–17.

Hein, J. (1987) 'Posse und Volksstück', in J. Hein (ed.) *Johann Nestroy. Der Talisman. Erläuterungen und Dokumente*. Stuttgart: Reclam, 80–90.

Kafka, F. (1970) 'Give it up' ('Gibs auf'), in *Sämtliche Erzählungen*. Frankfurt am Main: Fischer, 358.

Keller, R. (1996) *Karl Valentin und seine Filme*. Munich: Heyne Bibliothek.

Köhl, G. (1984) 'Karl Valentin und die Münchner Volkssänger', in G. Kohl, H. König and E. Ortenau (eds) *Karl Valentin in der Geschichte der Komiker*. Munich: Unverhau, 7–18.

Korowski, U. (1988) 'Die Erbschaft', in W. Stock (ed.) *Gauckler, Clowns und Komödianten. Tragikomödie im Film. Von Chaplin bis Fellini*. Gerolzhofen: Landesarbeitsgemeinschaft für Jugendfilmarbeit und Medienerziehung, 106.

Kuh, A. (1982) 'Der Vorstadthypochonder', in W. Till (ed.) *Karl Valentin – Volkssänger? Dadaist?* Munich: Schirmer, 18–21.

Mitchell, S. (1973) in W. Benjamin, *Understanding Brecht*, trans. A. Bostock. London: New Left Books, i–xx.

Münz, R. (1979) *Das ,andere' Theater. Studien über ein deutschaprachiges teateo dell'arte der Lessingszeit*. Berlin: Henschel Verlag.

Pemsel, K. (1982) 'Volksverbunden – falsch verbunden', in W. Till (ed.) *Karl Valentin. Volkssänger? Dadaist?* Munich: Schirmer, 54–69.

Quinones, R. (1985) *Mapping Literary Modernism*. Princeton: Princeton University Press.

Robb, D. (2001) 'Cities, Clocks and Chaos: A Modernist Perception of Time in the Comedy of Karl Valentin', in S. Marten-Finnis and M. Uecker (eds) *Berlin – Wien – Prag*. Frankfurt am Main: Peter Lang, 77–89.

Robinson, D. (1989) *Chaplin. Sein Leben. Seine Kunst*. Zurich: Diogenes.

Schechter, J. (1994) 'Brecht's clowns: *Man is Man* and after', in P. Thomson and G. Sack (ed.) *Cambridge Companion to Literature*. Cambridge: Cambridge University Press, 68–78.

Stevenson, R. (1992) *Modernist Fiction: An Introduction*. Hemel Hempstead: Harvester

Wheatsheaf.

Tichy, W. (1974) *Chaplin*. Reinbek: Rowohlt.

Valentin, K. (1978) *Alles von Karl Valentin*. Munich: Piper.

Wöhrle, D. (1984) *Die komische Zeiten des Herrn Valentin*. Munich: Schäuble Verlag.

## CHAPTER EIGHT

# The Bakhtinian headstands of East German cinema

Evelyn Preuss

The significance of François Rabelais as a writer and source of inspiration for a re-markable series of intellectuals had been sidelined for four hundred years, Mikhail Bakhtin laments in his seminal study *Rabelais and His World* (1984). As he blames the long history of neglect and misunderstanding on the loss of carnivalesque sensibility,[1] Bakhtin's own ability to recover the verve of carnival seems surprising. Yet why and how he could retrieve what supposedly had been lost to the social and aesthetic norms of modern society appears to be exempt from his scholarly scrutiny. While pointing out that the twentieth century has seen a 'new and powerful revival of the grotesque' (1984: 46), Bakhtin decidedly states that 'the analysis of these developments does not enter our picture' (ibid.).

However, in reading *Rabelais and His World* against its social and political context, Bakhtin's seeming lack of interest in his own time emerges as an omission. Professing to forego a direct reference to the present, Bakhtin implicates himself in his account of the past: the Soviet scholar's political agenda and literary strategy parallel those of his subject of study (Holquist 1984: xiv–xix). Like Rabelais' own works, Bakhtin's monograph on the Renaissance man 'carnivalises the present' (Holquist 1984: xxii). As Bakhtin dissimulates the relationship between his own text, its historical subject and the circumstances of his own writing, he addresses precisely what he claims to omit, and the gap between his stated intent and his actual project provides subterfuge for a politically-minded critique of his own era.

This critical edge is what defines Bakhtin's and Rabelais' common project. After all, it is not the singularity of the times through which they lived, the sense of revo-lution, upheaval and socio-political change, that most decisively shapes their texts (see Holquist 1984: xiv–xix), but the disenfranchisement and persecution – or worse – awaiting those whose texts threaten to disrupt the political order of any given era. To negotiate this threat, authors of the Rabelaisian, or Bakhtinian, kind overtly dis-avow the contemporary relevance of their texts and, at the same time, underscore it surreptitiously by resorting to historical foils and surreal landscapes. Precisely this political calculation and this fine balance between direct reference and *Verfremdung* (alienation) also characterises much of East Germany's cultural production and es-pecially the preoccupation of East German cinema with history and the fairytale. In what I will term, in the following, 'carnivalesque film', these two strands come together, forming a hybrid genre that not only exploits the carnivalesque propensi-ties of the cinematic medium, but that also incorporates elements of carnival into its plots and *mise-en-scène*. Popular with censors and audiences alike, the carnivalesque genre proved a convenient vehicle for filmmakers to voice their dissent with the regime and, consequently, constituted a sizable share of East German film production. Through its covert depiction of East German society, its politically-charged humour, its utilisation of the mass medium and its exploration of the carnivalesque tendencies of modern media, it upheld – and, as I will argue in this chapter, reinvented – the tradition in which Bakhtin and Rabelais are but two figures whom posterity has deciphered.

By the same token, however, carnevalesque film could be appropriated by the regime, in turn, inviting scholars' subsequent misunderstanding of the genre. Thus, it may become part of the vast cultural production that may never be read and recognised as carnival, or as an act of political resistance, because such discourse is susceptible to the capricious nature of the references that relate to historical reality, and also because historiography tends to interpret historical data in a way that acclaims rather than challenges institutions and political regimes.

Indeed, scholarship on East German cinema has not only overlooked the structural similarities between the films I will discuss under the heading 'carnivalesque film' and, instead, continues to use the same genre labels that East German authorities applied to these films – fairytale film (*Märchenfilm*), children's film (*Kinderfilm*) and historical comedy (*historische Komödien*). But, deeming these films to be merely for entertainment, scholars also fail to acknowledge their political import. As most scholarship on the former East German regime is interested in political partisanship, these films indeed have attracted little to no scholarly attention, despite the fact that they represent such an eminent part of the country's film production.

Moreover, a theoreticisation of the carnivalesque as a modern mode of expression and, especially, why it comes to bear in modern media is still wanting. While scholars have investigated the elements of carnival in films from temporal and spatial coordinates as divergent as Great Britain in the 1950s, India in the 1970s and Argentina in the 1990s, comparatively little scholarship has been devoted to theorising the carnivalesque as a genre or investigating the affinity of modern media with carnival. The most comprehensive study to date is Robert Stam's 1989 book *Subversive Pleasures*, which explores the applicability of Bakhtinian concepts to the analysis of contemporary mass media.

Many of the films Stam discusses certainly merit the label 'carnivalesque film' as I use it. However, Stam does not conceive of a film genre that could be called carnivalesque with the exception of the Brazilian *chanchadas*, which have been called 'filmes carnavalescos' ('carnivalesque films') because of their close association with Brazilian carnival (1989: 138).

Stam's main achievement is a titillating survey of mass media, finding, for instance, that 'Bakhtin has a contribution to make to the contemporary debate surrounding cinematic eroticism and pornography' (1989: 166) or discerning in US television a 'tendency to constantly serve up the simulacrum of carnival-style festivity as hyperreal palliatives for an enervated society' (1989: 224). At the same time, Stam avoids addressing questions as to the socio-political underpinnings and the cultural meaning of his findings: why does carnival have such an appeal to modern masses? Whom or what does mass media seek to address by integrating or imitating carnival? Why do supposedly democratic societies need carnival, a cultural phenomenon that Bakhtin associates with the socio-political order of the Middle Ages?

These questions pinpoint the larger problems underlying the politics of cultural production in the modern era, and indeed the few examples cited thus far show that, as in a hall of mirrors, the parallels between authors and times merge into a repetitive pattern: economically dependent on a totalitarian state apparatus, subject to comprehensive censorship and closely observed by secret service agents, artists working for the East German film industry found themselves as compelled to reproduce the regime's ideology as did Bakhtin when he started to work on *Rabelais and His World* during the height of the Stalin-era purges. Fulfilling their function in the regime with a twist that resembles Bakhtin's 'dialogic meditation on freedom' (Clark & Holquist 1984: 298), East German filmmakers adopted a strategy of simultaneously accommodating and defying the dominant ideology, as they capitalised on contradictions and ambiguities in the party's doctrine. Like Bakhtin some thirty or forty years earlier,[2] they celebrated carnival in order to recover artistic and political freedom and undermined their own propagandistic mission by following Bakhtin on his self-reflexive grand tour of the culture of Billingsgate, bodily excess and the ritual of turning hierarchy on its head.

However, East German cinema continued Bakhtin's project of resituating the carnivalesque into modernity with different means: it is the difference in the medium that sets Bakthin's work apart from that of the people involved in East German film production. While Bakhtin translated a predominantly graphic and performative culture into text (and, in dealing with Rabelais, even used a pre-existing translation), East German filmmakers cultivated the visual and performative character of carnival itself. Whereas Bakhtin's project targeted a group of academics with an elitist self-understanding,[3] East German film addressed a mass audience that, in the twilight of the screen, remained undifferentiated as to social status and aspirations. Finally, Bakhtin's reception was displaced in time and space: his book was published two and a half decades after its completion and received wider attention only after it was translated into English in 1968.[4] The volatile nature of this transmission process is illuminated by the publication history of another of his book-length manuscripts: its only copy went up in smoke during a bombing raid. Although some of East Germany's carnivalesque films share with *Rabelais and His World* the similar fate of belated popularity due to restrictions in distribution or outright censorship, most, in contrast to Bakhtin's text, had an immediate impact on society, as they were widely shown in movie theatres and on television, spontaneously turning their audiences into carnival communities.

In a way that was unfeasible for Bakhtin's bookish enterprise, modern media and in particular cinema reinvented carnival. Using East German film as a characteristic example, I will argue in this chapter that cinema very effectively translated and re-established the carnivalesque in modern society, because it shares a number of decisive features with carnival and because cinema, as a medium of the modern era, operates against a background of political ideologies that borrow heavily from the carnival spirit.

## Of the people, for the people, by the people: the carnival ideology of the modern state

Bakhtin's recovery of carnivalesque verve may not simply have been inspired by his knowledge of 'living in an unusual period', as Holquist puts it, for indeed history is full of times 'when,' as he states, 'virtually everything taken for granted … lost its certainty' (1984: xv). Doubtless, Bakhtin's project formulates a response to the ideology of the revolution with which the Soviet party leadership legitimised its political programme. According to this doctrine, the people had overturned their oppressors (and needed to be on guard lest they return) in order to rule themselves. But this contention is not unique to the Russian Revolution: it has characterised the legitimation of political movements, organisations and states since the onset of the French Revolution, and has led political scientists such as Francis Fukuyama to assert that liberal democracy is the ideological endpoint in the series of social experiments we call history (1993: xi).

Fukuyama's thesis certainly rings true to the extent that the so-called rule of the people – along with founding myths that detail how they usurped power from despotic and self-serving rulers – have become the pre-eminent ideology in the industrialised world. However, his assertion that liberal democracy 'conquered rival ideologies like hereditary monarchy, fascism, and most recently communism' (1993: xi) confuses actual political systems with their ideologies, for even the nastiest dictatorships of the twentieth century have legitimated themselves as liberal democracies that represent a final chapter in the development of the human race. In order to disguise and protect the socio-economic hierarchies and political chains of command that drive them, modern states need to identify themselves as democratic.[5] Hence, all modern states are, according to their ideologies, 'of the people, for the people, by the people', and the Soviet Union and East Germany were no exceptions to this rule.

To legitimise itself as a democratic government or *Volksregierung* (a people's government), the East German leadership translated Abraham Lincoln's definition of democracy into the slogan 'Arbeite mit, plane mit, regiere mit' ('Co-work, co-plan, co-rule'). To the extent that both Western and Eastern democracies were political instruments in the hands of the ruling classes who used them to promote their own interests, East German scholars reasoned, the two were indeed equivalent: 'Democracy always bears the stamp of class' (Böhme 1985: 166). At the same time, a major qualitative difference makes Western-style democracy inferior to that of the East: 'Bourgeois democracy is, independently of its forms, essentially a dictatorship of the bourgeoisie … The working class can only achieve real, feasible democracy through the dictatorship of the proletariat' (ibid.).

According to Marxist ideology, bourgeois democracy represents the social minority, whereas socialist democracy finally puts the social majority – 'the people' – into power and therefore embodies the only true democracy.[6]

But matching Marxist-Leninist theory with East German practice was not without challenge for East Germany's leadership. While the leaders claimed that, with socialism, they were building the first stage of communist society, they struggled to explain why certain problems characteristic of class society, such as crime, corruption and social differences, persisted in the East German state. Moreover, the absurd absolutism of the leaders' claim to perfection – 'the party is always right'[7] – could not but invite critique, because it set an impossible standard. In consequence, ideologues were pressed to make concessions, declaring, when necessary, their socialism to be still in its infancy, or reverting to Marx's definition of socialism as a transitional society. Caught in self-contradiction, the regime itself opened up loopholes in a tightly-knit web of doctrines.

History itself also did not conform entirely to the historiography projected by East German leaders. As the party's takeover resulted from Soviet occupation rather than democratic approval – let alone popular upheaval – even the regime's leaders had difficulty pronouncing the term 'Revolution'. To sustain the ideological construction, a more German-sounding equivalent with ambiguous connotations – *Umwälzung* – was used instead to refer to the sweeping social changes that enabled the founding of the GDR and the party leadership's rule (see Böhme 1985: 45).

In order to compensate for the regime change that could not be named a revolution, the East German regime constantly had to stage one. The ubiquitous propaganda – including banners, billboards, news media and school books – was brimming with phrases praising 'the creativity of the people', 'the revolutionary vigour of the masses' and 'the revolutionary achievements of the people'. Valorising the social contribution of what had traditionally been perceived as 'the lower classes', an ethnically cohesive group or an ill-defined social whole,[8] the regime portrayed itself as a virtual democracy driven by the revolutionary will and skill of the people. They, the 'folk', instructed by their party leaders, were the engine of society, the source of all ingenuity and progress.[9]

To challenge this ideology meant to challenge the regime – its self-representation as the endpoint in the development of mankind, its legitimation as a radical break with the past and as a democracy founded on the consensus of the people. Hence, East Germans heralded the collapse of the Soviet empire with the simple phrase 'We are the people!' By reclaiming publicly the reference of this contested term, the people on the streets declared themselves to be the political constituency that alone grants political legitimacy.

The East German demonstrations of 1989, which reached from the capital of Berlin via nerve centres of opposition such as Leipzig and Dresden to the smallest provincial towns, gave visible and vocal expression to a popular sentiment that, in a carnivalesque mode, had denied political leaders any kind of legitimation for the forty years of the regime's existence. This sentiment had found expression in the ubiquitous, but outlawed, East German jokes which contrasted the regime's idealistic self-portrayal with its material reality, revealed its striking continuity with the past, and pitted the regime's representatives against the people.[10] Following a robust tradition of folk humour that extends to antiquity, the jokes accompanied the East German regime in a laughing chorus that may have fallen short of a comprehensive political programme, but that articulated, as Clement de Wroblewsky claims, the political consciousness of East Germans (1990: 183).

The existence of these jokes illuminates how folk culture absorbs and exploits the carnival ideology of the modern state while competing and clashing with it. As true folk art (Wroblewsky 1990: 182), the jokes attest to the very same ingenuity and political acuity of the people that the regime proclaimed to be the cornerstones of its legitimation. But, at the same time, they also gleefully undercut the carnival ideology of the East German state, as they unveil its deceit in the face of a truly popular consensus. In a sense, the carnivalesque headstands of folklore put the regime on its feet again by analysing its hierarchical power structures, by exposing its economic foundations and by outlining its historical affinities.[11]

The political thrust of this folk culture came to bear in the fall of 1989, when the banners people carried through the streets featured joke-like slogans and epigrams that derided the regime. Indeed, according to Wroblewsky, the banner inscriptions represented East German jokes in their most specific form (1990: 183).[12]

Considering the vital importance of 'the people' to the rise and fall of modern political systems, it is no accident that both party ideologues and Bakhtin find their 'most comprehensive metaphor in "the folk"' (see Holquist 1984: xix). Nor is 'the folk' a mere metaphor: it is, first of all, a political argument. Indeed, Bakhtin recovers the spirit of carnival not only through living in a state that proclaimed itself as the world turned upside down, but also by reacting to an era in which all political legitimation derived from the people. Accordingly, Bakhtin conceives of the carnivalesque not only as a cultural phenomenon or a literary strategy, but in decidedly political terms when he calls Rabelais 'the most democratic among these initiators of new literatures' (1984: 2) and speaks of 'the revolutionary nature of folk humour' (1984: 138).

The paradigm of the world turned upside down – both in its use as official ideology and as a subversive practice – informed East German carnivalesque film in several ways. First of all, it formulated a response to the modern state, examining the regime's institutions in the light of its propaganda, and re-instituting the people as a political arbiter. Second, it mobilised the carnivalesque potential of the cinematic medium, especially by uniting the people in rounds of subversive laughter and thus providing a means to shake off anxieties, express taboo opinions and restore social bonds that were destroyed by the regime's atomising institutions (such as the ubiquitous threat of surveillance by the secret police and its informers). Thirdly, it bridged official policy and folk culture by using a state-sponsored industry to disseminate kernels of folk humour.

Assuming a special status in the cultural landscape of East Germany, carnivalesque film remained a favourite for almost the entire 46-year period during which East Germany produced films. In order to be able to show the films' texture within the limited space of a single chapter and yet give an impression of their paradigmatic quality, I will limit my analysis of carnivalesque film to the following examples: *Das Kleid* (*The Dress*, Konrad Petzold, 1961), *Hauptmann Florian von der Mühle* (*Lieutenant Florian of the Mill*, Werner Wallroth, 1968), *Jungfer, sie gefällt mir* (*Maiden, I Fancy Her*, Günter Reisch, 1969), *Wie heiratet man einen König* (*How to Marry a King*, Rainer Simon, 1969), *Sechse kommen durch die Welt* (*Six Make It through the World*, Rainer Simon, 1972), *Das blaue Licht* (*The Blue Light*, Iris Gusner, 1976) and *Wer reißt denn gleich vorm Teufel aus* (*Who's Afraid of the Devil*, Egon Schlegel, 1977). Bringing to bear the factors outlined above, I will argue that the special success of carnivalesque film resulted from its playful ambivalence, from its ability to uncover its own covert meanings without losing its cover.

## The logic of the reference

The carnivalesque must be appreciated for its duplicity and ambivalence. In the paradigm of 'the world turned upside down', the world might stand on its head, but it remains intact, forcing its laws, phenomena and interpretations onto the gestures of rebellion. Hence, the carnivalesque to some extent affirms the order it topples, preserving the original despite, or through, its negation. Bakhtin's own text, for instance, did not undermine the Soviet regime by contradicting outright the coercive pressure to conform to the regime's show of ideological uniformity, as Michael Holquist claims (1984: xix). Instead of putting forward an entirely opposed worldview, Bakhtin allowed for a vacillation in the meaning of his message. Depending on the perspective his reader takes, his scholarly celebration of the people's uncompromised union in *Rabelais and His World* echoed the party doctrine that members of the lower classes needed to disregard their differences and come together, and, at the same time, reconceived the concept of unity of the people in a way that sidestepped and even ridiculed the regime's ideological pressure to uniformity (see Preuss 2005). Opposed to the party's depiction of the people as soldered together by an idea, by a leader, and by a historical mission, he imagines the unity of the folk as a de-ideologised utopian merger of bodies in constant becoming and decay. Rather than disciplined, conscientious and sacrificing, the united folk, according to Bakhtin, is self-propelled, chaotically unruly and utterly dismissive of any kind of leadership.

However, while Bakhtin supplies the rationale for confronting the regime on the basis of its own ideology, he entrusts the reader with picking it up. Bakhtin's study is an invitation to make comparisons, draw conclusions and turn them into political actions, but an invitation only. His text resembles a picture puzzle in which one image eclipses the other although both are contained within the same frame (see Gombrich 2000: 5–7). Transporting and undercutting the regime's ideology at the same time, Bakhtin's ultimate message depends on the audience's disposition towards his text.

Similarly, carnivalesque film – and perhaps most of East German film production – affirmed the ideology of the regime while simultaneously contesting it, and relied on the spectator's political acumen to sort out the message of the films for themselves. On the one hand, carnivalesque film conformed to the ideology that constrained and permeated the public sphere. Set predominantly in more or less imaginary feudal eras, its heroes are the social underdogs who expose the ruling classes' mechanisms of exploitation, their inhumanity, their lack of capability, and their processes of legitimation. Thus, the films highlighted the injustices and inadequacies of class society and endorsed *ex negativo* the social order the East German regime was supposed to be. On the other hand, the just, equal and democratic society that the GDR aspired to be remained elusive, providing the licence for social critique. Commonly told jokes, like the one about the angry, bearded man waiting with a club at the entrance to heaven – 'That's nothing for you to be scared about. It's Marx waiting for the party leader' (Schlechte & Schlechte 1991: 138) – or those about the party leader's mother, who worriedly asks her son, after seeing his way of life, 'What are you going to do if the Reds come back?' (Wroblewsky 1990: 66), derived their punchline from the incongruity of party ideology and the socio-political reality of the regime. In many jokes, folk humour associated the party leaders themselves with feudal lords and an overwhelming number of jokes pit the people against the party leaders, finding ever new ways to articulate popular discontent. Carnivalesque film, living up to the regime's call for the *Volksverbundenheit* (closeness to the people) of the arts in a Bakhtinian way, adopted the structures of these jokes, in particular their way of summarising the regime's theory and practice into succinct absurdisms, their particular combination of surreal premise and naturalist depiction, as well as their sharp political pith.

Because the regime designed its ideological guidelines according to political exigency rather than with respect to narrative or logical cohesion, dogmatic stricture, in spite of itself, granted artists leeway. However great or small, this leeway sufficed for carnivalesque film to turn the regime's ideology against itself. For example, the duplicitous self-definition of the GDR nomenclature as both an integral part of the working class and as its leadership elite destabilised its own figurative placement in those narratives that were intended to support its rule. Carnivalesque film reflected the contradiction between the leadership's self-legitimisation as equal and its insistence on its superiority through the leaders' double signification. While a politically correct reading would have identified the party leaders with the films' revolting hero, their claim to superiority grouped them together with the hero's opponents, the feudal ruling class. Since the East German audience was thoroughly schooled in Marxism, which regarded the rulers of class society as the enemy of the working people, the regime's own teachings provided not only the means for referencing the East German upper class but also for critiquing it as an exploitative and deceptive clique, keen on self-enrichment, luxury and pomp, and with a way of life as anachronistic as it was immoral.

Hence, it comes as no surprise that GDR audiences, including the censors, discovered their rulers in the portrayals of abusive feudal lords and corrupt clergy, whether or not filmmakers made these associations explicit. For instance, censors complained that Eberhard Esche's portrayal of the frivolous king in Rainer Simon's *How to Marry a King* (a film based on the Brothers Grimm fairytale 'The Peasant's Wise Daughter') parodied Walter Ulbricht, who, at the time the movie was made, was to serve two more years as the leader of the party and four more as the head of state. While this resemblance had been unintended according to the film director who conceives of his films as parables (see Gehler & Schmidt 1990: 19–20), his colleague, Egon Schlegel, stopped just short of giving names. In the *mise-en-scène* of the king's court in *Who's Afraid of the Devil*, he ostentatiously used a letter so ambiguous that it reads as both an 'H' and an 'X'. The 'X' usually stands for a variable in a mathematical equation, a placeholder, and is used for a person who, for some reason, cannot be called by name. The 'H' might refer to the king's title in the film, 'Hoheit' (in English, 'Highness') or may stand for a name, which invites the association with Erich Honecker, who succeeded Walter Ulbricht in the early 1970s and stayed in power until the collapse of the regime in 1989. In East German media, he featured as ubiquitously as the 'H' or 'X' in the king's court of *Who's Afraid of the Devil*.

Parallelling carnival's parody of the cult and political order of the medieval church, as read by Bakhtin, carnivalesque films copied the institutions of the regime and turned the awe they inspired into ridicule. Although central to the regime's mainte-nance of power, these institutions did not fit the regime's portrayal of East Germany as a peace-loving country ruled by the working people. Hence, they were off-limits for public discourse, and openly speaking about them required tackling political taboos. In this respect, carnivalesque film alleviated the censors' concerns, because it allowed filmmakers to dress their references to East Germany's pervasive secret service, its militarism and its bureaucracy in a historical disguise – even though that disguise was more often than not ostentatiously flimsy. Under this whimsical camouflage, East Germany's most threatening institutions ironically make up the mainstays of repertory comedy. For instance, in *The Dress*, a surreal fairytale film based on the 1837 Hans Christian Andersen story 'The Emperor's New Clothes', secret police are omnipresent. Slipping out from behind the palace curtains, dashing down from the chandelier and even coming up from beneath the polar bear rug that lies in front of the throne, the shadowy figures give literally an all-round protection to the emperor. Trench coat-clad policemen appear on the streets out of sheer nothingness, ready to act on denuncia-tions and keeping the citizens in line. They even confiscate a deck of cards that seems to distract the people from watching the emperor's parade. In addition to the state surveillance that makes the people cautious of their every utterance, there are also two remarkably 'good citizens' who, alluding to the spying behaviour encouraged by East German authorities, do not hesitate to denounce their friends for their own economic advantage. As caricatures of the bourgeois type, from a Marxist point of view, their duplicity is marked as anachronistic. Thus, the film characterises the spying, falsehood and mistrust that marred the East German public sphere as the behaviour of the class enemy. Poetic justice has it that one ends up informing on the other: those who op-press the people are their own worst enemy.

The spies also end up working towards one another's downfall (literally) in *Lieu-tenant Florian of the Mill*, a historical comedy set in the post-Napoleonic era. The ubiquitous agent, Nepomuk alias 'the coachman' alias 'Ypsilon' ('Y'), adapts to his sur-roundings like a chameleon. An example of a pernicious spy turned ludicrous, his ever-changing disguises and awkward hiding places render him a laughing-stock. Priding himself on his cleverness and intuition, he is nevertheless always one or two steps behind the events. As he reasons about the case of high treason he has put to-gether, 'Something is still missing – the end of the affair, an unexpected effect. I bet I am very close to it', his words are rendered true by his rival at spying, a baroness, who approaches him from behind with a bread shovel and on his cue, 'It has to come with a bang', smashes it down on his head, literally knocking him – and herself – out of the frame for the remainder of the film. Hilariously inefficient and self-defeating, the car-nival stand-in for East Germany's infamous State Security dissolves the threat posed by the secret police into ridicule.

The same is true of the depiction of the military. Carnivalesque film permitted film-makers to take liberties with the subject matter that would not have been possible in any other genre or media. While the representation of the armed forces played a very prominent role in East German propaganda in justifying and promoting the militari-sation of society at large, their image in East German media was highly contradictory.

Depending on whether they were perceived as advancing the cause of social progress – and, of course, that of the party leadership – or were associated with the class enemy, they were either glorified for their uprightness, their fighting spirit and their readiness to sacrifice, or they were deplored for their docility, ruthlessness and atrocious conduct. This dichotomy of commendable versus threatening depiction excluded a third type: the military could never be a matter of mockery. Carnivalesque film short-changed this representational scheme through its mechanism of double referencing, which revealed East Germany's militarism in the guise of feudal militancy. The supposed other, the class enemy, served as a mirror for the repressed self and allowed for the otherwise impossible – namely, laughter. In *Maiden, I Fancy Her*, for instance, a film based on Heinrich von Kleist's play *Der Zerbrochene Krug* (*The Broken Jug*, 1807), obedience is mocked with scatological humour, as the military synchronises even the defecation of its recruits to the staccato of the command. Moreover, the army operates on a set of odd rules. On the command 'Fire!', for instance, half of the soldiers drop dead in a macabre sort of pretend play that is supposed to save men and ammunition by anticipating the expected number of casualties. When Licht, Adam's hapless secretary who ends up a soldier by mistake, explains to the officer in charge why this strategy might backfire in the field, his reasoning falls on deaf ears, or rather a dumb mind. The officer's fatuity owes a great deal to his schematic thinking and self-centred view of the world, which are precisely the traits that figure as the trademarks of party leaders in East German jokes, like the one about Walter Ulbricht having as many political enemies as Mao Tse-Tung, or the one about the East German Minister for State Security being the West German Minister for Economic Affairs.[13] Carnivalesque film takes up this kind of folk humour. For instance, in *Maiden, I Fancy Her*, the way in which the troops prepare for a potential deployment to New Zealand involves the same kind of schematicism and self-righteousness that folk humour ascribes to East German rulers: the soldiers train to walk on their hands, because the world in the Southern Hemisphere is presumably upside down. Employing East German folk humour, carnivalesque film portrays the military neither as a terrorist, savage and revanchist war machine nor does the latter emerge as the freedom-loving, civil and peace-keeping defender of a noble cause – it is simply ludicrously absurd.

Finally, carnivalesque film, as if aiming to render a comprehensive critique of the East German state, picks on the government bureaucracy. Staffed with careerists who subscribed to the slogans and phrases of the regime for privilege and profit, the East German governmental machinery did not comply the ideology of the state, which claimed to serve the citizenry and bring about a millennial change in the way society functions (Maaz 1990: 115–18). Likewise, the officials portrayed in carnivalesque film abuse law and ideology and pervert their mission. In *Maiden, I Fancy Her*, for instance, it is paradoxically the court that lacks any sense of justice. Judge Adam is the prototype of the bureaucrat in carnivalesque film: he does not only change laws and switch interpretations, depending on the situation and his interests, he is also the only one in the village who commits crimes: in addition to having a history of stealing money from his brothers-in-arms, he misappropriates the court's funds, blackmails Ev, his love interest, and attempts to rape her. Adam's secretary Licht, the emperor's ministers in *The*

*Dress*, the guard in *The Blue Light*, the king's steward and the taxman in both *How to Marry a King* and in *Who's Afraid of the Devil*, to name only a few, are all servile, insolent and self-serving administrators of power, and all meet with at least some degree of poetic justice. Most poignantly, the steward and the tax collector are chained, with their king, to the ferry that crosses the river to the underworld. The bureaucrats are the guardsmen of hell.

As the intermediaries of power, the bureaucrats embody the dialectic of victimhood and the perpetration of crimes: the violence on which power is based corrupts and finally harms those who administer it. The king's ministers in *Six Make It through the World* are literally wooden puppets. As soulless place holders of power, they receive decorations instead of the soldiers their pay. Yet their unreserved availability to the royal family makes them susceptible to its whims too. When the princess wants to fire the carnivalesque hero as her-husband-to-be, they are – again literally – burned.

In the end, the bureaucrats only transmit the faulty logic of their leaders. While much of East Germany's literature and film targeted only lower-level officials as pervertors of the system (and, justifiedly or not, prompted the generalised charge that East German artists only rendered a critique of surface phenomena), carnivalesque film shows that the corruption of reason starts at the top and affects the entire political system. For the king in *How to Marry a King*, for instance, contradiction is a governmental principle. In the blink of an eye, he rules that an ox gave birth to a foal and demands of his wife-to-be to come to the castle both naked and not naked, riding and not riding and with a present and without a present. The king in *Who's Afraid of the Devil*, like his taxman, again and again touts his standard phrases, letting no opportunity pass to assure everyone 'We are a merry government'. He even expounds this maxim to the carnivalesque hero as he plots the poor fellow's death. With the same effect, carnivalesque film subjected the self-delusion and self-acclamation of East German leaders to a deft mockery that, apart from telling names, rivalled the political defiance of jokes. Resounding the party leadership's claim to victory over the class enemy, the king in *Six Make It through the World* announces to his soldiers: 'I have won. I have won over the bloody great enemy. Completely. Entirely. Totally. I have crushed him. I will never be forgotten … I am taking your homage as thanks.' The king's emphatic repetition of the personal pronoun 'I' flies in the face of the weary soldiers who actually fought the war. Contrary to what he claims, they do not seem to honour their king in the least. They mumble tiredly 'Hurrah!' on command and seem to do so only because they are still waiting for their pay. The king's public acclaim is a contradiction in terms: it is a result of exercising authoritarian control.

Despite their circumlocutions, that is, their tacit agreement not to name names, carnivalesque films have a rapport with things East German that is palpable. Instead of emulating an aesthetic that conventionally denotes naturalism in costume dramas, filmmakers underscored the parable-like character of their films by emphasising artifice and a certain whimsical nature. In turn, the films' allegorical quality entailed, like a transitive verb requiring an object, a conceptual vacancy. Prompting the question, 'A parable *of what*?', the films coaxed the audience to search for comparisons, particularly among those issues and topics that could not be openly addressed in the public sphere.

From here it was only a small step for the audience to recognise the logical inconsistencies of the regime's ideology in the absurd arguments that the officials and feudal lords put forth in carnivalesque film. For instance, in *How to Marry a King*, the glaring paradox with which the steward preps the people for the king's hearing of their complaints, 'The king's grace is unending. Keep its limits in mind!', highlights the contradiction between the regime's claim to have liberated the people and ushered in a new era of democracy – in other words, the rulers' unlimited munificence – and its insistence on the use of force against political dissidents – in other words, the prohibitively slight leeway that the government actually granted people to express their views or even to relate matters of fact. Similarly incompetent in logical reasoning, the taxman in *Who's Afraid of the Devil* has difficulties justifying to the working people the reason why they have to pay taxes to fight robbers whom they have never encountered. He repeats, over and over, the same phrases and finally resorts to the tautological argument of power: 'The king has determined that there are robbers. Hence, there are robbers.' The robbers are as intangible as the class enemy that, according to East German propaganda, was ready to take advantage of even the feeblest show of non-conformity in order to seize the workers' achievements and abolish socialism. The audience could easily draw an analogy between the regime's ideologues and the taxman in *Who's Afraid of the Devil* as they both resort to formulaic statements and circuitous reasoning when they are unable to substantiate ideology with facts. As carnivalesque films render the contradiction between the regime's ideology and the lived experience of its citizens, they translate it into an aesthetic principle that, in turn, calls upon the audience to discern the truth. Similar to the point of the jokes, which relies on the audience's understanding and shared horizon of political perceptions, carnivalesque films leave it up to the audience to figure out the logic of their references.

In this way, carnivalesque films reverse the political process that they portray: they reintegrate the people – that is, the audience – into collective truth-finding and decision-making. As the arbiter of meaning, the audience can switch, in a carnival toppling of 'high' and 'low', the references of the folk heroes and their ruling-class opponents in contemporary coordinates. Instead of embodying the revolutionary leaders of the underclass, the party bureaucrats thus came to figure as the feudal caste. Their opponents, which according to GDR ideology should have been depicted as the oppressive class enemy of the underprivileged, are instead the carnivalesque heroes themselves. This inversion revealed the party elites as the oppressor class that they were, according to their own ideology, supposed to guard against. Like Bakhtin's *Rabelais and His World*, carnivalesque film left the storyline of the regime's master narrative unaltered, but changed its political meaning and, in this way, effectively denied the legitimacy of the regime by affirming its own ideology.

## Notes

1   See Bakhtin 1984: 3, 29, 58, 126–39.
2   His study *Rabelais and His World* represents, according to his biographers, Katerina
    Clark and Michael Holquist, 'Bakthin's most comprehensive critique to date of Stalinist

culture' (1984: 305).

3   See Katerina Clark's characterisation of the Russian intelligentsia (Clark 2004: 3).

4   Holquist notes 'the book's cool official reception in the Soviet Union and its extraordinary popularity in the West' (1984: xv).

5   May Sinclair, in her bestselling novel *The Divine Fire*, defines the modern era in these political terms: 'modernity simply means democracy' (1904: 415), and sees this form and doctrine of government as a political means to frustrate political dissent: 'when once democracy has been forced on us there is no good protesting any longer' (ibid.).

6   Since this argument diverges decidedly from Western ideology tinged by the Cold War, some elaboration of its underpinnings is necessary to define the political angle taken by carnivalesque film. Put plainly, the East German leadership derived its legitimation from the pretense of having created a society that finally corrected the wrongs of history. Hunger, war, exploitation, discrimination and every other kind of injustice or infringement of human dignity were supposedly overcome by the East German state. This claim received its theoretical backing from Marxist historiography which held that socialism would, albeit on a different social level, return to the egalitarian principles of primitive society. According to Marxist thought, technological advances had generated a surplus in production which, in turn, resulted in the uneven distribution of wealth. Those who owned the means of production started to rule those who did not. Thus, economics forged the hierarchisation of society into classes. As technology and human development progressed, they periodically clashed with social and political conditions, sparking revolutions that led to the formation of new social orders. Eventually, Marxists projected, the means of production would become so efficient that everybody's needs could be satisfied to the full. At this stage of technological development, the accumulation of surplus by the propertied caste would become anachronistic and the oppressed classes would overthrow class society altogether, propelling history forward to a return to mankind's original egalitarianism. Impressed by the rapid technological advance of the industrial revolution, Marx stipulated that the last day of class society had already dawned. Because capitalism would sooner or later outlive itself, the proletariat had the historical mission of ushering in a new era. By means of a revolution, it would first take dictatorial command over society and, after a transition period, finally fulfil the dream of mankind: communism. Considering the fascist regimes of the 1930s and 1940s to be the death throws of capitalism, East German rulers claimed that the regime change of 1945 marked the overthrow of the capitalist order as the final stage of class society and that, consequently, the German working class had accomplished its historical mission by founding the German Democratic Republic (GDR), the state in which the people ruled for the people.

7   Louis Fürnberg's 'Song of the Party' ('Lied der Partei') from 1950 summarised this axiom of East German politics in the refrain: 'Die Partei, die Partei, die hat immer recht' ('The party, the party, is always right').

8   The German notion of *Volk* comprises all three of these significations and was used by East German propagandists in this ambiguity.

9   The regime undertook a concerted cultural effort to substantiate this claim. Imitating similar measures undertaken by the Soviet leadership, it sponsored movements such

as folk dancing groups, folk singing groups and the 'Circles of Writing Workers'. Professional artists were sent into the factories to get in touch with, learn from and write about the folk. And the censors favoured folk motifs, 'folksy' style and narratives that revealed the exploitative character of class society, while granting poetic justice to the underprivileged, the true folk heroes.

10  Although the East German constitution guaranteed freedom of opinion and expression, the East German penal code essentially banned any kind of criticism of the state to the effect that people sharing these jokes risked imprisonment. Clement de Wroblewsky, albeit somewhat protected by his status as a celebrity artist, stopped adding to his collection of jokes after the first five pages, because he was afraid of being caught and incarcerated for the ten to twelve years that such 'crime' commanded (see Wroblewsky 1990: 50).

11  To cite one important example, the joke about Erich Honecker, the leader of party and state, and his secretary musing on how Honecker could bring joy to the people takes the leadership's omnipresent maxim 'Anything and Everything for the benefit of the people!' all too literally: 'Honecker stands at the window in the building of the State Council and looks down onto Marx Engels Square. "If I throw down a one hundred mark note, would someone rejoice?" – "Rather two hundred marks", his secretary says, "then two people would rejoice." – "Or five twenties" – "Comrade Honecker, then why not ten tens, then ten people rejoice." – "Or twenty times…" – "Comrade Head of the State Council," his secretary interjects, "the best thing would be for you to throw yourself down, then 17 million people would rejoice!"' (Schlechte & Schlechte 1991: 191). In strict reliance on the regime's own slogans and with conspicuous naïveté, the joke tells the story of a benevolent ruler and his eager and helpful secretary. Honecker wants to make the people happy and the way he goes about fulfilling his maxim – throwing money out of the window – fully corresponds to the professed materialism of the leadership. Even the regime's claim to bring happiness to everyone is relayed in the joke by the party leader's zeal to please as many people as possible. The secretary's suggestion also plays along with the leaders' self-portrayal as popular figures and folk heroes. She flatters Honecker that people prefer him over the money (especially, falling out of the window).

Yet, there is, of course, also a darker side to this politically correct story. First of all, the joke literalises the idiomatic expression for wasting money: 'Geld zum Fenster hinauswerfen' ('throwing money out of the window'). The inanity of Honecker's proposal is further underscored by the fact that as the leader of the state he should allocate funds based on need and merit, not according to whim or on the principle of pure chance. Moreover, the joke suggests that Honecker has the money that the people are lacking, thus pointing to the unequal distribution of wealth in East German society. Finally, Honecker also emerges as a stingy character unwilling to share his goodies with his people, since he does not respond to his secretary's suggestion to give more money to people, but instead proposes to throw down ever smaller bills. It is in response to his penny-pinching that his secretary comes up with a more economical idea: Honecker would even save his one hundred marks if he threw himself down.

Both readings of the story, the politically correct one and the one characterising

Honecker's insipidity and pettiness, proceed with stringent logic to the annihilation of the ruler. Honecker's death, the joke claims, would delight 17 million people – that is, the entire population of East Germany – and it puts him to the test: if he really wanted to do anything and everything for the benefit of the people, as his regime's ubiquitous propaganda claims, he would jump. As in the majority of East German jokes, the leader elicits a negative sort of popular acclaim: the only quality this kind of folk tale cherishes in the country's leaders is their mortality. Commonly expressing a wish for the leader's death, the jokes challenge the very existence of the leadership in the face of the common folk.

Finally, like many other East German jokes, the jest recommending Honecker to jump out of the window echoes a joke about Nazi leaders in which Hitler similarly wants to please the crowds and is advised to jump down from his high place (See Hillermeier 1980: 63). Whether adapted from an earlier version or reinvented under parallel ideologies and political circumstances, East German jokes pointed to a continuity in German history that the East German regime claimed to have broken. The historical memory they transported added to their perspicacity.

12 As a strategy of resistance, the witticisms proved more effective than a direct vilification of the regime. Not only did the laughter reduce the anxieties people felt when they openly challenged their regime (after all, the East German government had endorsed the massacre of Tiananmen Square of 4 June 1989 in which the Chinese government had crushed the pro-democracy movement with unspeakably sinister brutality), but in the puns on the regime's ideology, people could also articulate their own political vision rather than defining their endeavour purely in negating the old regime.

13 The self-centred perspective of the East German leadership became a matter of ridicule in popular slogans such as 'Wo wir sind, ist vorn' ('Where we are is the top'), which Wroblewsky uses as the title for his monograph on the East German joke, or 'die größte DDR der Welt' ('the greatest German Democratic Republic in the world', my translation; Wroblewsky 1990: 123, Maaz 1990: 106). The following two abbreviated jokes illustrate how East Germans poked fun at the schematic thinking of their political leaders and institutions. The first belongs to the era of Walter Ulbricht and almost certainly refers indirectly to Mao's short-lived policy of 'letting a hundred flowers bloom', which stood for a plurality of opinion and a brief, but powerful, discussion on the merit of party rule. The joke has Ulbricht ask Mao how many of the Chinese oppose him. Mao estimates about 17 million, and Ulbricht exclaims 'Just like in the GDR!', which only had 17 million inhabitants (Wroblewsky 1990: 55). Ulbricht's conceit and self-centredness make him oblivious to the fact that 17 million enemies mean for Mao 1.5 per cent of population, whereas for him it means 100 per cent. Taking the absolute number out of its context, he can equate himself with the leader who gained world-wide popularity through his audacity to defy the Soviet imperialism.

The second joke similarly compares Ulbricht's successor, Erich Honecker, to the West German Chancellor Helmut Kohl in an unfavourable way. Giving expression to the popular contempt for the regime's bureaucrats, the joke has Honecker ask Kohl how he had found such fine ministers. Kohl replies that he tests their intelligence and demonstrates the test to Honecker by asking the West German Minister for Economic

Affairs, Graf Lambsdorff: 'It is not your brother and it is not your sister and, yet, it is your parents' child. Who is this?' Lambsdorff thinks for a while and then says: 'It's me.' 'That's right,' answers Kohl. Upon returning to East Germany, Honecker summons the head of the East German intelligence service, the infamous Erich Mielke, and puts him to the test by asking him the same question: 'It is not your brother and it is not your sister and, yet, it is your parents' child. Who is this?' Mielke responds: 'Comrade Honecker, give me 24 hours and I will have that person tracked down!' In turn, Mielke gives his officers orders: 'It is not my brother, it is not my sister, and, yet, it is my parents' child. In 24 hours, I want to see that guy.' A scrupulous search starts. Each and every corner of East Germany is scrutinised. No one is found. The next day, Mielke has to admit to Honecker that the person described could not be found in the entire GDR. Honecker says: 'My dear comrade Mielke, the solution was really very simple: it is Otto Graf Lambsdorff' (Wroblewsky 1990: 12–13). The joke's punch goes in several directions: it mocks Honecker in the same way that the joke about the 17 million enemies poked fun at Ulbricht in that he thinks he can apply another ruler's circumstances to his own without making any adjustments. It also takes up the party leaders' ideology of being equal and yet superior: Honecker is higher in the chain of command and, therefore, has met a West German, which in turn makes him feel like he can tell Mielke the correct solution. Yet, as the discerning audience will register, he really indeed equals Mielke – in stupidity that is. Moreover, the joke ridicules the East German secret service as brainless muscle: the regime's hounds have the power to penetrate every corner of the country, but not the intellectual capability to use any of their power. According to the joke, the entire system is ridden with the rigid application of formulae and codes.

## Works cited

Bakhtin, M. (1984 [1965]) *Rabelais and His World*. Trans. H. Iswolsky. Bloomington: Indiana University Press.

Böhme, W. (1985 [1967]). *Kleines politisches Wörterbuch*. Berlin: Dietz.

Clark, K. (2004) 'The King is Dead, Long Live the King: Intelligentsia Ideology in Transition', in G. Freidin (ed.) *Russia at the End of the Twentieth Century*. Available online: http://www.stanford.edu/group/Russia20/volumepdf/clark_fin99.pdf (accessed: 15 May 2004).

Clark, K. and M. Holquist (1984) *Mikhail Bakhtin*. Cambridge, MA and London: Harvard University Press.

Fukuyama, F. (1993) *The End of History and the Last Man*. New York: Avon.

Gehler, F. and H. Schmidt (eds) (1990) *Rebellen, Träumer und 'gewöhnliche Leute*. Potsdam: Betriebsschule des DEFA-Studios für Spielfilme.

Gombrich, E. H. (2000) *Art and Illusion*. Princeton and Oxford. Princeton University Press.

Hillermeier, H. (ed.) (1980) *'Im Namen des Deutschen Volkes': Todesurteile des Volksgerichtshofes*. Darmstadt and Neuwied: Luchterhand.

Holquist, M. (1984) 'Prologue', in M. Bakhtin, *Rabelais and His World*. Trans. H. Iswolsky.

Bloomington: Indiana University Press, xiii–xxiii.

Maaz, H.-J. (1990) *Der Gefühlsstau: Ein Psychogramm der DDR*. Berlin: Argon.

Preuss, E. (2005) 'To See or Not to See?': Topographies of Repression in Konrad Wolf's *I Was Nineteen* (1968) and *The Naked Man on the Sportsground* (1974)', in W. Everett and A. Goodbody (eds) *Space and Place in European Cinema*. New York: Lang, 209–42.

Schlechte, H. and K.-D. Schlechte (1991) *Witze bis zur Wende: 40 Jahre politischer Witz in der DDR*. München: Ehrenwirth.

Sinclair, M. (1904) *The Divine Fire*. Westminster: Constable.

Stam, R. (1989) *Subversive Pleasures: Bakhtin, Cultural Criticism, and Film*. Baltimore and London: Johns Hopkins University Press.

Wroblewsky, C. de (1990) *Wo wir sind, ist vorn: Der politische Witz in der DDR* (second edition). Hamburg: Rasch und Röhring.

# CHAPTER NINE

# Shockumentary evidence: the perverse politics of the Mondo film
Mark Goodall

'Carnivalisation of life is the loss of the boundary between what is serious and what is performance.'
    – Umberto Eco (2002)

'We know that a text is not a line of words releasing a single "theological" meaning (the "message" of the Author-God) but a multi-dimensional space in which a variety of writings, none of them original, blend and clash.'
    – Roland Barthes (1977: 146)

About a third of the way into Haskell Wexler's newly reissued 1968 critique of the (American) news-gathering process, *Medium Cool*, the main protagonist and his lover are discussing the ethics of the making of news. The couple are using the 1963 documentary film *Mondo Cane*, which they have recently seen, as exemplary of the problematic practice of the creation of documentary news. *Mondo Cane*, a commercially successful Italian film, was made by a team led by journalists Gualtiero Jacopetti and Franco Prosperi. After debating the motives and actions behind one particular scene in the film (the effects of nuclear testing on the Pacific wildlife of Bikini Atoll), *Medium Cool*'s hunky protagonist wearily snaps: 'How the hell do I know what they did, those were *Italian* cameramen!'

It is precisely this kind of curtly dismissive and uninterested comment, typifying much about *Mondo Cane* and the many related films that subsequently formed what can be called the 'mondo cycle' that this chapter scarcely begins to counter. In the very many volumes written on the histories of feature film, scant attention is paid to *Mondo Cane* and to what has become known in cult circles as 'mondo film'. It is contended that this is not merely an act of neglect on the part of the esteemed critics, writers and academics who have shaped and continue to shape these histories; nor that mondo films are 'bad films' (as has been posited ever since they were released). Rather, as is argued here, mondo films have been ignored because they do not fit easily into the categorisations present in any of the broad aspects of such cultural historicisation. Mondo films currently have no proper status in the story of film (including the genre they are referent to most closely: the documentary film) precisely because they are 'transgressive' works of art. Moreover they are transgressive in accordance with both of the key aspects of Peter Stallybrass and Allon White's famous treatise on the politics and poetics of transgression: the 'blurring of boundaries' and the 'processes of inversion' (1986: 1–26). As we shall also see, mondo films contain aspects of exploitation and voyeurism that have jarred with political climates both social and cultural of the last thirty or so years and are indeed 'politically perverse'. Yet this in itself, as recent recuperations of many 'low' forms of film art show (what Jeffrey Sconce (1995) calls the 'paracinematic'), does not explain completely the absence of these works from the histories of film. The political perversity of the mondo film can arguably be viewed now more usefully as harbinger of many aspects of contemporary globalising media production and consumption. I think it is these qualities that make these films so meaningful in the context of world cinema today.

## Perverse politics

First it is necessary to examine how and why mondo films came about, and then became 'perversely political'. There were numerous 'sensational' documentary films made in the thirty or so years (if not since the advent of cinema itself) before the release of *Mondo Cane* that exhibited a misanthropic approach to the recording on film of the cultures of the world. Films like *Africa Speaks* (Walter Futter, 1930), *Goona Goona* (Armand Denis and Andre Roosevelt, 1932), *Karamoja* (William B. Treutle, 1954) and Elwood Price's *Mau Mau* (1954) provided Western audiences with a feast of ethnographic spectacle. Continuing trends developed by writers such as Jens Bjerre and Armand Denis, these films fused travel writing with the travelogue film under the guise of ethnographic research most often spuriously. The techniques used in *Mau Mau* (originally an account of anti-colonial 'terrorist' uprising in Kenya), for example, of combining field material with studio-staged sequences to increase the sex and violence quota was widespread. The arrival of *Europa di Notte* in 1959 made by Italian director Alessandro Blasetti began the mondo cycle as we know it today. *Europa di Notte* and other Italian follow-ups by Luigi Vanzi (*Mondo di Notte*, 1960) and Gianni Proia (*Mondo di Notte 2* (1962) and *Mondo di Notte 3* (1963), also known as *Ecco*) cemented the taste for the cinema of attractions, which

> solicits spectator attention, inciting visual curiosity, and supplying pleasure through an exciting spectacle ... theatrical display dominates over narrative absorption, emphasising the direct stimulation of shock or surprise at the expense of unfolding a story or creating a diegetic (fictional) universe. The cinema of attractions expends little energy creating characters with psychological motivations or individual personality. (Gunning 1990: 58–9)

Later films such as *Mondo Caldo di Notte* (Renzo Russo, 1962), *Mondo Freudo* (Robert Lee Frost and Bob Cresse, 1966), *Mondo Bizarro* (Robert Lee Frost and Bob Cresse, 1966), *Malamondo* (Paolo Cavara, 1964) and others luridly articulated a taste of exotic sexuality – a taste that Italian audiences gratefully received in their pursuit for 'sexy transgression' (Zamori 1999). This Italian intervention begins the perverse politics of the mondo film proper, effectively an intoxicating blend of what Christian Hansen, Catherine Needham and Bill Nichols describe as 'pornotopia' and 'ethnotopia' (1991: 212, 218), that cinematic position where 'representation as a semiotic operation confirms a ... voyeuristic pathology' (Nichols 1991: 63).

Pornography and ethnology share a discourse of domination over the subject who is presented as a primitive subservient. This has long been a critical question for the ethical study of film representation. The shaping of mondo films as (pseudo-)documentaries or 'shockumentaries' as they came to be known, recalls merely the 'pornography of knowledge' (Nichols 1991: 210) common to a wide range of photographic as well as cinematographic images: the deep desire *to know* that which seems at first incomprehensible. *Mondo Cane* was directed by Jacopetti and Prosperi at a precise time when the short newsreel became a cinema 'larger than life' and perfectly exemplified and exploited a growing fascination with such 'knowing' through the big screen. An American poster promoting the film promises 'a hundred incredible worlds where the camera has never gone before' and it is this promise of forbidden pleasures that the makers of the film exploited effectively and deliberately. The directors of mondo films took advantage of widespread changes in attitudes to sexuality, particularly in terms of film. In staunchly Catholic Italy, the beginnings of a social, cultural and political secularisation which in the early 1970s allowed a 'massive explosion of pornography' (Antonelli & Ortoleva 1999: 71) was exploited by filmmakers keen to serve up ever more risqué entertainment. For Carlo Antonelli and Peppino Ortoleva pornography 'Italian style' is 'an egotistic form of sexuality, disturbing to many in its brutal vulgarity' (ibid.); its powerful image refracted through the more perverse and sensational elements of mondo film through to such late twentieth-century television entertainment as the infamous *Italian Stripping Housewives*. Jacopetti, who had worked on the newsreels *Europeo Ciak* and *Ieri, Oggi, Domani* for the publisher Rizzoli and scripted part of *Europa di Notte*, had already observed not only how audiences flocked to these cinematic burlesques but that the life lived around or outside of these showy contexts was equally fascinating. The film was a clever compilation of thirty or so sequences from disparate parts of the globe dedicated to the notion of life as 'mondo cane', a Tuscan phrase honouring the peculiarities of life (often translated somewhat crudely as 'it's a dog's life'). The focus of the film, and of the camera-eye of the director and camera operator, was on the peculiar customs, rituals and lifestyles of the world's indigenous cultures. The huge success of *Mondo Cane* engendered a host of follow-up films such as those listed above all encapsulated by the proposition offer from the poster for *Il Pelo nel Mondo* (*Go! Go! Go! World*, Marco Vicario, 1964) of visions of 'primitive rites and civilised wrongs' where the sexualised image continued to reign supreme.

When in 1966 Jacopetti and Prosperi completed their 'masterpiece' *Africa Addio*, a sprawling and brutal account of decolonisation in the sub-Saharan continent, the 'text' for the film recalled not only the language of Western critiques of the 'society of the spectacle': 'all that was once truly lived has become mere representation' (Debord 1994: 12) but also that of African writers fully aware of the incursion now of Western cultural imperialism, after Western military, economic and political imperialism onto their territories:

the 'advanced' nations: the ambitious gigantism of the cinema, with its hunger for vast spaces, vaster than its screens can contain ... The cinema tries to depict the whole ocean, though it can't show at the same time the streams and rivers which run into that ocean. (Bemba 1971: 94)

Pornotopia and ethnotopia combine most strongly in Jacopetti and Prosperi's 1972 fictionalised documentary account of the American slave trade, *Addio Zio Tom*, when the 'travelling photographers', after arriving in the Deep South via helicopter, are given a grotesque guided tour of the many sexual exploitations of this disgraceful aspect of American history. Here the perverted dynamics of the male cinematic gaze is gleefully exposed in a sickening exposé of the justifications for such exploitation. Critical examination of such films probed the motives and methods of mondo directors paying particular attention to the sexual and violent content of mondo films. Bill Landis has dwelled almost exclusively and sensationally on the sexual and violent content of Jacopetti and Prosperi's films, casting the filmmakers as exploitative voyeurs. He describes *Addio Zio Tom*, for example, somewhat erroneously, as being 'far more sexually explicit and perverted than conventional pornography' (Landis & Clifford 2002: 166) and argues that 'in their inimitable way, Prosperi and Jacopetti have documented their own crimes against humanity by their imaginary reproduction of one of America's most shameful historical episodes' (ibid.: 170).

Subsequent mondo directors such as Alfredo and Angelo Castiglioni are also accused of exploiting sex, magic, mutilation and ritual as titillation (1998: 173). But Landis was not alone in pursuing the mondo aesthetic as a form of 'travelling perversion' (Landis 2000: 49). *The New Yorker* magazine's Pauline Kael famously described Jacopetti and Prosperi as 'perhaps the most devious filmmakers who have ever lived' (quoted in Gregory 2003). British reviews of the film were also accusatory: 'In the worst traditions of exposé journalism, it [*Addio Zio Tom*] merely exploits the exploited while pretending indignation and disapproval' (Jeavons 1973: 86). To these accusations of gross professional misconduct Franco Prosperi has stated 'we wanted to shock the audience. Shocking and alternating emotions by inserting soft scenes to allow the digestion of the violent scenes' (quoted in Gregory 2003). Elsewhere Prosperi has described watching *Africa Addio* as 'an assault' (ibid.). Jacopetti and Prosperi have always defined themselves as documentary filmmakers with serious intent: in *Mondo Cane* and *Africa Addio* as journalists; in *Addio Zio Tom* historical reconstruction, claims that have been supported somewhat in print. John Cohen identifies Jacopetti and Prosperi as 'movie-journalists' and their work as 'a new kind of journalism … presenting reality "as big as life"' (1966: 10). The more serious aspects of their work, the rare footage secured in Zanzibar for instance, is thus played down in favour of the pair's 'inauthentic' working methods and style. Meanwhile Angelo and Alfredo Castiglioni, who aim for a 'scientific' approach in their films, have acknowledged that their work is 'a compromise between spectacular effects and the needs of the ethnographer' (Novarin 1998: 52). This is supported somewhat by Charles Kilgore's reading of their *Mondo Magic* (1975) as a film that 'treats ritual with a certain amount of respect' (quoted in Staples 1995: 123).

A particular scene from *Addio Zio Tom*, set in a New Orleans slave market, presents the filmmakers, and thereby the audience, with an 'excessive' depiction of a range of commodified sexual entertainments: exotic mixed-race women, homosexuality, greased and massaged bodies, freaks. It is a deliberately grotesque moment of cinematic voyeurism, one of many in the film in which the viewer's complicity is made tangible and uncomfortable. In *Africa Addio*, in a sequence which represents a film crew making a 'documentary' on a Zulu tribe, the construction of fake representations is slowly exposed as the tribes people are revealed to be 'modernised' actors. Black Africans have 'gone native' for the presence and financial gain of a Western film crew; at the end of the shoot they dress back in modern apparel and drive off in fast and expensive-looking cars and motorbikes. However, a barbed and potentially subversive comment on the falsification of the real Africa by the imperial imaginary all too easily gives way to a montage of crude cultural stereotypes and then to a pornographic peepshow fragmentation and anatomisation of the female body. 'Third Cinema' advocates Fernando Solanas and Octavio Getino noted such representations as problematic: 'The more exploited a man is the more he is placed on a plane of insignificance. The more he resists, the more he is viewed as a beast' (Solanas & Getino 1971: 25). For Solanas and Getino films like *Africa Addio* epitomise a neocolonial methodology. Jacopetti is labelled a 'fascist'; in his films 'fantasy has been replaced by phantoms, and man is turned into an extra who dies so that Jacopetti can comfortably film his execution' (ibid.).

It is clear that within the context of the Italian film history, *Mondo Cane* and its predecessors were a violent repudiation of neorealist principles (Gregory 2003) and most of those of 'documentary realism'. Any drive for authenticity is dissolved into the construction of film images (and sounds) as part of a global spectacle. Artificiality replaced attempts at imaging the real; the deployment of new screen technologies such as lightweight cameras and Technicolor and widescreen merely hastened the act of spectacular-simulated representation towards an 'imperial imaginary' (Shohat and Stam 1994: 100), the 'panoptic' gaze (Foucault 1991: 195) and 'gendered spectatorial position' (Tseëlon 2000: 254). One can see why early reviewers of the Italian cycle, imbibed with the ethics of '*cinema vérité*' and 'direct cinema' and the revolutionary critique of the various 'new waves', were moved to be dismissive about the apparent exploitation techniques employed by the directors and producers of this material (this is particularly noticeable in the reviews of mondo films published in the British periodical *Monthly Film Bulletin* between 1963 and 1976). Nevertheless this process of representation has remarkably continued until the present day as films with increasingly violent and disturbing imagery derived from the 1960s originals continue to emerge from countries like the US and Japan as well as from Italy.

## Transgression

*Mondo Cane* and the films that followed can be seen to express many of the aspects that articulate a perverse politics. Yet through further examination, and keeping in mind the theory of the politics and poetics of transgression, it is possible to reveal some aspects of the mondo film, particularly the films of Jacopetti and Prosperi, that at least problematise any critical dismissal and simplistic categorisation.

In an important and useful essay entitled 'Documentary Modes of Representation', Bill Nichols outlines and illustrates four generic types of the serious business of documentary practice (1991: 32–75). If as an experiment in transgression we try to map the mondo film onto Nichols' theories, we can see that, although mondo films reflect some of the characteristics of documentary films quite closely (Cohen 1966: 10–26; Rondi 1966: 214), others, particularly those of Jacopetti and Prosperi, regularly transgress such 'rules'. The following table identifies on the left some of the characteristics of Nichols' documentary modes; the column on the right identifies how the modes of the mondo films compare to these:

| Characteristics of the 'expository' mode: | Characteristics of mondo film: |
|---|---|
| • 'Voice-of-God'<br>• Editing continuity<br>• Linear<br>• Causal meaning for audience | • 'Voice-of-God'<br>• 'Shock cuts'<br>• Non-linear<br>• Meaning ambiguous |
| Characteristics of the 'observational' mode: | Characteristics of mondo film: |
| • Attempt at 'reality' (or neo-reality)<br>• Ethical<br>• Author anonymous<br>• Synch sound<br>• Long takes<br>• Purist | • Surreal<br>• Misanthropic<br>• Author 'visible'<br>• Non-synch sound<br>• Rapid edits<br>• Artificial |
| Characteristics of the 'interactive' mode: | Characteristics of mondo film: |
| • Interview style<br>• Encounter with author<br>• Directed 'on-screen' | • No interviews<br>• Author off-screen<br>• Directed to audience (subjects mute) |
| Characteristics of the 'reflexive mode: | Characteristics of mondo film: |
| • Film about the 'act of representation'<br>• Self-conscious<br>• Filmmaker-viewer *not* Filmmaker-subject<br>• Ironic | • Film about the 'act of representation'<br>• Self-conscious<br>• Filmmaker-viewer *and* (perverted) Filmmaker-subject<br>• Ironic (but satire/parody rather than 'self-critical') |

Four modes of documentary representation (Nichols 1991: 32–75)

The mode of the reflexive is, perhaps unwittingly, the 'nearest fit', especially in terms of the very powerful use of music in mondo films as an ironic, manipulative instrument of control. The tendency towards the self-conscious, the stylistic and poetic, the voyeuristic, the ironic and a clear lack of 'truth' is also evident. Perhaps most significantly there is a strong sense of parody and satire evident in mondo films, an aspect that Nichols codifies as radical and 'underdeveloped in documentary where the prevalence of the discourses of sobriety and a Calvinist sense of mission ... particularly in English-speaking countries' (1991: 69–70) has prevailed.

In *Addio Zio Tom* there are some dialogues between the filmmaker and the subject (usually the exploiters of the slaves, the intention obviously being to make these characters, some real historical figures, look ridiculous) but most other interaction remains voyeuristic (rape, prostitution, torture, and so on). Jacopetti and Prosperi, throughout their film works, certainly enjoy the use of irony, effective both linguistically (narration) and semiotically (imagery). This irony manifests itself, as 'ironic representations inevitably have the appearance of insincerity since what is overtly said is not what is actually meant ... as a tone or attitude irony comes after romance, tragedy and comedy; it sets them all on edge; it undermines their solidarity and sobriety' (1991: 73). Further 'the trope of irony ... provides a linguistic paradigm of a mode of thought that is radically self-critical with respect not only to a given characterisation of the world of experience but also to the very effort to capture adequately the truth of things in language' (White 1973: 37–8).

The concept of the 'traditional' spectacle of the film document is partially subverted to form a 'critical' spectacle where representative modes are turned on their head and the thriving cultures of Western capitalism are instead subjected to the cinematic gaze and power relationships between viewer and viewed. This does not 'even things up' but nevertheless indicates a critical position concerning modes of representation:

| 'Traditional' Spectacle: | 'Critical' Spectacle: |
|---|---|
| •'Other' cultures | • Western cultures |
| • Women | • Men |
| • Rituals | • Rituals |
| • Exchange | • Consumerism |
| •'People' | • Filmmakers |

As is evidenced explicitly in the 'film crew' sequence from *Africa Addio*, and implicitly in the slave-market section of *Addio Zio Tom*, the process of filmmaking, what to do with people, the 'signification of subjects in other people's discourse' (Nichols 1991: 39) itself was acknowledged and critiqued.

Jacopetti and Prosperi have regularly mocked and criticised the values of Western capital, drives for consumption (of food and drink; German drunks on the *Reeperbahnstrasse* in *Mondo Cane*), technological 'progress', 'scientific' exploration or 'high' concepts and ideologies such as modern art (French conceptual artist Yves Klein being savagely ridiculed, much to his consternation, in *Mondo Cane*). In *Africa Addio*, unreconstructed representations of black Africans are countered somewhat by the grotesque imaging of colonial powers, especially the British colonisers and ludicrously idealised, spectacularised whites in Capetown. As these commentaries form no overarching narrative aim (as in the expository documentary mode, for example) their meaning is often obscured or muddled in the collage of images and expositions. Through their narrative the filmmakers were also sceptical of the validity of certain

African governance taking over from the colonising powers, predicting bloodshed as equally disastrous as that which had come before. This was a message frankly unwanted at the politically sensitive time of the film's release, yet one that in light of recent events in the Democratic Republic of Congo and Zimbabwe, has some historical authority. Similarly, a crude retelling of the sexual perversity of the American slave trade in *Addio Zio Tom* was too much for many audiences and critics in the early 1970s, despite a bizarre and bloody coda depicting a 'black power'-style slaying of whites which would not be out of place in a blaxploitation film. The mondo film thus evades the modes of documentary filmmaking, the mondo film's transgressiveness problematising simplistic categorisation and readings. The motives, meanwhile, of the mondo directors are as varied and inconclusive as the films are diverse.

## Conclusion

Certain aspects of the mondo film transcend 'distinctions' such as popular/serious, ethnographic investigation/pornographic spectacle, reality/*mise-en-scène*. Mondo, perhaps more than any other film genre, 'extracts, shuffles and reinserts Others back into the mainstream of Western popular culture and imagination' (Staples 1995: 111). It is also ever more difficult to justify stratifications of media: production, style, content and most importantly *meanings* as impervious. Our faith in the film as a record of the world has dissolved; the 'Blair Witch phenomenon' – the blurring of fact and fiction in the world of the integrated spectacle arguably began with films like *Mondo Cane*. The obsession for and with 'reality' and 'actuality' television was arguably a taste also developed by the makers of the mondo film. Cable and satellite television schedules are augmented by 'real' footage of car crashes, accidents, murders, suicides, man-made and natural disasters that continue to exploit audiences' curiosity in the grotesque. Television news and the critical satires of television news are virtually indistinguishable. In a recent interview, Jacopetti (2001) identifies his work as a precursor to the spectacular news satire of *Striscia La Notizia*, a particular favourite of Italian television audiences where political comment merges easily with soft porn. This 'exhibitionist impulse' where mondo-style 'displays of attractions' (Nichols 2001: 87) mimic hard-core scenes from pornography is increasingly prevalent in contemporary media output.

After its own period of invisibility *Medium Cool* has emerged bristling with critical praise and replete with useful reconstituted concepts for new anti-globalisation movements and mass media critics. Aspects of the mondo film, in particular those of Jacopetti and Prosperi, may soon emerge from their current place in the dustbins of film history. Mondo films will not give us any 'accurate' or 'true' representations of historical time, but they can tell us much about the problems of attempting such representations in the first place. Mondo films will still be 'perversely political' but may also offer messages of a politically perverse agenda frighteningly apposite to our modern media age. For this reason we need to look again at these films. As another Italian once remarked: 'Truth it is, many things seem at first sight good, which are ill: and many ill, that notwithstanding are good' (Castiglione 1975: 151).

# Works cited

Antonelli, C. and P. Ortoleva (1999) 'The Italian Way to Modernity', in G. Malossi (ed.) *Volare: The Icon of Italy in Global Pop Culture*. New York: Monacelli Press, 66–75.

Barthes, R. (1977) 'The Death of the Author', in *Image, Music, Text*. London: Fontana. Press, 142–48.

Bemba, S. (1971) 'The Dark Room', in R. Larson (ed.) *Modern African Stories*. London and Glasgow: Fontana Books, 83–97.

Castiglione, B. (1975) *The Book of the Courtier*. London: Dent.

Cohen, J. (1966) *Africa Addio*. New York: Ballantine Books.

Debord, G. (1994) *The Society of the Spectacle*. New York: Zone Books.

Eco, U. (2002) 'Don't Smile When You Say That', *Guardian*, 22 June.

Foucault, M. (1991) *Discipline and Punish: The Birth of the Prison*. London: Penguin.

Gregory, D. (2003) *The Godfathers of Mondo*. New York: Blue Underground.

Gunning, T. (1990) 'The Cinema of Attractions: Early Film, It's Spectator and the Avant-Garde', in T. Elsaesser (ed.) *Early Cinema*. London: British Film Institute, 56–62.

Hansen, C., C. Needham and B. Nichols (1991) 'Pornography, Ethnography, and the Discourses of Power', in B. Nichols (ed.) *Representing Reality*. Indiana: Indiana University Press, 201–28.

Jacopetti, G. (2001) Interview on Japanese DVD of *Addio Zio Tom*. Tokyo: Spike.

Jeavons, C. (1973) 'Zio Tom', *Monthly Film Bulletin*, 40, 471, 86.

Landis, B. (2000) 'The Private Perversions of Gualtiero Jacopetti', *Sleazoid Express*, 3, 49–59.

Landis, B. and M. Clifford (2000) 'Taking Their Show on the Road: Times Square Mondo Movies', in B. Landis and M. Clifford (eds) *Sleazoid Express: A Mind-Twisting Tour Through the Grindhouse Cinema of Times Square!* New York: Fireside, 154–76.

Nichols, B. (1991) 'Documentary Modes of Representation', in B. Nichols (ed.) *Representing Reality*. Indiana: Indiana University Press, 32–75.

_____ (2001) *Introduction to Documentary*. Indiana: Indiana University Press.

Novarin, A. (1998) 'Angelo e Alfredo Castiglioni' (interview), in *Helter Skelter: Mondo Extremo*. Bologna: Alex Papa, 42–55.

Rondi, G. L. (1966) *Italian Cinema Today*. London: Dobson Books.

Solanas, F. and O. Getino (1997) 'Towards a Third Cinema', *Afterimage*, 3, 16–35.

Sconce, J. (1995) '"Trashing" the Academy: Taste Excess and an Emerging Politics of Cinematic Style', *Screen*, 36, 4, 371–93.

Shohat, E. and R. Stam (1994) *Unthinking Eurocentrism: Multiculturalism and the Media*. London and New York: Routledge.

Stallybrass, P. and A. White (1986) *The Politics and Poetics of Transgression*. Ithaca: Cornell University Press.

Staples, A. (1995) 'An Interview with Dr Mondo', *American Anthropologist*, 97, 1, 110–25.

Tseëlon, E. (2000) 'Woman and the Gaze', in D. Fleming (ed.) *Formations: 21st Century Media Studies*. Manchester: Manchester University Press, 252–60.

White, H. (1973) *Metahistory: The Historical Imaginations in Nineteenth-century Europe*. Baltimore: Johns Hopkins University Press.

Zamori, R. (1999) Sleeve notes for *Mondo Caldi di Notte*, LP record. Prato: Plastic.

PART FOUR

# Performing Stardom and Race

# CHAPTER TEN

# 'Telling the truth can be a dangerous business': stardom, race and Isabelle Adjani[1]

Guy Austin

The frame of reference for this exploration of how race functions in Isabelle Adjani's star image is the pioneering work of Richard Dyer on stars and on whiteness. As Dyer tells us, the white woman is idealised in Western culture as 'the most prized possession of white patriarchy' and 'the envy of all other races' (1986: 43). Traditional symbolism of 'light and chastity' affords her a central place and makes of her 'the light of the world' (1986: 44). As a star, the white woman becomes 'a light source', 'shining', 'golden', 'glittering' with a 'stellar luminescence'.[2] In *White*, Dyer stresses that even in contemporary cinema, 'glow remains a key quality in idealised representations of white women' (1997: 132). The French film star Isabelle Adjani, in a publicity still used for *La Reine Margot* (1994), is chosen by Dyer to illustrate this symbolic cinematic 'glow'. Whiteness is certainly crucial to Adjani's star image. Because she is dark-haired rather than blonde, her whiteness is symbolised principally by her pale, 'porcelain' skin, the 'radiance' of her face and her blue eyes.[3] These elements of her star image are emphasised verbally in articles and visually in posters, film stills and magazine photos. The monochrome cover of a 1995 issue of *Time Out* for example, publicising the British release of *La Reine Margot* (Patrice Chéreau, 1994), shows Adjani's face in extreme close-up as perfectly white. The only colour in the photo is the tinted blue of her eyes, which exaggerates further her status as visibly white. The photos inside, although in colour, still emphasise the pallor of Adjani's face by contrast with her black hair, red lips and blue eyes.[4]

In the image from *La Reine Margot* that Dyer (apparently unaware of Adjani's ethnic origins) uses to illustrate filmic conventions, 'light constructs the relationship' within the straight romantic couple, so that 'the man [is] illuminated by the woman' (1997: 134). Hence Vincent Perez is of a noticeably much darker skin tone than Adjani, and is represented staring down at her as she almost literally beams up at him. *La Reine Margot* is one of several films starring Adjani in which this convention is evident. Most of these luminous roles are in fact from the first decade of her career, before her star image underwent a hysterical modification in the mid-1980s. Adjani's pale, radiant characters are contrasted with darker male co-stars who are often in need of salvation through the qualities of innocence, goodness, charity and virtue that are symbolised by her visible whiteness. In André Téchiné's *Barocco* (1976), for example, Adjani – dressed throughout in yellow and surrounded by the positive symbolism of gold and light – protects and redeems a dark-haired killer by dyeing his hair blonde and falling in love with him.

Adjani plays the 'white maiden' again as Lucy Harker in Werner Herzog's horror, *Nosferatu the Vampyre* (1979). Once more the themes of chastity, purity and love are expressed through her appearance: in this case, her exaggeratedly pale make-up (contrasting with her black hair and the kohl round her eyes), the iris effects of the lighting, and the white nightgowns she wears.[5] The early scenes between Lucy and her husband Jonathan (Bruno Ganz) conform to the romantic paradigm of light woman/dark man and also offer, in the visual contrast between her glow and his gloom, a suggestion that his future is over-shadowed by darkness. He will become the vampire's victim; she his destroyer. This is Adjani the vampire slayer, the apogée of the white woman, the devoted wife, embodying goodness and purity, resisting the plague (the *Black* Death which decimates her hometown but spares her) and fighting the forces of evil as the 'woman of pure heart'[6] who alone can destroy Count Dracula. She is the light and Dracula the darkness; she sacrifices herself to kill him, asking him into her bed and keeping him there until daybreak. As she waits on the white bed, dressed in white, with a white vase of white flowers above her, she is purity incarnate, whiter than white and confident of triumph.

But ambiguity also informs Adjani's image. Is she as unproblematically white, pure and radiant as first appears? Is she a 'white maiden' or a 'dark French beauty'?[7] This ambiguity first became apparent in the representation of origins and identity in her early stardom. Hence, in 1974 *Paris Match* had noted innocently that although born in the working-class Parisian suburb of Gennevilliers, Adjani had the name of a princess from the *Arabian Nights* (her second name is Yasmine).[8] In the film that made her a star a year later, *L'Histoire d'Adèle H.* (François Truffaut, 1975) Adjani's performance as Adèle centres on the attempt to deny her identity as the daughter of Victor Hugo, the most famous man alive. This film and others, such as *L'Eté meurtier* (Jean Becker, 1983) and *Camille Claudel* (Bruno Nuytten, 1988) feature characteristically melodramatic performances from Adjani in which breakdown or regression is often linked to questions of origin and identity, and they repeatedly dramatise the transfer of identity from father to daughter in an almost hysterical register. These suggestions of excess, ambiguity and resistance were soon to become central to Adjani's star image, and crystallised around the vexed question of racial identity.

Adjani was *the* French female star of the 1980s. The decade began with her winning her first César and being voted favourite actress by the readers of *Paris Match*.[9] It ended with another César, an Oscar nomination, and the confirmation that she was a global star.[10] But another development in her stardom during this time was much more unexpected and controversial, and concerned her newly-revealed status as, in the words of *Paris Match*, France's first major *beur* (Arab) star.

Up until the mid-1980s, it seems, Adjani's ethnic origin had not been common knowledge in France. But in October 1986 Adjani spoke in an interview with Harlem Désir, the president of SOS-Racisme, about her racial identity, declaring that 'I always felt like a *Beur*' (quoted in Rosen 1990: 24). Adjani's statement was provoked by her father's own struggle to come to terms with his ethnic identity near the end of his life. She explained that her father was Algerian and her mother was German. In response to the revelations, the writer Philippe Sollers noted in an open letter to Adjani that there were 'two hidden powderkegs in France: the Occupation and the Algerian War. By some unlikely chance, you were born at the exact juncture of these two secrets.' The

French public's favourite actress had in one stroke become 'a foreigner in their midst' (ibid.). Moreover she was not just foreign but *Algerian* (this line of descent proved to be much more problematic than her German roots). As the *Revue française de sciences politiques* reported in 1987, as far as image was concerned, Algerians occupied the lowest rung of the social ladder (see Stora 1998: 356). In the eyes of French public opinion, Adjani had joined the lowest of the low.

According to subsequent rumours, apparently spread by the Front National, Adjani became a diseased foreign body, infected with AIDS: 'The French have long regarded foreigners as an infectious body within the nation, and of course that's like AIDS. So to the right-wingers like Le Pen I became a good target' (Adjani quoted in Rosen 1990: 25). In late 1986 it was reported that Adjani had died of an AIDS-related illness. Finally, on 18 January 1987, Adjani appeared on the TF1 evening news to prove that she was alive and well, literally presenting her star body to the public for their scrutiny; hence the significance of the moment, commented on in a *Paris Match* exclusive, when she moved her left hand away from her cheek to reveal 'smooth' (that is, healthy, lesion-free) skin underneath.[11] *Paris Match* celebrated Adjani's public return to life by reanimating the symbols of her whiteness. The first indication that all is well is her 'radiant smile'; the magazine also comments on her 'blue eyes' (twice), her 'dazzling look' and her 'radiant beauty'. It concludes that Adjani is 'shining with brilliant health', contrasting these luminous qualities with the darkness of the rumours, which are repeatedly characterised as 'shadows'. The darkness has in effect been defeated by her stellar luminescence. Adjani was healthy and glowing again.

A few weeks later, in April 1987, Adjani was once more on the front of *Paris Match*, in a photo which celebrated her 'radiance' (*son éclat*) and yet perhaps hinted at her recently-revealed ethnicity by showing her head wrapped in a towel. This apparent hint was followed that year by Adjani's appearance in a film which explicitly referenced her racial identity, the universally-slated Hollywood comedy *Ishtar* (Elaine May, 1987). Here Adjani plays Shirra Assel, a revolutionary fighter in the 'people's movement' of Ishtar (a fictitious North African state for which one might read Algeria). Shirra is pitted in armed anti-imperialist struggle against the corrupt Emir, who is backed by the CIA (a situation which has some parallels with French support for the regime in Algeria). Because the film is a comedy, with two big Hollywood stars (Warren Beatty and Dustin Hoffman) playing a couple of inept American singers, the political narrative and Adjani's performance have both been marginalised. But far from being just the 'love interest' in the film, Adjani is in fact an embodiment of various racial and political positions previously not associated with her star image.

The most striking of these is the fact that Adjani is identified with Africa in the film and not with France. She appears either in disguise (as a man) or in combat fatigues and the foulard throughout the film, until the very last scene. (This allowed some parts of the French press to trade on fears of an association between AIDS and Africa, evident in the suggestion that Adjani wore scarves in the film in order to hide signs of ill-health – that is, AIDS – on the 'infamous left cheek' that had been covered by her hand during the television appearance in January 1987.)[12] The action plot sees Adjani, Beatty and Hoffman stranded in the desert, using bazookas to fight off CIA helicopters.

Their victory assures 'social reforms in Ishtar as dictated by Shirra Assel' (plus a live album and worldwide promotion for the two singers). It is only in the final sequence, the live concert, that Adjani is seen in Western clothes, and hence 'dressed like a girl' as Beatty puts it. But although the gender ambiguity is therefore resolved, the political tensions remain, and are celebrated when, in the presence of the American military, Hoffman dedicates a song to Shirra, 'a very lovely lady of the Left'. As for Adjani's ethnic identity, notwithstanding her change of costume, she remains strongly identified with Ishtar/Algeria, while on a more personal level the hysteria surrounding her star image in 1986 is encapsulated by the title of the theme song dedicated to Shirra: 'Telling the truth can be a dangerous business'. This Adjani knew to her cost.

Despite the hysteria of the mid-1980s, her performance in *Ishtar*, and her subsequent interventions on foreign policy and immigration – in 1988 she visited Algeria for the first time, in order to 'struggle against the wall of silence' surrounding human rights abuses and to support the student movement (see Cojean 1997: 8) – ethnicity has not become an explicit part of Adjani's star image. Or rather, her star ethnicity remains of the unmarked kind: visible whiteness, stellar luminescence. Hence her appearance in *White*. After *Ishtar*, there have been hardly any other performances that play on Adjani's ethnic origins. A recent exception is her role in *La Repentie* (Laetitia Masson, 2002), where she plays a second generation Maghrebi, and where her ethnicity is signalled in a sequence where she dances barefoot on the Promenade des Anglais in Nice.[13] More noticeable have been the performances, like those in *La Reine Margot* and on stage in *La Dame aux camélias* (2000), which have played upon the association

Isabelle Adjani embodies North Africa in *Ishtar* (1987)

between her star image and AIDS. *La Reine Margot* considers an entangled network of blood, sex, poison and death, and includes a scene in which Adjani as Margot embraces the dying king, his poisoned blood soaking her white dress.[14] Her stage role as *La Dame aux camélias* was interpreted as being about AIDS rather than consumption because, via her public statements and her on-stage performance, 'Adjani wanted to make this into a modern play about a present-day disease' (Joucla 2000: 52; my translation). She could thus be said to have renegotiated the meaning of the racist association made in the 1980s between herself, Africa and AIDS in a positive way, to grant her performance in the play a contemporary resonance.[15]

To a large extent Adjani seems to have been recuperated as a white star, as the examples of her public image that we began with tend to show. The hysteria surrounding her ethnicity was redirected in the 1990s towards her private life (principally her relationship with Daniel Day Lewis). In 1995 she won a César for *La Reine Margot* and in 1997 became the youngest ever President of the Jury at the 50th Cannes Film Festival.[16] A yardstick of Adjani's status in the 1990s as a reassuring and uncontroversial icon is that she was chosen to replace Emmanuelle Béart as the face of Dior after Béart had become the all-too-visible face of the *sans-papiers* movement in 1996–97. But Adjani remains a star who has been perceived hysterically because she lived out in her star body the complex racial make-up of her society. Adjani – like a true star – has transcended the hysteria and the ambiguity. She has done so in a manner which seems to reiterate whiteness but which also, as we have seen, manages to accommodate the foreign body.

## Notes

1   My thanks to the Arts and Humanities Research Board (AHRB) (now called the AHRC – Arts and Humanities Research Council) for providing me with a research grant and also research leave funding, both of which facilitated the preparation of this chapter.

2   These are all terms taken from media descriptions of Princess Diana; see Segal 1998: 132.

3   See for example Andrew 1995, Cojean 1997 and Loiseau & Rouchy 1997. The most famous idealised white women are usually blonde (Marilyn Monroe, Brigitte Bardot, Princess Diana).

4   See *Time Out*, 11–18 January 1995, 1, 23 and 25.

5   The first two effects are deliberate allusions to silent cinema and to F. W. Murnau's *Nosferatu* (1922), of which Herzog's film is a remake. It is noticeable that several of the shots of Adjani illuminated at night are 'impossible' in terms of realism: light appears to shine on her from outside, that is, from the dark.

6   This epithet is stressed throughout the film in readings from a book on how to kill vampires.

7   See www.imdb.com/Bio?Adjani+Isabelle for the use of this term to describe Adjani.

8   *Paris Match*, 7 December 1974, 102. The fact that Gennevilliers housed a largely immigrant population was not picked up on in the feature, nor was any mention made of her exotic surname.

9   See *Paris Match*, 5 March 1982. The César was for *Possession* (Andrzej Zulawski, 1981).

10  See *Voici*, 104, 6–12 November 1989, 4–9, for a report on the global success of *Camille Claudel* and Adjani's 'international career'. The César and the Oscar nomination were also for this film.

11  See *Paris Match*, 30 January 1987.

12  See for example *Le Nouveau VSD*, 537 (17–23 December 1987), 102.

13  Many thanks to Alec Hargreaves and Keith Reader for bringing this film to my attention.

14  Jean-Hugues Anglade, playing the king, had just starred as a man infected with HIV in *Killing Zoe* (Roger Avery, 1994). This scene perhaps also recalls the famous embracing of an AIDS victim by Princess Diana.

15  This racist identification between AIDS and Africa was (ironically, perhaps unwittingly) mobilised in Gérard Depardieu's defence of Adjani published in *Lettres volées* in 1988; see Goldin 1990: 42.

16  Although her film appearances were scarce during the late 1990s, this is attributable to Adjani's own decision to reduce her workload and bring up her second son, who was born in 1995.

## Works cited

Andrew, G. (1995) 'Isabelle époque', *Time Out*, 11–18 January, 23–6.

Cojean, A. (1997) 'Les Protestations contre le projet Debré', *Le Monde*, 22 February, 8.

Dyer, R. (1986) *Heavenly Bodies: Film Stars and Society*. London: British Film Institute.

_____ (1997) *White*. London and New York: Routledge.

Goldin, M. (1990) 'The Story of Isabelle A.', *Interview*, 20, 1, 40–3.

Joucla, F. (2000) 'Isabelle Adjani: "Vivre avec la mort aux trousses"', *Le Nouvel Observateur* 1881, 23 November, 52.

Loiseau, J.-C. and M.-E. Rouchy (1997) 'Adjani: questions d'image', *Télérama*, 2468, 30 April, 26.

Rosen, M. (1990) 'Isabelle Adjani: The Actress as Political Activist', *Cinéaste*, 17, 4, 24–5.

Segal, N. (1998) 'The Common Touch', in M. Merck (ed.) *After Diana: Irreverent Elegies*. London and New York: Verso, 131–46.

Stora, M. (1998) *La gangrène et l'oubli: la mémoire de la guerre d'Algérie*, Paris: La découverte/Poche.

# CHAPTER ELEVEN

# The new Brazilian Bombshell: Sônia Braga, race and cinema in the 1970s

Stephanie Dennison

A few years ago when the director Fina Torres was choosing the female lead for her film *Woman on Top*, she said she was looking for the new Sônia Braga, whom she defined as having an innocent way to her but with a fondness for sin.[1] A couple of observations can be made here which will serve to form the basis of this chapter. First, Torres' comment suggests the extent to which Sônia Braga has over the years become associated with the characters she has played on screen. And secondly, the Venezuelan director's description of Sônia Braga is strikingly reminiscent of the way dark-skinned women have traditionally been portrayed in Brazilian culture.

I will illustrate these issues with reference to two films: *Dona Flor e seus dois maridos* (*Dona Flor and Her Two Husbands*), directed by Bruno Barreto in 1976, and *A dama do lotação* (*Lady on the Bus*) by Neville d'Almeida, from 1978. Both films were sleek and expensive productions for their day, both were what can be loosely termed erotic movies, and both starred the frequently naked Braga, who was already in 1976 one of Brazil's biggest and sexiest television stars.

Sônia Braga was born in 1950 in the south of Brazil to a part-black father and part-Indian mother.[2] Outside of Brazil she is perhaps best known for her role in Hector Babenco's Academy Award-winning *Kiss of the Spiderwoman* (1985), as well as her numerous roles as the sultry *latina* in Hollywood movies such as *The Rookie* (Clint Eastwood, 1990) and *From Dusk Till Dawn III: The Hangman's Daughter* (P. J. Pesce, 2000) (we can see that in the United States she is as much a victim of racial lumping as any other Hispanic-American actor), and she is also known for the leading men with whom she has been linked over the years, including Robert Redford, Clint Eastwood and Marcelo Manstroianni. She was most recently seen in Britain in the popular US television series *Sex and the City*, in which she played the sultry *latina* lesbian lover of the sexually rampant Samantha. Having recently admitted to lesbian relationships in the past, Braga has become Brazil's latest gay icon, thus continuing to mirror in a large number of ways the career of the first Brazilian bombshell: Carmen Miranda.

## Socio-political and cinematic context

By the time the films under discussion were being made, Brazil had begun the officially sanctioned but very gradual move towards a return to democracy, commonly referred to as *abertura*, after years of strict authoritarian rule. Censorship laws were loosened, a political amnesty was declared, and the more unpleasant features of dictatorship, in place since 1968 and the so-called 'coup within the coup', were removed. In the interim years of severe political censorship, home-grown erotic comedies, or *pornochancha-das*, had become the most popular national cinematic form. To simplify, the reasons for the *pornochanchada*'s popularity were three-fold: the inevitable censorship of more politically motivated films, the fact that foreign porn was banned, and, more significantly, that compulsory screen quotas resulted in exhibition groups producing their own films, the result of which were cheap, mass-produced soft-core porn films, many of which were partly financed by Embrafilme, the State film production and distribution agency.

In the 1970s a close relationship between Brazilian television and film was forged, as illustrated in, for example, the influence of the *pornochanchada* on the gradually more sexually suggestive soap operas, and the influence on the mainstream Brazilian film industry of TV Globo's production values and star system.[3] Occasionally at this time actors and directors associated with mainstream cinema and television would wander into the territory of erotic comedy, usually in an attempt to tap into the huge commercial success that such films were enjoying at the time. With their big budgets, famous actresses and models and high production values, they created a cleaned-up version of the *pornochanchada* (Bernardet 1978). They tended to rely on the nudity (or promise of nudity) of the leading actresses, especially if the public was used to seeing them in more 'respectable' roles in television soap operas, for example. Thus the element of transgression of these films is clear from the outset and even in the choice of actress for the leading role. This element of transgression arguably attracted viewers to the cinema as much as the promise of nudity associated with such films.

## Sônia Braga and race

Braga was catapulted to stardom in Brazil in 1975 by her appearance in the title role in TV Globo's adaptation of *Gabriela*, a novel first published in 1958 by the nation's most successful and prolific writer, Jorge Amado. She would go on to play Gabriela in a film version in 1983, as well as two more of Jorge Amado's heroines on the big screen, including arguably Brazilian cinema's biggest ever role for a female lead, Dona Flor. In 2001 on Jorge Amado's death, Braga acknowledged the debt she owed to the writer, declaring that his name alone represented her whole career. Earlier she had declared: 'He loves our people so much and he helped the Brazilian woman to understand that our beauty is how we are, brunette with brown eyes, it doesn't matter, we don't need to have blonde hair or blue eyes!'[4]

When examining the star text and racialised sexuality of someone like Sônia Braga, we must be careful not to fall into the trap of understanding race as it is understood in Britain or the United States, for example. That said, it is impossible to deny the 'structuring absence' of blacks and mixed-race people in Brazilian visual media, particularly when we contrast these with other popular cultural forms, and particularly when we consider the extent to which many of the surviving and transformed Africanisms in Brazil have become part of the national culture, rather than an Afro-Brazilian ethnic culture (Telles 1999: 83). Michael Hanchard points out that the Africanisation of the female bodily aesthetic as a national standard of beauty is a distinctive feature of Brazil, where scant attention is paid to breast size and emphasis instead is placed on large hips, buttocks and thighs and a narrow waist (Hanchard 1999: 68). While this bodily aesthetic has slowly changed since the 1970s (consider, for example, the recent trend in breast enlargements, possibly as a result of the success of Brazil's curvaceous Germanic supermodel Gisele Bundchen), it is interesting to observe how few black or mixed-race pin-up girls there have been in Brazil, a country with such a large mixed-race popula-tion,[5] beyond the world of hard-core porn.

Racial definitions in Brazil are flexible and negotiated, and there is a strong ten-dency to identify as white persons near the white/brown colour boundary (Telles 1999: 84). Emphasis is placed on how people perceive themselves, just as much as on how people are perceived by others. Therefore racial background, unlike, say, in the United States, does not always determine one's race and/or colour.[6] Brazil's (white) president Fernando Henrique Cardoso, in office from 1995 to 2002, illustrated the difference between the nation's understanding of race and that of the home of the 'one-drop rule', by declaring, in a classic example of Brazilian political incorrectness when discussing race, that like most Brazilians he too had 'one foot in the kitchen', a reference to the country's domestic slave-holding past.

Angela Gilliam points out that people who struggle to pass for white in the United States may not pass for black in Brazil, citing as one example the actress Lena Horne (1992: 177–8). In this context, Sônia Braga's whiteness, in Brazil at any rate, is not open for discussion.[7] The racial definition most frequently applied to Braga is not *mulata* but *morena*.[8] Nevertheless, with her black wiry hair, wide hips and dark skin she stands out, even among the new generation of stars, as physically one of the most Africanised of Brazil's successful white actresses. In an interview given in the US, Braga described herself in the following terms: 'I am a typical Brazilian. I have a typi-cal Brazilian bottom, typical Brazilian colouring, even a bit Africanish, and a typical Brazilian style.'[9]

## Dona Flor and Her Two Husbands

In 1976 Bruno Barreto released *Dona Flor and Her Two Husbands*, the hugely popular film based on Jorge Amado's 1966 novel of the same name that was set in Salvador on the east coast of Brazil in the 1940s. It still holds the record for the largest (recorded) number of spectators for a national film, and as a result many contemporary Brazilian directors use it as a model of how to get the public back to the cinemas.[10] In the film Braga plays Flor, a middle-class woman who longs for the return of her dead husband, Vadinho, who had collapsed during carnival after a short and over-indulgent life. Her second husband – decent, honest and hard-working – cannot offer her the intense sexual gratification of her late husband. She therefore consults a *macumba* (or voodoo, for want of a better term) priestess and Vadinho returns, naked and visible only to her, so that she can enjoy the best of what both men have to offer.

The film's link with carnival, inversion, transgression and Afro-Brazilian culture is established from the beginning, when Vadinho appears cross-dressed as a *baiana* (the social type associated with the Northeastern black woman) at a street carnival, dances with a *mulata* and drops dead. It is therefore carnival that generates the situation that forms the focus of the plot: the death of Vadinho. The tale is set in Salvador, Brazil's most Afro-Brazilian city. Flor, too, is associated with Afro-Brazilian culture in the sense that she is a cookery teacher, invariably preparing Afro-Bahian cuisine.

Given the general absence of people of colour from television and cinema screens in Brazil, it is my contention that the *morena* frequently fills the role assumed by the *mulata* in other art forms. Braga's 'whiteness' did not prevent her from playing the lead in films with titles such as *A moreninha* (Glauco Mirko Laurelli, 1970) (which roughly translates as 'little dark girl') and *Mestiça, a escrava indomável* (Lenita Perroy, 1973) (about an indomitable mixed-race slave girl) earlier in her career. The screen *morena*, of which she is the most celebrated example, is very sensual, dark-skinned, with long wavy hair and European features. Flor's *morenice* (those attributes associated with the *morena*) is emphasised when she is naked, skin colour, according to Homi Bhabha, functioning as the most visible of fetishes (1983: 30). Therefore, in the scenes in *Dona Flor* in which she makes love to Vadinho, she appears much darker-skinned than when she is with her second husband (she has sex with him beneath the bedclothes), which returns us once again to the cliché of the lascivious dark-skinned Brazilian woman or *mulata*.

Jorge Amado, the self-styled 'man of the people', was one of Brazil's most successful writers and one of its most successful exports. His novels of the 1960s and 1970s, for which he is best known, were commonly set in Bahia, Brazil's most African of states and had exotic, sexy, mixed-race females as their protagonists (the character Dona Flor, for example, is a mixture of the three races romantically believed to make up the

Sônia Braga as a mixed-race slave in *Mestiça, a escrava indomável* (1973)

typical Brazilian: white, Indian and black).[11] It is worth noting that the work of Gilberto Freyre, the sociologist most associated with the myth of Brazil's racial democracy, provided the inspiration for Amado's heroines and his interpretation of Brazilian culture. Freyre's description of the myth in turn is strikingly similar to his description of Sônia Braga, whom he considered to be the typical Brazilian woman. He described her as *the* Brazilian muse, and maintained that her mixture of blood gave her her beauty.[12]

## Lady on the Bus

The second film to be discussed is Neville d'Almeida's *Lady on the Bus* from 1978. At the box office it was the second most successful Brazilian film of all time. In it Braga plays Solange, a sexually frustrated and recently married woman, incapable of making love to her husband, who finds solace on Rio's busy buses, picking up strangers, like a carioca 'Belle de Jour'. In her quest for sexual satisfaction, she also beds her father-in-law and her husband's best friend. On discovering his wife's philandering, the husband Carlos retreats to his bed and remains there, in a kind of living death, while his wife both dutifully assumes the role of nurse by night, and continues her sexual sojourns by day. Sônia Braga here is playing a racially unmarked upper-middle-class housewife, but race and sexuality are still relevant in the film, as revealed in one scene in particular. In the scene, which in fact is a parody of a scene from Luis Buñuel's *Belle de Jour* (1966), an erotic game of footsie takes place between Solange and her husband's best friend Assunção as they and their respective partners watch a *mulata* show in Rio de Janeiro's Oba Oba nightclub.

The scene serves to remind us of the extent to which Braga's character is caught between two worlds – the world identified with the *mulata*, traditionally considered to be the seductress, sexual initiator, who is promiscuous, has loose morals and enjoys sex, and the virginal, frigid, white wife. The dichotomy reminds us of the extended family of traditional Brazilian society: the wife/slave frigid/whore dichotomy that, according to Gilberto Freyre, dates back to plantation times. Freyre's views on the extended family of masters and slaves (and by extension landowners and indentured workers and patrons and servants), and how they influenced the nation's social and sexual practices, were well known at the time and widely believed to be true. Just as in plantation times, each group of women (middle-class housewives and *mulata* dancers) has its own space and function. Sex is all around in a place like Rio de Janeiro, but despite the images of chaos, of freedom captured by Neville's camera, we see that, in terms of sex, there is an order of sorts. For example, Solange takes strangers to open spaces, but her father-in-law and husband's best friend are taken to a motel.

Even though Braga plays a racially unmarked woman in *Lady on the Bus*, her descent and incapacity to be 'decent' (that is, her unbridled lasciviousness) reflect values traditionally associated with Brazilian *mulatas*: they were destined to be fallen angels, and this is clearly how Solange is portrayed in the film. The film also deliberately sets up a contrast between Solange and Séverine in *Belle de Jour*, which arguably marks her as a racial Other.

## Braga and cultural nationalism

Sônia Braga has often commented that her appearance on the acting scene in the 1970s marked a new aesthetically nationalist period in that people saw for the first time that they, with their dark skin and brown eyes, could be beautiful too. With this she endeared herself to millions of Brazilian women. Just as Jorge Amado promoted himself as a 'man of the people', so too could Braga's star persona be read as populist. I would not suggest with this that the choice of Sônia Braga as actress in these two blockbusters heralded a new era for mixed-race actresses, as Braga has not broken down as many boundaries as she might like to think. Instead, I would argue that during the 1970s in Brazil notions of racial harmony and national unity were being promoted more than ever by the military dictatorship.[13] In a climate of cultural nationalism, the promotion of the racial democracy myth and the popularity of cultural representations of sexual transgression such as those seen in the *pornochanchada*, the dark-skinned Brazilian woman came to symbolise Brazilian culture in the 1970s. It is surely no coincidence that the other big commercial hit of the mid-1970s that had a female lead, Carlos Diegues' *Xica da Silva* (1976), starred the black actress Zezé Mota playing a sexually rampant slave. Evidence of how attractive a notion the assertion of the dark-skinned character of Brazil can be, and how it is often unavoidably linked to the myth of racial democracy, can be found in respected sociologist Roberto Da Matta's (2002) dismissal in 1999 of the need for the introduction of affirmative action in the country because, he argued, in Brazil practically everyone is a *mulatto*.

Given that *Dona Flor* and *Lady on the Bus*, Brazil's two biggest films, appeared at the time of political *abertura* and given that they marked a kind of shift in social and sexual terms, as well as in terms of representation, Sônia Braga became associated with the transgressive and liberated mood of the period, and this must be one of the reasons why these two films were so successful upon their release. Also, given the commercial success of the writers on whom the two films were based, Jorge Amado and Nelson Rodrigues, Braga's association with Brazilian popular culture and identity were firmly established during this period, and as we have seen, the successful *pornochanchada* genre that in part influenced these two films was consciously associated by audiences with transgressive and debauched behaviour so that they arguably served to undermine the conservative morality of the dictatorship.

Throughout the *abertura* period, in interviews at home and abroad, Braga actively sought to link herself with the boom in popular Brazilian culture, the Brazilian masses, good times, freedom (not necessarily in political terms) and hope for the future. At times it becomes difficult to distinguish between Braga the woman, the roles she has played, and the nation itself. In a lengthy interview to Brazilian *Playboy* magazine in 1982, she evidently considered herself to be the flag bearer for popular Brazilian cinema (Almeida Filho 1982). The journalist who interviewed her, Hamilton Almeida Filho, said of her: 'She reminds me of Brazil smiling, I don't know why.' Braga declared in the same article that she represented an unconscious desire for liberty, that she had been an ugly child, which had helped her be beautiful in adulthood, and that she had lived in poverty for a while – 'that's the story of Brazil'.

Within the context of cultural nationalism in the 1970s, it is interesting to note the importance placed on the notion of syncretism in the *Política Nacional de Cultura*, a national cultural policy developed by the dictatorship in the first half of the 1970s with the aid of a number of cultural producers. This policy, which signalled an attempt at the industrialisation of cultural production that was similarly taking place in other countries at the time, favoured popular culture and a positive historical re-examination of the development of the nation from the point of view of what we nowadays call hybridity. In the same year (1975) film director Nelson Pereira dos Santos appeared to echo one of the features of the *Política Nacional de Cultura* when he wrote the following words: 'Gilberto Freyre has taught us that there are two cultures in Brazil: an imported one that imitates Western culture, and another, more natural one, which is spontaneous, has much stronger roots, and is repressed' (quoted in Ortiz Ramos 1983: 130; my translation). It is interesting to note that Dona Flor keeps both husbands rather than settle for one and Solange keeps the husband she loves as well as an array of bus passengers. According to Da Matta, it is this third way or middle path that most fittingly describes the dynamics of Brazilian culture (1991: 168). Sônia Braga herself, in terms of her racial background and how she portrayed herself and was portrayed in the media at the time, fitted comfortably into notions of syncretism, hybridity and middle paths. She was often described in terms of contrasts: beauty and the beast, reality and fiction, a mixture of innocence and carnality. Dona Flor was described as being an ideal role for Braga to exhibit her ambiguity, a mixture of the standard of Brazilian womanhood and carioca sophistication (Simões 1976). And based on his reading of the film version of *Gabriela*, also starring Braga, Bruce Williams wrote: 'the archetypal Brazilian woman is at once *magna mater*, Amazon, Madonna and whore' (1990: 30).

## Conclusion

Sônia Braga in the 1970s was government-approved in the sense that she made expensive, Embrafilme-produced films that did well at home and abroad and that were not, strictly speaking, *pornochanchadas*. She was also seen by everyone at the time as being very Brazilian, as if there was something almost patriotic in her colouring and personality. She appeared at a time when there was a need to produce 'an authentic national culture for the people, a category both vague and all-embracing' (Oliven 2000: 63), and the *morena*, as we have seen, is a widely encompassing term. She was also anti-establishment, in that she appealed to people partly because of her libertarian and transgressive qualities, on- and off-screen.

It is interesting that in the post-*abertura*, post-modern period (after Braga starred in *Gabriela*) the offer of film work in Brazil dried up and media attention seemed to turn almost immediately to Xuxa Meneguel, the blonde, blue-eyed and wholesome children's television host and film actress, and later, media mogul.[14] Xuxa has practically built a career on a carefully constructed image of whiteness and all that Richard Dyer (1997) tells us this represents. Sônia Braga, on the other hand, in her spontaneity, vitality, energy, exaggerated sensuality, alternative lifestyle, willingness to get naked on screen, 'natural' beauty and 'Africanised' body, came as close to representing the *mulata* on screen as Brazil's briefly nationalist but ultimately racist visual media of the 1970s would permit.

## Notes

1 Quoted in 'Diretora de "Sabor da paixão" procurava nova Sônia Braga'. Available online at: www.terra.com.br/cinema/noticias/2000/10/27/000.htm (accessed: 20 May 2002).

2 Some sources refer only to Braga's part-Indian ancestry. In an interview in 1982, she described her entire family as being from the state of São Paulo and of Portuguese and Indian origin (Almeida Filho 1982).

3 TV Globo is best known for producing and exporting glossy soap operas or *telenovelas* and both its allegedly ruthless star system and the so-called Globo standard of quality, by which all visual media are judged in Brazil. The reach of the Globo empire, one of the largest media organisations in the world, is such that it has dominated the country's television, radio and the press for at least two decades.

4 In *Dona Flor* press notes (undated, microfiche on Sônia Braga, British Film Institute, London).

5 According to the 2000 census, out of a population of just under 170 million, a little over 66 million citizens declared themselves to be *pardos* or of mixed race, with 90.5 million self-identifying as white and 10.5 million as black (IBGE 2002).

6 'One of the most striking consequences of the Brazilian system of racial identification is that parents and children and even brothers and sisters are frequently accepted as representatives of quite opposite racial types' (Harris 1964: 57).

7 Braga was criticised in some circles in Brazil for being too white to play Gabriela in the 1970s soap opera, while by contrast a review of *Dona Flor* in New York's *Variety* (14 September 1977) described the title character as a 'lovely mulatto woman'.

8 The term *morena* means olive- or dark-skinned or brunette white woman but is often used (not necessarily in Braga's case) as a euphemism for *mulata* or woman of mixed black and white race. *Mulata* in turn is used to signify black. This use of euphemisms also complicates racial definitions in Brazil.

9 Quoted in *Dona Flor* press notes.

10 In terms of the humour and debauched elements, overpowering female sexuality and glossy values, see Carla Camurati's *Carlota Joaquina* (1995), which kick-started the so-called *retomada* or rebirth of Brazilian cinema in the 1990s.

11 It is interesting that despite her racial mixture as described by Jorge Amado, in the film version of *Dona Flor* the title character is marked in one scene as being white. In the scene, suspicious Flor confronts a black woman who had borne a child with a man called Vadinho. The black woman explains that he could not be Flor's husband, as her Vadinho does not like white women. Flor seems therefore to be a classic example of the process of 'whitening' which marks Brazil's racial formation, as discussed earlier.

12 Quoted in *Dona Flor* press notes.

13 'The military adopted the racial democracy myth *tout court*, denouncing any anti-racism activity as a species of leftist subversion' (Winant 1999: 103).

14  Xuxa was careful to remove evidence of a not so wholesome past when she became a star.

## Works cited

Almeida Filho, H. (1982) 'Playboy entrevista: Sônia Braga', *Playboy* (Brazil). Unmarked magazine clipping, MAM Film Archive, Rio de Janeiro.

Bernardet, J. (1978) 'Uma pornô grã-fina para a classe média', *Última Hora*, São Paulo, 29 April.

Bhabha, H. K. (1983) 'The Other Question: the Stereotype and Colonial Discourse', *Screen*, 24, 6, 18–36.

Da Matta, R. (1991) *A casa e a rua: espaço, cidadania, mulher e morte no Brasil*. Rio de Janeiro: Guanabara Koogan.

_____ (2002) 'Cores: Homenagem a Oracy Nogueira'. Available online: http://www.jt.estadao.com.br/noticias/99/09/05/cdamatta.htm (accessed: 3 March 2002).

Dyer, R. (1997) *White*. London and New York: Routledge.

Gilliam, A. (1992) 'From Roxbury to Rio – and Back in a Hurry', *African-American Reflections on Brazil's Racial Paradise*. Philadelphia: Temple University Press, quoted in J.W. Warren (2001) *Racial Revolutions: Antiracism and Indian Resurgence in Brazil*. Durham and London: Duke University Press.

Hanchard, M. (1999) 'Black Cinderella: Race and the Public Sphere in Brazil', in M. Hanchard (ed.) *Racial Politics in Contemporary Brazil*. Durham and London: Duke University Press, 59–81.

Harris, M. (1964) *Patterns of Race in the Americas*. New York: Norton.

IBGE (2002) 'Brazilian Institute of Geography and Statistics Website'. Available online: http://www.ibge.gov.br (accessed: 1 March 2002).

Oliven, R. J. (2000) 'Brazil: The Modern in the Tropics', in V. Schelling (ed.) *Through the Kaleidoscope: The Experience of Modernity in Latin America*. London and New York: Verso, 53–71.

Ortiz Ramos, J. M. (1983) *Cinema, estado e lutas culturais: anos 50/60/70*. Rio de Janeiro: Paz e Terra.

Simões, I. (1976) 'Cinema de cama e mesa', *Movimento*. São Paulo: 20 December.

Telles, E. (1999) 'Ethnic Boundaries and Political Mobilisation Among African Brazilians', in M. Hanchard (ed.) *Racial Politics in Contemporary Brazil*. Durham and London: Duke University Press, 82–97.

Williams, B. E. (1990) 'A Captive of the Screen: Archetype and Gaze in Barreto's *Gabriela*', *Film Criticism*, 14, 2, 24–32.

Winant, H. (1999) 'Racial Democracy and Racial Identity: Comparing the United States and Brazil', in M. Hanchard (ed.) *Racial Politics in Contemporary Brazil*. Durham and London: Duke University Press, 98–115.

PART FIVE

**Interrogating Gender**

# CHAPTER TWELVE

# Canonising sexual image, devaluing gender performance: replacing the *onnagata* with female actresses in Japan's early cinema[1]

Hideaki Fujiki

In a Japanese motion picture magazine of 1917, a two-page spread photogravure epitomised a historical moment in Japanese cinema, highlighting the differences between the representation of American female actress Myrtle Gonzales and that of Japanese male actor Tachibana Teijirô playing a female role (which is either called *onnagata* or *oyama*). On the left page, a close framing showcases Gonzales' face. She is turned toward the camera with her naked shoulders on a slight diagonal under low-key lighting. Such photographic stylisation, which was a typical representational method for portraying American actors at that time, effectively aestheticises the surface and configuration of her body. By contrast, on the right page, a distant framing displays the *onnagata*. He is wearing a female kimono and wig, sitting erect with his legs folded under him and casting down his eyes. Such a tableau-shot does not emphasise his

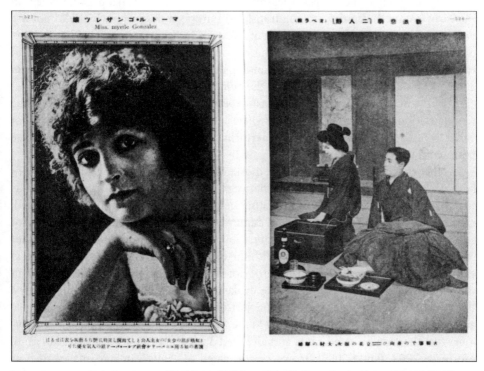

Two-page spread photogravure of Tachibana Teijirô and Myrtle Gonzales in *Katsudô gahô* (1917)

natural physique; in the photogravures, not until the late 1910s did close-ups begin to represent Japanese actors. Such a visible imbalance between the American and Japanese portraits marks the historical circumstance in which *onnagata* was still a mainstream practice in Japanese films, while images of American female stars gained a wide currency through films and photographs in Japan. By 1923, however, female actresses almost completely replaced the *onnagata* in Japanese films.

In this chapter I will discuss why such a replacement occurred during this period. Specifically, why did *onnagata* remain an orthodox practice in Japanese films until 1920, so that such dissimilarity was visible between Japanese and American star images? What led to the shift from *onnagata* to female actresses? How was this transition related to the historical and cultural context? Recent studies eschew the teleological account that regards *onnagata* as unnatural and cinematically underdeveloped. Instead, they point out that the removal of *onnagata* was due to the rising popularity of female actresses in 1920, efforts to modernise domestic films, or the demand for psychological realism and natural acting styles by filmmakers and critics (Komatsu 1990; Deguchi 1991; Bernardi 2001). Such accounts, however, have hardly explored two important factors: the inflow of personnel from theatres into cinema and the canonisation of Western actors' images. For personnel, by the late 1910s the source of film actors was no longer limited to *kabuki* and *shinpa* theatre – or the 'new school' that arose in the late nineteenth century and dramatised contemporary issues – both of which largely adopted *onnagata*. Rather, it extended to other newly emerging theatrical types, such as the *shingeki* theatre – or the 'New Theatre' that became salient in the early twentieth century, staging translated European dramas – which did not use *onnagata*. In addition, the canonisation of 'Western' images was promoted by an influx of American films and photographs. This allowed Japanese practitioners and critics to recognise differences between American female actresses and the Japanese *onnagata* and conceptualise differences between the *onnagata* and actresses in terms of the specific quality of the medium, the relationship between performance and image, and the reorganisation of gender and sex. These new conceptualisations propelled the shift of value from the *onnagata* as a gender performance to the female actress as an image representing the sexual body.

As theorists of gender and sexuality, most notably Judith Butler (for example, 1990), have discussed, the simple dichotomy between sex as biological nature and gender as social construction is problematic. Neither gender nor sex is essentially determined; rather, each is historically formed and culturally defined. Sex should be captured not as a person's fixed bodily biological nature, but as a signification based on his or her somewhat plastic, physical features. With the replacement of the *onnagata* by actresses, however, sex was essentialised as the performer's innate, physical nature rather than the performative quality that he or she evoked. In *kabuki* of the eighteenth century, the *onnagata* was conventionalised as a sort of gender performance insofar as male actors attempted to adjust their bodies to the feminine costumes, gestures and behaviours that the men imitated, cited and idealised during that time (see Kano 2001: 5–6; Morinaga 2002; Fujiki 2005). However, instigated by American star images such as that of Gonzales, reform discourses and the new fan culture in the mid-1910s increasingly posited that on-screen gender roles must be subordinate to the performer's sex, and that photographic and cinematographic images necessarily reflected their innate nature.

## Maintaining gender performance

*Onnagata* remained an orthodox practice in theatres and films until the 1910s, when it became controversial and underwent transformation. It follows that the gender performance dominated early Japanese cinema. Institutional and conventional connections with *kabuki* and *shinpa*, as well as critical discourses and fan culture, enabled films to preserve the *onnagata*.

One reason for the *onnagata*'s supremacy in early Japanese films was that the two types of theatre, *kabuki* and *shinpa*, were the major sources of personnel. Unlike the British theatre, in which female actresses emerged in the late seventeenth century (Howe 1992), Japanese plays persistently relied on cross-dressed actors. Certainly, the newly emerging theatrical type, *shingeki*, cast female actresses for all female roles when staging translated European and Russian dramas, including those of Shakespeare, Ibsen and Strindberg, but it had yet to establish a sufficient stock of actors in the first half of the 1910s (Ôzasa 1985: 71–135). The more established *kabuki*, however, had a symbiotic liaison with the film industry. Because this theatrical form – with minor exceptions like the newly forming women's *kabuki* – retained all-male casting, the presence of the *onnagata* in the film genre called *kyûgeki* or *kyûha* (the old drama or old school) was maintained. For low-ranking actors, films were lucrative as a part- or full-time job (Kairaishi 1911: 3; see also Fujiki 2004). As the domestic film industry became more established, with the vertical integration of the Nikkatsu Company in 1912 and the Tenkatsu Company in 1914, even the celebrated theatre *onnagata* signed long-term studio contracts (see Anon. 1916a: 29).

Just as *kabuki* supplied actors to old drama films, another type of theatre, *shinpa*, did the same for *shinpa* films. In the late nineteenth century, *shinpa* theatre became popular. Unlike *kabuki*, early *shinpa* theatre consisted of amateur actors, including both the *onnagata* and female performers. Despite its emergence with its innovative traits, *shinpa* became more politically conservative and stylistically conventional by the 1910s, with recourse to elements reminiscent of the established 'classic' theatre, *kabuki*, such as music, dance and *onnagata* (Kano 2001: 57–8). This legacy further influenced cinema, particularly in the 'melodramatic' genre called *shinpa-higeki*. The *onnagata* appeared in *shinpa* films throughout the 1910s, when *shinpa* actors began to work for film companies, either as part-time or long-term employees. They did this despite the prohibition against film appearances by some associations of actors – most notably, the Theatre Guild of Tokyo in 1915 – which probably aimed to prevent its personnel from flowing into the cinema and to resist the rising popularity of the new medium (Shigeno 1915: 4; Hagii 1974: 126–8, 141–4).

Yet the 1910s did see the appearance of female actresses in a type of *shinpa* film called *rensageki*, which alternated stage acts with screen scenes. Affiliated with *shinpa* actor-troupes that had a contract with a film company, Nakamura Kasen, Kinoshita

Kinoshita Yaoka in *Katsudô Gahô* (1917)

Tachibana Teijiro in *Katudô no sekai* (1916)

Yaoko and Miho Matsuko represented the *sensageki* actresses, though the latter two also had experiences in *shingeki* (Kinoshita 1915: 18; Tsukuda 1915b: 15; Okamura 1916: 178–83). These performers, however, did not replace the *onnagata* but rather coexisted with them. Unlike American stars, the *rensageki* actresses were not discursively canonised as an exemplary model for Japanese films. In addition, their presentation was not so much a powerful alternative to gender performance, as a kind of reproduction of it, particularly because these performers relied more on gender-based performance than on physicality-based sexuality. For one thing, the *sensageki* actresses attempted to restrain their body-based sexuality due to fears that they might have been regarded as sexual practitioners equal to *geisha* and prostitutes (Kinoshita 1917: 156–7). Also, as theatre historians note, early female performers imitated the existing performance styles, especially that of *onnagata* performances, since no other acting model existed for them (see, for instance, Kano 2001: 32). While some photogravures of Kinoshita showcased her body in a medium-long shot with few traits of gender performance like that of the *onnagata* (see *Katsudô gahô* 1917b), others were extremely similar to the *onnagata*'s representation. In their magazine photogravures, Kinoshita and Tachibana Teijirô – one of the post popular *onnagata* – were both posed in a typical *shinpa* tableau, in which a female character stands with a male character under an umbrella (*Katudô no sekai* 1916; *Katsudô gahô* 1917a).

Indeed, the stylistic form of Japanese motion pictures and photogravures of the time was another reason for the preservation of *onnagata* as a mainstream practice. Although few films of the 1910s survive today, magazine photogravures of the time suggest that the visualising techniques hardly served to accentuate a performer's bodily surface and configuration. Instead, the distanced framing contributed to positioning his or her pose in the picturesque tableau. What signifies femininity here is not the body, per se, but the ways of using the body, that is, the conventional posing and attitudes, such as downcast eyes and so-called 'willowy' standing (in which the bodily line from the shoulder to the hip gently curves). Likewise, *onnagata* and *rensageki* actresses both usually wore *kimono*, or occasionally a loosely-shaped Western dress covering most of the bodily skin, so that his or her costume functioned as a sign of gender identity without drawing on the articulation of anatomical, sexual difference.

Not only such representational forms but also critical discourses and fan culture played a part in retaining the gender performance. While reformist critics began to place primary importance on the cinematic representation of actors' 'natural' features and movements in the latter half of the 1910s, other reviewers hardly differed from their critiques of theatrical performance when describing an actor's characterisation and acting style. One of the earliest film critics, Yoshiyama Kyokkô, for instance, praised Tachibana's expression of the heroine's strong will without mentioning the filmic representation of his physicality (1915: 105–6). Other reporters noted some traits of Tachibana's body, such as his 'slenderness', 'vocal tone' and 'the shape of his hands on his knees', but these first and foremost pointed to how Tachibana conformed to *onnagata* roles rather than emphasising his sexual identity (Urashima 1916: 58–9; Taguchi 1917: 28–30).

The fan culture of the *onnagata* also did not problematise the 'incongruity' between the actor's gender role and sexual identity. Although little record of audiences' voices survives, their inclination can be extrapolated by the fact that critics recognised most fans of Tachibana as weepy, fanatic females. That is, regardless of whether the fans were fascinated by Tachibana's masculine sexuality or his narrative roles, they neither repudiated his cross-dressing nor required that the representation of him be based on his anatomical nature. Rather, they were involved with the narrative role enacted through his performance skills, beyond heterosexual affection. For them, Tachibana's attraction lay in that gender and sexuality were ambiguously blended in his character roles, performance and physique (Tamahitsu 1917: 100–5; Tekkamen 1917: 174). Thus, though the fans and some critics had different reasons, neither required that the representation of gender be subordinated to body-centred sexuality.

## Forming sexual image

Meanwhile, however, the *onnagata* increasingly became problematic in both theatre and cinema. Newly formulated theatrical forms such as operas, all-female revues, and *shingeki* adopted female actresses, instead of the *onnagata*, for female narrative roles, and almost all films did so by 1923. In the late 1910s and early 1920s, there were still few film actors who had not had theatrical experiences before appearing in films. The sources of personnel, however, were no longer dominated by *kabuki* and *shinpa*, but were expanding to include new types of theatres. This was the case for the first female film stars, such as Hanayagi Harumi (from *shingeki*), Hanabusa Yuriko (from Asakusa Operetta), Azuma Eiko (from Takarazuka Revue) and Kurishima Sumiko (who formerly had experiences both in *shingeki* and *shinpa*). One of the difficulties for women who became actresses in legitimate theatres before the 1910s was the fear that they might have been regarded as overt sex practitioners equal to *geisha* and prostitutes. In the late 1900s and early 1910s, however, the establishment of modern acting schools and the legitimisation of actresses (as in the all-female play of the 'Imperial Theatre' initiated in 1911) helped dilute the prejudice against actresses, resulting in their acceptance (Ôzasa 1985). Accordingly, the replacement of the *onnagata* by actresses in films coincided with the theatrical situation in which female actresses arose in new types of theatres while the *onnagata* were confined to *kabuki* and *shinpa*, which then became regarded as classical or special.

The transformation of this material condition was sustained by the canonisation of female actresses. This process comprised reformist discourses on theatre and cinema which both modelled Euro-American practices and theories and appraised Japanese ones from a 'Western' standard. In the case of the theatre, reformist practitioners and critics shared three main concerns: the naturalness of acting, the bodily essence of sex and social respectability. Espousing natural acting, *shingeki* theorist Shimamura Hôgetsu, for instance, insisted that an actress must reflect her psychology in her physical expression on-stage and strive to master this skill by training off-stage (cited in Kano 2001: 138). This naturalising process necessarily posited the notion that the performer must attribute his or her sexual identity to the biological nature of the body. In another essay, Shimamura suggested that performers in European films like *Film d'Art* were excellent models for his student-actress Matsui Sumako to imitate so as to master 'natural' acting (1916: 18). This indicates his presuppositions that Western actors' performances were the canon for natural acting and that cinematic images automatically transmitted naturalness. Similarly, in a debate on the need for female actresses in the theatre magazine *Engei gahô*, despite the debaters' opposite opinions, all assumed that female actresses were 'natural' whereas the *onnagata* were 'artful'.

Significantly, both Shimamura's thoughts and the debate on actresses were placed in the larger historical context, in which Japanese intellectuals and governors attempted to establish the social respectability of the Japanese theatre compared with the European theatre. Since the Meiji government replaced the Edo government in 1868, knowledge imported from Europe increasingly became the canon for evaluating cultural value. On a general level, as historians argue, influenced by European sexology and Christian religious notions, medical and scientific discourses essentialised biological difference, while legal and political codes legitimised the norm of heterosexual monogamy (Ueno 1990; Frühstück 2003: 55–115). As a result, unless *onnagata* was considered an 'art', it began to be identified with the imported concept of 'homosexuality' and thereby with an unnatural, perverted person (*hentai*) (Hasegawa 1920; see also Furukawa 1994). On a level more specifically related to the theatre, visits to London, Paris and Berlin by government officials and entrepreneurs led to the formation of the Theatre Reform Society in 1886. The society promoted the removal of *onnagata*, aiming to 'improve' the quality of Japanese plays by making them comparable to European theatre. One consequence was the advent of actresses' plays in the 'Imperial Theatre' established in 1911 (Ôzasa 1985: 32–7). Ayako Kano aptly positions the New Theatre movement in relation to the world powers, stating that 'theatre was one of the most conspicuous sites for the new government to display Japan's legitimacy as an advanced nation, one that could not only avoid colonisation by nations such as the United States, Britain, Germany and France, but one that would eventually become a colonial power itself' (2001: 6).

Although the government was not as involved with cinema as the theatre, reformist film critics were engaged with the canonisation of female actresses in Western, especially American, films. Without recognising the differences between Japanese and Western films, and without valuing the latter over the former, *onnagata* was not denied. The expanding deluge of films (especially serials and a moderate-budget brand, Universal's Bluebird) from the United States after the outbreak of World War One likely urged film critics to compare them with domestic motion pictures (see Thompson 1985: 74; Fujiki 2005). Coinciding with the development of printing technology, such as offset and half-tone printings, the diffusion of photographic American star images through multiple media, including magazines, postcards and photographic cards, seemed to push forward this cognitive activity.

The visual differences between Japanese and American performers are clear, both in the racial and sexual traits of their bodies and in the styles of their visual representation. In an American portrait, *mise-en-scène* devices such as twisted posing, low-key lighting, revealing costumes and abstract backgrounds centre on highlighting the bodily surface and proportions that the American white celebrity embodies. These elements work in co-operation with photographic and cinematographic techniques like closer framing, a focus on the face and level camera angles. In contrast, deriving from a still photograph of a tableau-like film scene, Japanese representations of the *onnagata* rarely focused on bodily features. Instead, they were reminiscent of Japanese portraits of *geisha* and prostitutes conventionalised in woodblock prints (*ukiyoe*) and, by extension, early photographs. Here the signification of sexual difference depended less on bodily features and more on other *mise-en-scène* elements, like the way of wearing *kimono*, accessories, the wig, posture, and props such as mirrors (Saeki 1993; Sakuma 1995: 234; Wakakuwa 1997: 20–32). In effect, situated by their visible contrast with Japanese conventional portraits, the American star images showed a marked emphasis on the sexuality of physical bodies.

Reformist critics never neutrally interpreted such visible distinctions. Rather, while canonising American acting techniques or star images, they problematised *onnagata* in terms of its unconformity to the medium, its performativity-oriented images and the inconsistency between its gender and sex. Like the Theatre Reform Society, the new film critics, often called the Pure Film Movement (*Jun eiga-geki undô*), attempted to criticise and improve the domestic culture from a 'Western' standpoint, urging Japanese films to adopt more American and/or European styles of filmmaking (for example Kaeriyama 1921: 18–37; see also Bernardi 2001: 84–5, 110–15). Yet unlike the debate on *onnagata* in theatre, which accepted its coexistence with actresses to a certain extent, the film critics almost all pressed for its abolition, although a few suggested that it might continue for the fans of *shinpa* films or be preserved as a 'traditional' culture (Saginoya 1917: 198–9). For them, female actresses were indispensable because of the nature of film. The three distinguished critics of the time, Gonda Yasunsuke, Mori Iwao and Kaeriyama Norimasa, all compared film with the theatre, and then ascribed an imperative of naturalness to the former, especially due to its mechanical properties, ability to provide close framing and photographic representation with no sound. Gonda argued that, whereas the theatre was a conceptual medium and hence allowed the conventional practice of *onnagata*, film portrayed concrete objects and thus necessitated actresses (1922: 180–2). Mori emphatically reiterated the critical cliché that a closer framing would expose the *onnagata*'s 'unnaturalness' (1976: 66). The same was also true for Kaeriyama, who more systematically explained the indispensability of authentic character expression for film. Although he stressed his preference for symbolic construction over realistic representation, both of these directions nevertheless shared the common premise that film must show the 'true nature' of the performer's physique (1921: 92–3, 111).

This assumption regarding the medium's specificity suggests another point in favour of female actresses. That is, for the reform discourses and fan culture, cinematic images should mediate actors' bodies and personalities prior to their performances. The critics thus urged film productions to depart from theatrical acting and staging, and to compose images conveying the actor's natural behaviour and attitude. Yet they faced the conflict of how they themselves should evaluate film acting without drawing on earlier conventions of theatrical criticism, which admired virtuoso stylisation of both acting and characterisation (such as Tamahitsu 1917: 105). Two trends of criticism concerning the *onnagata* and female actresses emerged and struggled to overcome the old form of criticism. One was to either poetically appreciate or analytically describe the shapely beauty of a performer's bodily parts, including face, waist and legs. The 'beauty issue' of film magazine *Katsudô kurabu* in September 1919, for instance, epitomised the criticism of actresses' bodily proportion and features, mostly modelling American white stars. Another trend was concerned with the 'naturalness' of expressions, paying attention to how the acting functioned to naturally express psychology and how it was not stylised. This form of evaluation was new. One critic, for example, criticised one of the first female actresses, Nakayama Utako, for imitating the *onnagata*'s 'unnatural' performance style (Ôuchi 1921: 11), while another critic applied this new criterion of 'naturalness' to a critique of *onnagata* (Tsukuda 1915a: 11–12). Both trends – the appreciation or description of the performers' bodies and the criticism of the performers' naturalness of acting – continued to intricately intermingle in the 1920s, although the former tended to appear in popular magazines and the latter in more intellectual journals. In both cases, it was assumed that the cinematic and photographic image was optimal for conveying the actors' bodily nature and realistic acting, rather than accentuating virtuoso manipulation of their body.

At the same time, in the new discourses, American star images had a more symbiotic relation with actors' body-based sex identities than with the performance of gender. One male film critic in the 'high-brow' journal *Kinema Record* noted, 'For the film, a female actress with a poker face is better than an *onnagata* with a sweet facial expression' (Anon. 1916b). This quote succinctly indicates that anatomical bodily features must define any expression of femininity and sexuality in films. For the reform discourses, the subordination of gender to sex was natural, while the reverse case was presented as unnatural and grotesque.

Moreover, in the late 1910s, when the critics delimited the essence of the photographic cinematic image to the transmission of body-centred sex, the wide range of discourses and practices concerning American female stars began to construct fantasies of heterosexual commitment for male audiences in an unprecedented way. Certainly, it is implausible to think that the female fans of the *onnagata* suddenly stopped their sexually ambiguous affection for the performers and were inclined exclusively toward heterosexual relationships (Anon. 1917a). But it became increasingly remarkable that the new star discourses were addressed to male fans on more clearly heterosexual grounds. As American films and their stars' photographic images gained a wider currency from the mid-1910s, critics increasingly noticed that male fans were fanatically collecting photographic cards foregrounding actresses' bodies (Anon 1920; Kaeriyama 1928: 26). Such ardent male spectators were absent in discourses surrounding the *onnagata*. Whereas the cross-dressed actors of the Edo period were performance commodities who often provided male or female audiences with off-stage services, including direct sexual contact (see Leupp 1995: 72–7), cinema actresses were image-based commodities that were well-suited to be collected and gazed upon by male spectators. Reformist critics admonished such monomaniac audiences for engaging in 'wrong spectatorship' and criticised the star system for its commercialism. At the same time, however, they admitted that male audiences found the actresses' body-based sexuality more attractive than the *onnagata*'s skilful performance of gender, even though their acting was awkward (Gonda 1922: 183–4; Kaeriyama 1928: 22–9, 122–8). In any case, they either sanctioned the heterosexual relationship between stars and audiences or attempted to guide audiences to a de-sexualised spectatorship beyond sexual affection (Anon. 1917). Accordingly, their guidance emphasised restraining the filmic image from a representation of the performance of gender in favour of a direct reflection of sex difference that was essentialised on the basis of the performer's physical body.

## Conclusion

The replacement of *onnagata* by female actresses was an uneven and complex process. Two forces were involved in this shift. On the one hand, the cinema's connection with *kabuki* and *shinpa*, both in production and reception, contributed to the preservation of the *onnagata*'s conventions until the 1910s. On the other hand, changing circumstances, like the rise of new theatrical movements and the spread of American star images, led reform discourses and the newly-emerging fan culture to call for female actresses. This struggle concerned the definition and management of gender and sexuality. It is particularly significant that this transition occurred in conjunction with an influx of visual images from the United States, bringing about a visible contrast between Japanese performers as 'unnatural' and American performers as 'natural'. With a nationalistic aspiration, which was to authorise their domestic culture by equating it with 'Western' white culture, reformist critics drove Japanese performers to imitate the American stars' images in their representations, instead of mastering the conventions of the *onnagata*'s gender performance. And yet, of course, this is not to say that the Japanese film actresses were represented in completely the same way as American actresses. In the first half of the 1920s, Japanese actresses often wore *kimono* in their photogravures, and the film industry began to differentiate their stars from American ones by foregrounding Japanese uniqueness while assimilating some American ways of representation (see Fujiki 2005). Nevertheless, it is clear that, from the 1920s onwards, as a variety of indigenous female actresses arose, gender performers like the *onnagata*, aside from some 'queer' performers, were almost entirely eradicated in Japanese films. The fact that the Shôchiku Kinema Company and other new film companies established in the early 1920s began using actresses in all of their films should be understood in this historical context. The replacement of *onnagata* by female actresses in films occurred in the context of circumstances in which Western, especially American, star images were circulated, recognised, conceptualised and canonised in contraposition to the Japanese domestic practice of gender performance.

## Note

1   I would like to thank Hiroshi Kitamura, Donna Maurer, Sara Ross and Ben Singer for their comments and advice during the various stages of the preparation of this chapter.

# Works cited

Anon. (1916a) 'Nippon no katsudô haiyû hanagata zoroi' ('All film stars in Japan'), *Katsudô no sekai*, August, 28–34.

_____ (1916b) 'Gujin no gugo ka aruiwa nihon eiga no ketten ka' ('Is it my silly talk or the Japanese film's deficiency?'), *Kinema Record*, October, 427.

_____ (1917a) 'Gendai no fujin no mitaru katsudô shashin' ('Motion pictures that women watch today'), *Kinema Record*, May, 218–19.

_____ (1917b) 'Gendai no fujin no mitaru katsudô shashin' ('Motion pictures that women watch today'), *Kinema Record*, June, 278–9.

_____ (1920) 'Genga no hanashi' ('Story about the original pictures'), *Kinema junpô*, 1 February, 1.

Bernardi, J. (2001) *Writing in Light: The Silent Scenario and the Japanese Pure Film Movement*. Detroit: Wayne State University Press.

Butler, J. (1990) *Gender Trouble: Feminism and the Subversion of Identity*. New York: Routledge.

Deguchi, T. (1991) 'Naniga hakujin konpurekkusu o umidashitaka' ('What brought about the complex about the white?'), in K. Iwamoto (ed.) *Nihon eiga to modanizumu 1920–1930*. Tokyo: Riburopôto, 104–23.

Fujiki, H. (2004) 'Dual Persona: Onoe Matsunosuke as Early Japanese Cinema Star', *ICONICS*, 7, 157–80.

_____ (2005) 'Multiplying Personas: The Formation of Film Stars in Modern Japan', unpublished PhD dissertation, University of Wisconsin-Madison.

Furukawa, M. (1994) 'The Changing Nature of Sexuality: The Three Codes Framing Homosexuality in Modern Japan', trans. Angus Lockyer, *U.S.-Japan Women's Journal*, 7, 98–123.

Frühstück, S. (2003) *Colonizing Sex: Sexology and Social Control in Modern Japan*. Berkeley: University of California Press.

Gonda, Y. (1922) *Minshû goraku no kichô*. Tokyo: Dôjin-sha.

Hagii, K. (1974) *Shinpa no gei*. Tokyo: Tokyo shoseki.

Hasegawa, S. (1920) 'Hentai seiyoku kara mita onnagata' ('The *onnagata* seen from the viewpoint of perverted sexual desire'), *Engei gahô*, November, 155–9.

Howe, E. (1992) *The First Actresses: Women and Drama, 1660–1700*. New York: Cambridge University Press.

Kaeriyama, N. (1921) *Katsudô shashingeki no sôsaku to satsuei hô* (second edition). Tokyo: Seimitsu-sha.

_____ (1928) *Eiga no seiteki miwaku*. Tokyo: Bunkyû-sha shobô.

Kairaishi (1911) 'Senmon teki katsuhai o naze yôsei nasazaru ka' ('Why do they not train actors specialising in the film'), *Katsudô shashin kai*, September, reprinted in R. Okabe (ed.) *Nihon eigashi sokô*, 7, *Shiryô nihon no haiyû gakkô*. Tokyo: Firumu raiburari kyôkai, 358.

Kano, A. (2001) *Acting Like a Woman in Modern Japan: Theater, Gender, and Nationalism*. New York: Palgrave.

*Katsudô gahô* (1917a) July.

*Katsudô gahô* (1917b) October.

*Katudô no sekai* (1916) December.

Kinoshita, Y. (1915) 'Joyû ni naru made' ('Until becoming an actress'), *Katsudô shashin zasshi*, December, 18–20.

_____ (1917) 'Aruyo no hanashi' (Story one night), *Katsudô gahô*, July, 96–101.

Komatsu, H. (1990) 'The Fundamental Change: Japanese Cinema Before and After the Earthquake of 1923', *Griffithiana*, 38/39 (October), 186–96.

Leupp, G. (1995) *Male Colors: The Construction of Homosexuality in Tokugawa Japan*. Berkeley: University of California Press.

Mori, I. (1976 [1919–20]) 'Nippon eigaki no jôkyo' ('Circumstances of Japanese Film Culture'), in I. Mori and Y. Tomonari (eds) *Nihon eiga-shi sokô bessatsu, Katsudô shashin taikan, 2, Nihon katsudô shashin kai no kenkyû*. Tokyo: Firumu raiburari kyôkai.

Morinaga, M. (2002) 'The Gender of *Onnagata* as the Imitating Imitated: Its Historicity, Performativity, and Involvement in the Circulation of Femininity', *Positions*, 10, 2, 245–84.

Okamura, S. (1916) *Katsudô haiyû meimei den, jô*. Tokyo: Katsudô shashin zasshi-sha.

Ôuchi, S. (1921) 'Hikaku' ('Comparison'), *Kinema junpô*, 21 January, 11.

Ôzasa, Y. (1985) *Nihon gendai engeki shi: Meiji, Taishô hen*. Tokyo: Hakusui-sha.

Saeki, J. (1993) '"Bijin" no jidai' ('The period of the beauty'), in H. Tôru (ed.) *Bunmei toshite no tokugawa nihon*. Tokyo: Chûôkôronsha, 416–41.

Saginoya (1917) 'Tachibana Teijirô jô ni' ('To Mr. Tachibana Teijirô'), *Katsudô gahô*, April, 198–9.

Sakuma, R. (1995) 'Shashin to josei: Atarashii media no tôjô to "miru/mirareru" jibun no shutsugen' ('Photography and women: The advent of the new medium and the emergence of the "seeing/seen" self'), in A. Okuda (ed.) *Onna to otoko no jikû: Nihon josei shi saikô, 5, Semegiau onna to otoko: kindai*. Tokyo: Fujiwara shoten, 187–237.

Shigeno, Y. (1915) 'Waga katsuhai no yûki to doryô' ('The courage and tolerance of our film actors'), *Kinema Record*, February, 4.

Shimamura, H. (1916) 'Katsudô shashin no shin ni sakan na jidai' ('The period when the motion picture genuinely flourishes'), *Katsudô no sekai*, May, 18–19.

Taguchi, Ô. (1917) 'Onnagata to Joyû to' ('The *onnagata* and actresses'), *Katsudô gahô*, December, 28–33.

Tamahitsu, S. (1917) 'Byôshô no Tachibana Teijirô shi ni' ('To Mr Tachibana Teijirô sick in bed'), *Katsudô gahô*, January, 100–5.

Tekkamen (1917) 'Boku no kangae' ('My ideas'), *Katsudô gahô*, December, 174–5.

Thompson, K. (1985) *Exporting Entertainment: America in the World Film Market*. London: British Film Institute.

Tsukuda, F. (1915a) 'Naigai haiyû roku' ('The database of film actors inside and outside Japan'), *Kinema Record*, March, 11–13.

_____ (1915b) 'Naigai haiyû roku' ('The database of film actors inside and outside Japan'), *Kinema Record*, April, 11–15.

Ueno, C. (1990) 'Kaisetsu' ('Exposition'), in S. Ogi, I. Kumakura, C. Ueno and S. Katô (eds) *Nihon kindai shisô taikei, 23, Fûzoku, sei*. Tokyo: Iwanami shoten, 519–35.

Urashima, S. (1916) 'Tsukioka to Tachibana to Fujino' ('Tsukioka, Tachibana and Fujino'), *Katsudô no sekai*, March, 58–60.

Wakakuwa, M. (1997) *Kakusareta shisen: Ukiyoe yôga no josei rataizô*. Tokyo: Iwanami shoten.

Yanagawa, S. (1912) 'Joyû wa ôi ni yûbô' (Female actresses are really promising), *Engei gahô*, January, 45–8.

Yoshiyama, K. (1915) 'Kakukan shashin tanpyô' ('Short reviews of playhouses'), *Katsudô shashin zasshi*, November, 103–14.

## CHAPTER THIRTEEN

# Troubled masculinities: questioning gender and sexuality in Liu Bingjian's *Nannan nünü* (*Men and Women*)

Louise Williams

Liu Bingjian's 1999 film, *Nannan nünü* (*Men and Women*), is a story of conflicting desires and sexualities in a rapidly changing Beijing. China after Mao's death had not only undergone economic changes, but had also seen shifts in cultural and social attitudes, which were mostly concentrated in its large, east-coast cities. Unlike previous (city-based) cinematic representations of homosexual masculinities from Mainland China, such as Chen Kaige's *Bawang bieji* (*Farewell My Concubine*, 1993) or Zhang Yuan's *Donggong xigong* (*East Palace West Palace*, 1996), *Men and Women* does not exoticise, theatricalise or pathologise same-sex desire, but treats homosexuality as part of this contemporary complex cultural atmosphere. Most of the actors in Liu's film are gay and non-professional (Yu Bo plays Xiao Bo), except for the more recognised actress, Yang Qing (playing Qing). The director perceives the film as a personal response to changing ideas of sexual roles in Chinese society, hypothesising that his protagonists' sexual 'subculture' provides them with a space to move outside prescribed codes of gender and sexuality.[1] However, while the main character, Xiao Bo, acts as an object of desire and a narrative catalyst, his indeterminate masculinity prevents him from occupying the central position expected of main male protagonists. This ambiguous sexuality serves to undermine the social and sexual certainties of the men and women whom he encounters.

This chapter will focus upon the manner in which homosexual masculinities are represented in *Men and Women*. The plot of Liu's film hinges on a series of assumptions and coincidences, which serve to satirise the dichotomies to which multiple sexual identities are often reduced. Firstly, I will examine Xiao Bo's position within his two substitute families, one heterosexual and one homosexual. Secondly, I will explain how Xiao Bo's characterisation as a sexual object challenges traditional politics of representation. However, for a film that explores the possibilities of sexuality, *Men and Women* represents surprisingly little actual sex. In fact, when they are presented, sexual encounters are invariably destructive. The third section of this chapter will explore this apparent anomaly. Finally, I will assess the implications of Liu's representation of members of a Mainland Chinese gay community. In his definition of the way that 'queer theory' works through film, critic Ellis Hanson argues that films that represent homosexuality in the West often feel the need to present positive images or to respond to political agendas through their gay protagonists (1999: 11). Do Hanson's observations equally apply to Liu Bingjian's film, since 'positive' agendas and images may carry very different meanings in a Chinese context?

## Synopsis

*Men and Women* begins when its main male protagonist, Xiao Bo, walks into a small clothes boutique in a busy shopping district of Beijing looking for his contact in the city and a job. Although his connections let him down, in that he never finds the mysterious Mr Li for whom he is looking, the owner of the boutique, Qing (a smart woman in her thirties) gives him a job and a spare room in her tiny apartment, which she shares with her husband, Kang. Qing takes her new charge under her wing, and eventually arranges a blind date for him with her best friend, Ah Meng. However, Ah Meng tells Qing that she suspects that Xiao Bo may be gay. Qing confides her worries about Xiao Bo's sexuality to her husband, who tells her not to worry unduly. Nevertheless, when Xiao Bo is alone in the house with Kang, Kang attempts to rape him, only to insult Xiao Bo when he is rejected.

As a result of Kang's advances, Xiao Bo leaves Qing's apartment and walks out on his job. Bereft of a place to stay, he calls Chong Chong, a new friend who publishes a magazine called *Lavatory Literature* that collects lavatory graffiti and 'fables' and, presumably (though left unsaid), is a lifeline for the cottaging community of Beijing's gay scene. Unknown to Xiao Bo, he lives with Gui Gui, his partner who records a programme called *Lavatory Time*, the audio equivalent to Chong Chong's magazine. However, the arrival of the good-looking Xiao Bo puts a strain on the relationship between the pair, and leads Gui Gui to walk out when he discovers Chong Chong's indiscreet infidelity with their house guest. Meanwhile, Qing's relationship with Ah Meng deepens, until Qing announces to her husband that she is leaving him for a lesbian relationship with her friend. As a final gesture, Gui Gui delivers his final edition of *Lavatory Time* into Chong Chong's answer phone, and declares his intention to leave Beijing.

## Xiao Bo and substitute families

Superficially, the young and attractive Xiao Bo is an obvious main protagonist. However, his surface beauty and amiability does not so much serve to define his role in the drama to come, but instead obscures it. Essentially, Xiao Bo is all things to all men (and women). He is in possession of a malleable masculinity that impacts upon the various relationships that he encounters. After he has made the initial decision to buy a bus ticket to Beijing, the choices that he does make (and which propel the narrative into new directions) are all sexual – he chooses which partner to reject, and which to accept. This emphasis displays the extent to which Xiao Bo is important as a vehicle to question ideas of sex and sexuality, even though other aspects of his personality remain enigmatic. For example, he first appears in Qing's shop as a shy young man. He enters almost unnoticed, appearing at the side of the frame with arms crossed, shifting repeatedly from foot to foot. Xiao Bo appears to be a typical country bumpkin lost in a threatening and anonymous city. As a migrant from the country, his sexual indeterminacy is accompanied by economic marginality, further displacing his personality from importance. Xiao Bo simply falls into situations; he is a connecting circuit to whom past histories and motives need not be explained. Xiao Bo miraculously stumbles upon a steady job in which he is trusted (no mean feat for an unknown from the country; city prejudice towards migrant workers is conspicuous by its absence in this film)[2] and lands a nice room in a clean flat in which he is waited upon hand and foot. In fact, he fits into two substitute families: one heterosexual and one homosexual.

Firstly, Xiao Bo reveals the weaknesses behind many heterosexual relationships by taking on the role of a son in the home of Qing and her husband Kang. Qing runs a fairly successful business in downtown Beijing. She is a member of a new generation of female entrepreneurs, making her way in a business world previously dominated by men. Nonetheless, when she brings Xiao Bo home, her need for something outside her job and immediate home circumstances is revealed. Qing and Kang are a rarity for a middle-aged couple in that they are childless, leaving a gap that Xiao Bo is flexible enough to fit into. Chris Berry points out that cinematic representations of homosexualities in East Asia often focus on finding a place for a gay protagonist inside a family setting, whereas homosexual characters in Western film are excluded from, or operate without, such domestic structure (1996: 172). Despite the absence of his actual parents, Xiao Bo spends the film playing the role of a son in his two 'homes' for the benefit of his two sets of carers.

As soon as Xiao Bo enters her apartment, Qing selects a towel for him, insists on making his new bed and tells him which toiletries to use. Moreover, Xiao Bo's new room is clearly meant for a child in the original plan of the apartment; he even has a kite on his wall. The presence of Xiao Bo allows Qing to play a mothering role that she previously has not had the opportunity to act. She even assumes the role of a mother in Xiao Bo's love life. Much as a parent would, she attempts to find a suitable match for her substitute son. Qing is the active partner in the mother/child relationship, whilst Xiao Bo is passive, the recipient of Qing's attentions and the object of her wishes. Unconsciously, Qing indicates the parameters of their relationship through her order to Xiao Bo that he should accompany her out to dinner: 'Xiao Bo, I'll bring you to meet a friend of mine tonight.'[3] The French title of the film, *Le Protégé de Mme Qing*, perhaps more accurately conveys the nature of Qing and Xiao Bo's relationship. That is to say, Xiao Bo is Qing's protégé as well as her *didi*, or younger brother, whom she nurtures and protects.[4]

When Xiao Bo is homeless after he has thwarted Kang's rape attempt, he turns to Chong Chong, and enters his second family of the narrative. The first time that the two men encounter each other is in an anonymous public lavatory, where Xiao Bo is one of the users to whom Chong Chong courteously hands his business card. However, this mysterious editor is the first person to whom the destitute Xiao Bo runs for help. When Xiao Bo finally arrives at Chong Chong's tiny apartment, Chong Chong reassures his friend that 'the folding bed is still there', confirming their acquaintance, and maybe a possible flirtation. Did Xiao Bo, the geographical and emotional tourist, decide to take an interest in Chong Chong and his *Lavatory Literature* magazine? Once more, Xiao Bo has wandered into another narrative that has occurred behind our backs. Such secrecy may be in sympathy with the lives of gay couple Gui Gui and Chong Chong, and the community that their journalistic activities suggest; connections are made and friendships forged away from a dominant heterosexual narrative.

Xiao Bo's relationship with Chong Chong shares characteristics with that of his bond with Qing – in both narrative strands, his presence is random and unexplained, yet is a catalyst to upheavals in the protagonists' lives. Chong Chong also looks after Xiao Bo. On his way to deliver issues of the magazine *Lavatory Literature* in local bars, Chong Chong puts Xiao Bo on a bus. Xiao Bo is, literally, a lost paperboy who is being sent off on his round. Xiao Bo's childlike qualities are reinforced when he is asked what sort of food he would like to eat one evening. When given a choice of restaurant, he answers that he wants to eat at McDonald's. His choice may be understandable for a young migrant new to the city and its cosmopolitan (Western) taste of an affluent lifestyle, but he also chooses the place where parents take their indulged offspring for a weekend treat. Chong Chong's actions towards Xiao Bo are consistently protective. He takes off his guest's coat tenderly, he tucks him up in bed at night, and kisses him. However, this kiss is not merely substitute 'paternal' affection, it is also sexual, as Chong Chong reveals when he revisits Xiao Bo's bed the following night.

## Xiao Bo and sexuality

When Chong Chong next walks in on his sleeping house guest, he is naked. He climbs into bed and begins to kiss Xiao Bo passionately. Is this sexual experience (implied but unshown) an affirmation of Xiao Bo's previously ambiguous sexuality? However, this 'coming out' experience has serious (and destructive) ramifications for Chong Chong's relationship with Gui Gui. Just as Qing's husband Kang assumes Xiao Bo's passivity in his rape attempt, Chong Chong takes it for granted that Xiao Bo is sexually available. Once more, Xiao Bo has propelled another narrative into crisis. Chong Chong's indiscreet infidelity has sent Gui Gui noisily packing his bags, revealing Chong Chong's naïve idea of the boundaries of their partnership. As Chong Chong hears Gui Gui's recorded voice on the answer phone, Xiao Bo is nowhere to be seen. Any details of a future for Chong Chong and Xiao Bo are left to speculation.

Xiao Bo's position as a sexual object had been foregrounded in an earlier extended sequence. When Xiao Bo first arrives at Qing's apartment, he takes a shower. However, instead of stopping at the door, the camera lingers as Xiao Bo undresses, while the bathroom mirror lends us an alternative view of his face. A cut to Qing chopping vegetables is short-lived, as we once more return to the bathroom while Xiao Bo shampoos his hair. Such a focus not only literally and metaphorically exposes Xiao Bo, but also highlights his vulnerability and corporeality. He is a blank canvas upon which the protagonists and the audience may project their gaze. In Laura Mulvey's (1975) influential hypothesis, women on screen are 'to be looked at' by the male spectator, whose voyeuristic desires sublimate his psychological anxieties. Steve Neale offers a counterpoint to Mulvey's arguments, since he observes that men in Hollywood cinema may in fact be the ones 'to be looked at' by a male audience, although the success of mainstream cinema depends on this same-sex desire being displaced or masked (1993: 19). In Liu's film, this homo- (and, indeed, hetero-)sexual looking is not concealed.

Xiao Bo's objectification places theories of the gendered gaze into doubt by displacing 'conventional' politics of looking. Through this device, we are encouraged to interpret Xiao Bo as a sexual being; that is, we are placed in a spectatorial position in which we cannot fail to interpret Xiao Bo's body as a visual object. Having nowhere else to look, we are forced to focus upon Xiao Bo's physicality, and to contemplate him in terms of conscious (or unconscious) desire. In comparison, we see relatively little of the female body during the film. For example, Qing does not reveal herself to us to the same extent, undressing under her bedcover in the shadows. Instead, *Men and Women* firmly places men (and Xiao Bo in particular) as objects of sexual desire.

## *Men and Women* and homosexual masculinities

To the end of the film, Xiao Bo never makes an open statement concerning his sexuality. It is almost as though his sexuality is speculated into existence by the observations of Qing's friend, Ah Meng – if Xiao Bo shows no interest in her (and is not even attracted to Gong Li, the famous Chinese actress) then he *has* to be gay. From this remark, Qing's reactions to Xiao Bo visibly change. In a comic scene, perhaps poking fun at the stereotypes of 'feminisation' that are placed on homosexual men, Qing eyes Xiao Bo quizzically, as he rearranges a mannequin in the window of the shop, as though seeing him for the first time. Qing's scrutiny confirms what she has decided already – Xiao Bo (who works in a clothes store on her own initiative) is showing an 'unhealthy' interest in fashion, and any heterosexual masculinity that Qing has formulated for Xiao Bo is compromised.

In part, Xiao Bo resembles what Richard Dyer has described as the 'sad young man' in the context of novels of the 1950s and 1960s; like Xiao Bo, these melancholy protagonists served to represent urbanism as a process of alienation (1995: 77). He is the vehicle for the anxieties of a society in the process of social, cultural and moral transformation. Xiao Bo's youth and vulnerability, like Dyer's 'sad young man', contributes to his sexual and sympathetic appeal, both inside and outside the plot. That Liu places this responsibility for representing the concerns of an uncertain community (in a sexual sense and in the context of increasing abandonment of old social priorities) on such a sexually ambiguous figure as Xiao Bo is significant. If Xiao Bo does choose a homosexual life, this choice demonstrates how far representations of masculinities and male desires have come from the worker/peasant/soldier tropes of the past.

Nonetheless, Liu is careful not to present Xiao Bo in terms of a series of camp stereotypes. Xiao Bo accompanies Kang on a mission to extract money from a recalcitrant debtor, and he does not hesitate to use his fists to persuade the man to honour his debt. Later, Qing questions Xiao Bo, and he admits that he has been boxing since he was a child. While the press-ups that Xiao Bo performs before bed allow his body to be displayed, they also modify his masculinity, in that they are a symbol of physical strength and negate stereotypes of 'weak' or 'unmanly' homosexual men; that is, Xiao Bo fails to perform the new homosexual role expected of him. In the words of Judith Butler, he fails to 'conform to the gendered norms of cultural intelligibility by which persons are defined' (1999: 23).

However, Chong Chong and Gui Gui appear to reinforce many stereotypes that the film seems to have been busy dismantling. For example, Chong Chong's promiscuity inside his relationship with Gui Gui only acts out popular myths about gay sexuality. Gui Gui himself is a loveable diva figure, whose 'femininity' is repeatedly inferred. His recording of his radio 'broadcast' at the beginning of the film could almost be taken for an everyday public service announcement, read by a suitably well-heeled female presenter. If Gui Gui can be said to perform a 'feminine' role, Chong Chong expresses a more masculine persona. He is in charge within the flat, and takes an active, outside role in promoting his magazine. Despite his later infidelity, Chong Chong is also portrayed as the rational partner in the relationship, whilst Gui Gui reacts to situations in a more emotional, stereotypically 'feminine' way.

But if Liu seems to adhere to certain representational stereotypes, he might employ cultural forms of expression that can reach audiences both inside and outside China. For example, although the film was made outside the studio system, screenwriter Cui Zi'en hopes that it will eventually be shown in his native China.[5] Since representations employ what Richard Dyer describes as 'the codes and conventions of the available cultural forms of presentation' (1995: 2), the lack of representations of male homosexuality in China in recent times may impact on the types that Liu chooses to be embodied on screen.[6] Song Hwee Lim comments on the pitfalls of the critical disparagement of 'negative' representations of homosexualities, couched as they are in the dichotomies and assumptions that many critics apparently sensitive to issues of sexuality and identity seek to avoid (2002: 61). In her discussion of the need for recognition of hybridity in the formation of sexualities in Taiwan, Fran Martin also recognises that homosexual lives are not easily reducible to a linear tradition that emanates from dichotomies, whether they pit China versus the West, or place 'gay' against 'straight' (2003: 32). If Chong Chong and Gui Gui have traits that are perceived to be effeminate, such as Chong Chong's ballroom dancing, these may simply represent one expression among many homosexual masculinities rather than a negative comment upon their characters or a clue to their 'essential selves'. For example, when Gui Gui noisily walks out on Chong Chong, he does so not because he is a temperamental 'queen', but because his partner has cheated on him. If Chong Chong has slept with Xiao Bo, this promiscuity is not linked to his sexuality, but to the fact that he is the type of man who finds it easy to be unfaithful.

I believe that instead it is important to focus on the ambiguities that Liu Bingjian's main protagonists articulate, since I contend that they are part of a deliberate project to dismantle preconceptions surrounding sexualities. Liu outlines a series of social types, which present multiple narrative possibilities, and which make visible the homosexuality that has previously been *invisible* in Chinese cinematic history. Liu creates a liberal environment in which male homosexuality can be acknowledged in everyday discourse. Qing and Ah Meng imply that homosexuality *per se* is not a problem, but that the possibility of Xiao Bo, the substitute son, actually being gay may cause concrete problems for the 'family' in the future. There *is* a gay community, since *Lavatory Literature* clearly sells, Gui Gui reads out personal ads on his broadcasts, and Chong Chong meets with a transsexual who is a regular contributor to his journal. However, this 'community' beyond Chong Chong and Gui Gui is largely unseen, perhaps commenting upon its official condemnation. Despite the ironic title of his 'radio station' ('International Red Star radio station'), Gui Gui is also aware of the limits imposed by the same authorities that he ridicules, hinting on several occasions that 'the political climate is always changeable.' At the conclusion of the film, his final telephone call to Chong Chong is a private affirmation of the homosexual community that his radio broadcasts have attempted to coalesce.

## Men and Women and sex

Of all the diverse relationships portrayed in *Men and Women*, the heterosexual partnership between Qing and Kang is the weakest in the film. The couple share a sterile life, in which each acts out their expected obligations towards the other. Kang is non-expressive, and is the least likeable (and least physically attractive) of the characters. However, he does what is expected of a good husband and appears to have fixed ideas about appropriate gender roles. He beats moneylender Yang because he has tried to 'cheat a woman', for example. Nevertheless, the obligations that he requires of Qing remain unfulfilled – the couple have a non-existent sex life, with Qing viewing sex with Kang as a 'bother'. In this platonic relationship, Kang seeks fulfilment by attempting to rape Xiao Bo. Kang appears to have shown no homosexual behaviour; however, with hindsight, his desire for Xiao Bo may have a precedent. After Xiao Bo's initial, disastrous date with Ah Meng, Kang takes Xiao Bo along with him to play pool. On the way out of the pool hall, Kang decides to go to the lavatory, and Xiao Bo briskly follows him in. Do the pair exchange looks as they stand next to each other? In the context of the film, lavatories are not merely amenities, but meeting places for the gay community, where connections are forged and previously unsaid meanings articulated. Xiao Bo's (mundane) conversation with Kang prequels the manner in which homosocial ties between men (formed in the competition involved in the pool game) can extend into the homoerotic and how supposedly neutral spaces can be transformed into sites for the expression of (in the context of Mainland China) subversive desires.

Kang's rape attempt is prefigured by his spectatorship as Xiao Bo performs his press-ups. The camera responds to Kang's desiring gaze and rests on Xiao Bo's body, although Kang is still seen within the frame. Kang visibly fidgets, and does not only watch Xiao Bo, but also physically looks him up and down. Kang *thinks* about his desire for Xiao Bo, and considers before he grabs the young man and forces him down on the bed. However, he does not reckon on Xiao Bo's strength. As he is pushed away, Kang feels betrayed when Xiao Bo does not act out his fantasies of a gay sexuality. In his aggressive reaction after he has been rejected, Kang gives voice to conventional views of homosexuality as somehow separate to 'masculinity', which he claims to embody ('You stink, *looking like a man*'). As Kang's explanations quickly turn to hostility ('I just wanted to try something new … What a shame for men'), he reveals the sexual curiosity inside his own, uninspiring relationship.

When Xiao Bo steps out of his role of compliance, Kang feels that he has to defend his own masculinity. On account of Xiao Bo's status in the household, this attack is arguably virtual incest, with a father-figure taking advantage of his subordinate substitute son. Kang's authoritative role inside the home has been compromised, destroying the family structure as a site of safety. However, Kang is not only hostile, he is also *afraid*. Xiao Bo threatens to kill him if he repeats his accusations, and Kang cowers behind the wall as he fumbles through a final attempt to salvage some face. While Kang has decided that he will act out a masculine role, Xiao Bo's reaction has confirmed that his guest is unwilling to act as a compliant 'female'/androgynous figure. Xiao Bo is a *man*, and Kang's certainties about gender roles, particularly his own, have been shattered. His tirade against the moral evils of homosexuality is an attempt to convince himself of the sexual boundaries that he once set. Through his protest, Xiao Bo has exposed the complex desires inside this apparently heterosexual relationship, and his ambiguous sexuality has thrown words like 'men' and 'women' into free-fall.

Whilst censorship limits what is shown on screen (although Liu must have hardly expected the state censors to embrace his second film), sex in the film is invariably destructive, even in the homosexual relationships towards which it is sympathetic. Although both *Lavatory Literature* and *Lavatory Time* undoubtedly address Beijing's cottaging scene (Gui Gui includes advertisements for men seeking well-endowed partners in his programme), no overt cruising is shown, nor is the magazine revealed to concentrate on it. At the end of the film, Chong Chong's impulsive infidelity destroys his relationship with the sensitive (though well-meaning) Gui Gui. In fact, the only relationship left at the end of the film is a lesbian one (between Qing and Ah Meng), although, again, the relationship develops away from our eyes.[7] In *Men and Women*, women seem to survive as a self-sufficient community. In contrast, men end up devastating their relationships, and seem on a path to self-destruction. Liu presents masculinities that are on the margins, fragmentary and solitary, and underlines the extent to which desire can also be a disruptive force. If conventional (homosexual and heterosexual) partnerships only stifle alternative desires (whether they are for another partner or for another way of life), Liu's film calls for a freer conception of bonds between individuals.

## Conclusion

The beginning of this chapter questioned to what extent Liu Bingjian, as a director representing homosexual protagonists, may feel a responsibility to present positive images, or to respond to the cultural or political agendas raised by Ellis Hanson in the context of American film (1999: 11). I have demonstrated that *Men and Women* deals with both the visual and the political ideas of representation to which Hanson refers. In visual terms, Xiao Bo's objectification places traditional formulations of gendered spectatorship into doubt. Politically, although Liu Bingjian may carry certain burdens of representing gay and lesbian relationships, we have seen that *Men and Women* ends in questioning such categories, whether or not they are employed in repressive ways. Curiosity about Xiao Bo's uncertain sexuality is the catalyst for the destruction of two substitute families, and the constancy of human relationships are tested to the extreme. Xiao Bo has demonstrated both the importance of set, filial relationships for men in contemporary China, and the difficulties for those who choose to reject these hierarchical ties. Through this refusal to present stable and predictable sexualities, Liu Bingjian questions the extent to which individual behaviour is determined by identity categories, whether these are labels of homosexuality and heterosexuality, of masculinity and femininity, and even of men and women.

## Notes

1   Liu Bingjian's statement can be found on www.pardo.ch/1999/htm/press/art/filmSUR/ eng.htm (accessed: 26 April 2004).

2   As the state relaxed controls on entrepreneurship and population movement, under-employed rural dwellers began to travel to larger towns and cities in search of casual work in order to support families or to save up for a more certain future. Xiao Bo is just one of many young men traveling to the capital in search of a brighter future. However, without roots and urban household registration status, permanent city dwellers resented the extra strain on resources brought by migrants, along with a popular belief that rootless migrants (especially young single men) posed a risk to social order (the influx of rural dwellers was frequently represented as an uncontrollable tide). The recent Li Yang film, *Mang jing* (*Blind Shaft*, 2003) dramatises the isolation felt by many young migrants, one of several, more positive, representations of rural people in big cities (see also the documentary *Tielu yanxian* (*Along the Railroad*, Du Haibin, 2001)).

3   Earlier, Qing bestows Xiao Bo's job upon him in much the same tone: 'You can work for me here then.'

4   *Didi* means 'younger brother'. Qing uses this title to address Xiao Bo throughout the film. To Xiao Bo, Qing herself is addressed as 'older sister' (*jie*), and Kang is an 'older brother' (*ge*). Whilst these are family relationship titles, they also confer the general nature of relationships between people, in which younger more inexperienced members of society respect their older and wiser superiors.

5   Cui Zi'en chose the title of the film in preference to more explicit possibilities, in the hope that the film might one day be shown in China.

6   Song Hwee Lim also observes that characterisation that may be interpreted as derogatory in one time and place may have very different connotations in other cultural contexts (2002: 60). While Chong Chong and Gui Gui express 'effeminate' traits that may be perceived as 'negative' in one cultural milieu, these expressions may not have the same connotations in the Beijing gay underground scene that Liu Bingjian portrays. The comments of Cui Zi'en (a protagonist in *Men and Women* as well as its screenwriter) and Ye Guangwei (a worker at an advice centre for Beijing homosexuals) suggest that effeminacy and a 'feminine' persona are often equated with homosexuality on the Mainland. Considering prejudice from the heterosexual majority, Cui comments that 'I can understand a heterosexual being startled at seeing a very effeminate man', while Ye states that 'a man who isn't masculine is disdained. And for him to take on a female role during a sexual act is unthinkable and a disgrace in people's eyes.' Interviews from www.unesco.org/courier/2001_07/uk/doss24.htm (accessed: 22 September 2003).

7   However, in sympathy with the themes of *Men and Women*, the relationship does not

begin auspiciously, since the taxi that is supposed to carry Qing away to her new life with Ah Meng breaks down, and the women are forced to get out and push.

## Works cited

Berry, C. (1996) 'Sexual DisOrientations: Homosexual Rights, East Asian Films, and Post-modern Post-nationalism', in X. Tang and S. Snyder (eds) *In Pursuit of Contemporary East Asian Culture*. Boulder, CO and Oxford: Westview Press, pp. 157–82.

Butler, J. (1999) *Gender Trouble: Feminism and the Subversion of Identity* (second edition). London: Routledge.

Dyer, R. (1995) *The Matter of Images: Essays on Representation*. London: Routledge.

Hanson, E. (1999) *Outtakes: Essays on Queer Theory and Film*. Durham: Duke University Press.

Lim, S. H. (2002) 'Contesting Celluloid Closets: Representing Male Homosexuality in Chinese Cinemas', *Tamkang Review*, 33, 2, 55–75.

Martin, F. (2003) *Situating Sexualities: Queer Representation in Taiwanese Fiction, Film and Public Culture*. Hong Kong: Hong Kong University Press.

Mulvey, L. (1975) 'Visual Pleasure and Narrative Cinema', *Screen*, 16, 3, 6–18.

*Nannan nünü* (1999) Press release available online: http://www.pardo.ch/1999/htm/press/art/filmSUR/eng.htm (accessed: 24 September 2003).

Neale, S. (1993) 'Masculinity as Spectacle: Reflections on Men and Mainstream Cinema', in S. Cohan and I. R. Hark (eds) *Screening the Male: Exploring Masculinities in Hollywood Cinema*. London: Routledge, 9–20.

PART SIX

# Hollywood's Others

# CHAPTER FOURTEEN

# Orientalism or occidentalism? dynamics of appropriation in Akira Kurosawa

Rachael Hutchinson

Until recently, the study of Japanese cinema has been largely concerned with essentialised representations of 'Japaneseness' on film and the struggle of Japanese directors to make use of Western film technology for the expression of indigenous cultural values and ideas. Criticism of Japanese cinema has often been dominated by an Orientalist construction of 'Japaneseness' as Other to a homogeneous West, and has tended to focus on how 'Japanese' or 'Western' a given film or director may be. Studies of Akira Kurosawa (1910–98) and his films lie at the centre of this trend, where Kurosawa has been constructed as anything from the 'most Westernised' or 'least Japanese' director in Japan, to the personal representative of a national discourse of Japaneseness. This chapter responds to recent calls to get away from the essentialising tendencies of such criticism (Yoshimoto 1993, 2000; Freiberg 2000) by reading Kurosawa, his films and their reception in terms of critical theory on Occidentalism. In investigating issues of 'world cinema' Kurosawa is interesting precisely because he is at once set up as a manifestation of 'Japaneseness' and at the same time hailed as the great '*sekai no Kurosawa*', or 'the world's Kurosawa'. The way in which we refer to this director (Kurosawa Akira or Akira Kurosawa?) reflects the dynamic of interplay between 'Orient' and 'Occident' both within his own oeuvre and in the way the world has appropriated it. This chapter examines the dynamics of appropriation both in and of Kurosawa's films in terms of Orientalism and Occidentalism, exploiting these theoretical frameworks to make sense of the apparent contradiction between Kurosawa's 'Japaneseness' and his longstanding universalist image.

Many Kurosawa films are based on other texts, ranging from Japanese *kabuki* and *Noh* dramatic texts,[1] to Shakespeare, to Japanese and Western novels of the modern period. This chapter seeks to offer an alternative reading of 'adaptation' by demonstrating the agency, self-reflexivity and constructedness in Kurosawa's filmic act. By reading Kurosawa's adaptation in terms of appropriation, we can analyse his films as discursive act rather than as part of some mythic national discourse of 'Japaneseness'. As adaptation and appropriation involve questions of power, the fact that Kurosawa worked under the constraints of Occupation censorship provides the opportunity to examine further questions of power structures and the possibility of counter-discourse in the filmic text. This chapter will argue that, by reading Kurosawa's films in terms of Occidentalist appropriation, we can begin to reconcile notions of adaptation and translation, the universal and the local, which underlie much of the field of Japanese cinema studies and studies of world cinema in general. The academic reception of Kurosawa's films in the West, particularly in the United States, raises further questions about continuing stereotypes and power structures still inherent in Area Studies, where Japan has not been seen as subject or agent but as the object of study. This approach is reinforced by an asymmetrical power structure which has continued to operate between the United States and Japan since World War Two and the Occupation.[2] By using the framework of Occidentalist theory we may acknowledge the totalising, Orientalist approach of postwar Area Studies on Japan, and move on to reconcile the study of Japanese cinema with the wider theoretical frameworks employed in cultural and world cinema studies now.

## Interrogating Japaneseness: orientalist criticism versus 'self-reflexivity'

The study of Japanese cinema has traditionally focused on two related issues – the perceived struggle of the indigenous artist to express a truly 'Japanese' sensibility using the foreign technology of the film medium; and the question of how successfully this Japanese aesthetic has been transposed into any given film. Evident in Donald Richie's work in particular is an emphasis on struggle for the Japanese filmmaker. Richie adheres to the *wakon-yōsai* formula of the Meiji period, which sought to combine the two elements of 'Japanese spirit, Western technology'. The essentialising nature of this approach is seen in his recent statement that 'the Japanese have a particular genius for assimilation and incorporation. Thus any influence … is swallowed, digested and turned into something sometimes rich, often strange, and always "Japanese"' (2001: 11). The discourse about adaptation of the Western film medium is usually couched in similar terms of conflict, struggle, assimilation and imitation. The Japanese cinema is set up as confined, limited and in need of techniques and ideas from the West, achieving success when it assimilates or incorporates Western cinema. This model is then applied to individual directors, including Kurosawa.

Kurosawa's talent is often seen to lie in his ability to 'amalgamate' or 'assimilate' the Western model. Richie argues that 'it is this genius for amalgamation which one may find typical of Kurosawa and very Japanese of him' (2001: 170). Noël Burch states that Kurosawa is distinctive because 'after Kinugasa, he was only the second filmmaker in the history of the Japanese film who, after thoroughly assimilating the Western mode of representation, went on to build upon it' (1979: 291). The argument then moves on to discuss Kurosawa in terms of whether he is a more 'Western' or 'Japanese' director. Richie agrees with the idea that Kurosawa is the 'least Japanese' of the Japanese directors: 'The description is understandable in that he is "Western" enough to be openly individual … he has gone beyond the confines of cinematic language as the Japanese understood them and, in so doing, has broadened them. Consequently, perhaps, his films have been widely accepted in the West itself' (2001: 176). The West is constructed as judge on Kurosawa's films, which gain acceptance by achieving the standards of individualism, creativity, originality and 'breadth' so prized by the Western audience. What stands out in this discussion is firstly the de-historicisation of filmmaking in Japan, conflating contemporary filmmaking with that of the Meiji period, and secondly the construction of hierarchical binary structures in which the West holds power, technological superiority and right of judgement over the national Japanese cinema, which is essentialised as particular, exotic and engaged in struggle to successfully adapt. Underlying the debate is the assumption that 'Westernness' and 'Japaneseness' exist as absolutes. This hierarchical binarism and timeless essentialisation are key features of Orientalism.

Such Orientalist structures are clear in much criticism of Japanese cinema, which judges a particular film or director on how successfully the indigenous 'Japanese spirit' has survived the transposition to the Western film medium (Richie 1994; Rimer 1994). The best example of this kind of criticism may be seen in Noël Burch, who takes the basic premise that every aspect of Japanese culture, from *kana* script through to *kabuki* drama, infuses the modes of representation in Japanese film.[3] Studies of Kurosawa have also tended to scrutinise his films for evidence of the 'Japanese aesthetic'. The extent of Kurosawa's 'Japaneseness' has traditionally been found in the frequency with which he employs aspects of *Noh* drama, seen in the set expressions of character's faces and their slow, exaggerated movements; in the staged geometric formalism of the set design; and in the frequent use of long, slow camera movements to emphasise the ritualistic aspect. Films such as *Kumonosujō* (*Throne of Blood*, 1957), *Kagemusha* (1980) and *Ran* (1985) are often used as examples for this argument.[4] In these analyses the *Noh* masks, props and minimalist sets are explained as manifestations of the Buddhist values of mutability or 'simplicity-as-complexity'; the films held up as representative of Japan's national cinema. The role of the critic is to explain and interpret these aesthetics, to 'teach a Western audience how to "read" a Japanese film' (McDonald 1994: 321).

Satō Tadao and Yoshimoto Mitsuhiro counter such Orientalist approaches by arguing that such preoccupation with essential cultural aspects of 'Japaneseness' ignores the historical specificities of source dramatic forms such as *Noh* and *kabuki* (Satō 1994: 185–6; Yoshimoto 2000: 101–6). The importance of taking specifics into account becomes evident when we consider Kurosawa's use of *kabuki* and *Noh* plays as source texts for his films. For example, *Tora no O o fumu otoko-tachi* (*Men Who Tread on the Tiger's Tail*, 1945) is extremely complex in its playful intertextual references to the *Noh* play *Ataka* ('The Ataka Checkpoint') and the *kabuki* play *Kanjinchō* ('The Subscription List'), both based on historic events of the twelfth century.[5] Yoshimoto argues that, by emphasising the intertextual aspect of certain scenes through referential dynamics, Kurosawa is making 'a critical commentary on the relationship between *kabuki* and Japanese cinema' (2000: 111). McDonald provides a thoughtful treatment of this intertextuality, arguing that Kurosawa's parody of the traditional tale, playing on specific details of the original texts, makes for a 'radical departure' from formulaic wartime films based on similar stories of feudal loyalty. By insisting on the value of the human individual, rather than that individual's role in a hierarchical society, Kurosawa undercuts the traditional loyalist reading of *Kanjinchō*. This departure was a challenge to the Japanese censors in patriotic 1945, however it was the 'blinkered' American authorities who banned the film on its completion, and it was not released in Japan until 1952 (1994: 171, 180). The complex referential aspect to Kurosawa's films based on *Noh* and *kabuki* source texts, and the effect of referentiality on the censorship and reception of those films, make it evident that ideas of mere 'influence' or 'adaptation', or the straightforward 'incorporation' of elements from *Noh* and *kabuki*, are too simple to serve as a useful interpretative model.

Another popular approach to finding evidence for Kurosawa's 'Japaneseness' is to emphasise his evocation of the samurai spirit and the ethics of *bushidō*, focusing on the *jidai-geki* films (period action dramas) such as the Venice Grand Prix-winning *Rashōmon* (1950) and on the 'samurai films' such as *Shichinin no Samurai* (*Seven Samurai*, 1954), *Yojimbō* (1961) and *Sanjurō* (1962).[6] But Kurosawa's so-called 'samurai films' do much more than simply invoke the spirit of *bushidō* to portray a Japanese ethos. Looking more closely at *Rashōmon*, a story of rape and murder told from three different perspectives, we find that the tale told from the samurai's point of view is just as suspect as the tales told by the woman and even by the bandit, so that the samurai ethic of truth, courage and steadfastness is laid open to doubt. Even more clearly, the fight scenes between the samurai and bandit are shown in two very different ways: the first fight is noble, grand and choreographed, while the second is scrappy, cowardly and more 'realistic'. The second fight shatters the image of the first, and with it is shattered the samurai ethic. Moreover, the main character of *Yojimbō* and *Sanjurō*, played by Toshirō Mifune, is a *rōnin* or masterless samurai. While he holds to his samurai ethic of frugality, endurance and protection of the weak in the case of women and children, he also shows himself to be a ruthless and manipulative mercenary, auctioning his swordsmanship to the highest bidder – thus undercutting the samurai's traditional disdain for monetary matters. Kurosawa's problematisation of *bushidō* and the samurai ethic is also seen in the deviation from generic norms in these films. The realistic, desperate violence of *Rashōmon* and *Seven Samurai*, coupled with Kurosawa's insistence on historical accuracy, differed greatly from generic conventions of the *jidai-geki* films in Japan at the time.[7] It is also worth noting here that Kurosawa was inspired to make *Yojimbō* on the model of the western genre. A complex intertextual aspect may be seen in the menacing use of the gun, the many long shots of the wide centre street, and the desolate wind that blows incessantly through the ghost-town setting. Kurosawa's appropriation of the western genre in the 1960s built on the generic deviations of *Rashōmon* and *Seven Samurai* to reinvent and problematise the Japanese period drama. Kurosawa's *jidai-geki* films do not show us so much a preoccupation with displaying 'Japanese' ethics, but with experimentation and the desire to ask questions of the film industry as a whole.

This questioning aspect of Kurosawa's films is borne out by the analysis of Darrell William Davis, who examines Kurosawa's *jidai-geki* films in relation to the 'monumental style' of 1930s Japanese cinema. The main purpose of 'monumental style', which elevated traditional Japanese aesthetics to the level of spiritual heritage, was to whip up nationalistic fervour and galvanise support for the coming war. The pictured 'Japan' was contextualised in historical fact, decorated and embellished with traditional Japanese arts and aesthetics, and ordered by the hierarchical structures of feudal and court ritual. These films presented '"transitive" Japaneseness, a matter of being Japanese *for* some purpose rather than just being Japanese' (1996: 7). Davis argues that this sense of purpose is evident in Kurosawa's two films which are made in this style, *Kagemusha* and *Ran*. Kurosawa uses the tactics of monumental style to construct a certain picture of 'Japaneseness', only to play with its conventions and ultimately undermine them. In *Kagemusha*, the Lord to whom so much respect is being shown throughout the film is actually a 'shadow double', a sham, so that the court ritual and hierarchy which play so important a role in monumental style are shown to be meaningless. As Davis argues, 'since *Kagemusha* does not "belong" in the monumental style so much as make an issue of it, the film reveals itself to be a most critical, yet rueful, vehicle of Japanese cultural identity' (1996: 236). Similarly, *Ran* appears to be a monumental *jidai-geki* film on the surface, but constructs a mythologised, theatrical idea of 'Japanese history' where nothing is as it should be. Everything in *Ran*, from the depiction of *bushidō*, Buddhism and traditional aesthetics, to the details of character, set design and costume, is exaggerated to the point of abstraction. Davis argues that through this abstraction and theatricalisation of history, *Ran* purposefully 'unravels the indigenous associations of monumental style itself' (1996: 244). Through the appropriation of monumental style Kurosawa brings the whole issue of 'national identity', and its expression through the medium of film, into question.

In his appropriation of *kabuki* and *Noh* sources, his self-reflexive use of intertextuality, and his deconstruction of the conventions of *jidai-geki*, Kurosawa demonstrates an awareness of film as a medium within which to experiment and ask questions about genre and convention. This awareness is also reflected in Kurosawa's self-conscious use of editing techniques throughout his career. A celebrated example is seen in *Rashomon* as the camera follows the woodcutter walking into the forest. A sequence of shots focus on the woodcutter from above, from behind, from underneath, at a range of distances and from a number of different angles. When the woodcutter stops to stare at something, the following shot, which we expect to show his point of view, is revealed instead as a mirror image, the camera pointing back at him as he unexpectedly appears in the shot (Desser 1992a: 61). The triangular geometry of *Rashomon*, too, calls attention to itself throughout the film. We not only see three characters at the gate, three characters in the forest, three settings and three narratives, but also a repetition of shots framing three actors in a triangle, and equal time given to close-ups, medium- and long-shots when depicting dramatic sequences. The direct focus on the sun and the breaking of the 180-degree rule in the forest of *Rashomon* were both groundbreaking techniques for the period (see Kurosawa 1983: 185). At a time when other directors had long since turned to soft wipes and dissolves, Kurosawa made increasingly frequent use of the hard-edged wipe from *Rashomon* onwards. Frequent use of the hard-edged wipe in *Tengoku to jigoku* (*High and Low*, 1963), coupled with a staged geometric formality, similarly calls our attention to the constructed nature of film, while the use of taped voices calls attention to the medium's double function as audiovisual representation.[8] With these techniques Kurosawa draws our attention to the editing process itself, 'thereby exposing the elements most essential to the production of the strong diegetic illusion' (Burch 1979: 298). By foregrounding the mode of representation, Kurosawa calls attention to the signifier, rather than the signified.[9] Such evident self-reflexivity suggests another way of looking at Kurosawa's films that does not rely on cultural essentialisation. In the theoretical framework of Occidentalism, Kurosawa may be seen as calling attention to the signifier not only within his films but also with the wider discursive filmic act.

# Kurosawa's occidentalism: self-appropriation and counter-discourse

Xiaomei Chen defines Occidentalism as 'a discursive practice that, by constructing its Western Other, has allowed the Orient to participate actively and with indigenous creativity in the process of self-appropriation, even after being appropriated and constructed by Western Others' (1995: 4–5). Examining the components of Chen's definition in relation to Kurosawa shows how this may be a useful model with which to analyse his films. The main component of Chen's definition of Occidentalism is the process of self-appropriation on the part of the Orient. Kurosawa may be seen as an active participant in the affirmation of the Japanese Self, which on the surface is evident in his use of *Noh*, *kabuki*, past history and court ritual – elements of the 'monumental style'. But we have seen that constructions of 'Japaneseness' are called into question by Kurosawa through his selection and parody of source texts, the abstraction and exaggeration of *Ran* and his manipulation of genre. Kurosawa was interested in actively questioning, problematising and investigating the idea of Japanese identity, and also in taking advantage of the possibilities of the Japanese cultural heritage and Japanese cinematic conventions in the making of new films. This deep interest in utilising Japanese culture for his own purposes, while at the same time subverting and improving Japanese cinema, shows a director who was indeed engaged in a process of 'self-appropriation'.

Kurosawa's problematisation of 'Japaneseness' is emphasised by Yoshimoto, who argues that 'what his films show is his obsession with the problematic of Japanese modernity' (2000: 326). Yoshimoto argues persuasively that Kurosawa makes a strong statement in his films on the topic of war memory and the disjunctive version of Japanese history created by the American Occupation (1945–1952). Yoshimoto argues that in the 'Occupation version' of history, the date 15 August 1945 stands as a point of complete rupture between Japan's militaristic past and its new role as emerging democratic nation. The continuity of Japanese history is erased, and with it, the role of Japan as colonialist aggressor and America as imperialist Occupying force. In *Waga seishun ni kuinashi* (*No Regrets For Our Youth*, 1946), Kurosawa undermines this disjunction and dichotomy, by hinting at the continuity of the Japanese experience through the character of Yukie (see Yoshimoto 2000: 133–4). In doing so, Kurosawa would have been covertly resisting the Occupation version of Japanese history. In Chen's model of Occidentalism, the process of self-appropriation takes place 'even after being appropriated and constructed by Western Others'. Self-appropriation is thus bound up with the idea of counter-discourse against the Other. *No Regrets For Our Youth* may be read as an example of self-appropriation and counter-discourse, because by reconstructing the continuity of Japanese history, Kurosawa reclaims that history from its erasure by Occupation forces.

A more subtle critique may be read in three other films made by Kurosawa in the immediate postwar period. At a time when SCAP (Supreme Commander for the Allied Powers) censorship forbade any depiction of the ravages of war, the Occupation forces, or Japan's own imperialistic aggression, Kurosawa worked just within the limits to depict a society thrown into chaos by war and at odds with itself over the rebuilding process. Continuity between pre- and post-1945 is shown in the individual struggles of characters to make a living or fall in love on the one hand, or to drink themselves into oblivion on the other. In *Subarashiki Nichiyōbi* (*One Wonderful Sunday*, 1947), the couple trying to enjoy their date in the city are met with difficulties at every turn – the city of Tokyo, suspended between ruins and renovation, reminds them of their historical situation and the impossibility of transcending the war to start afresh. The environment of *Yoidore tenshi* (*Drunken Angel*, 1948) allows neither the audience nor the inhabitants of the slum to forget the war, giving a bleak picture of poverty and degradation as the strength of the *yakuza* gangsters rises in the power vacuum created by the handover to Occupation forces. In his autobiography, Kurosawa recalls how the depressing image of the sump in *Drunken Angel* was developed from an image of a derelict concrete ship, 'a kind of parody of defeated Japan', while the intense focus on the *yakuza* engendered an equal focus on their environment, the 'black markets that sprang up everywhere like bamboo shoots after a rain in postwar Japan' (Kurosawa 1983: 155–6). In *Stray Dog* the foregrounding and problematisation of the returned war hero calls attention to the fact that he is now alienated from the wider Japanese society that desperately wanted to forget about the war and its aftermath (Yoshimoto 2000: 177–8). Many of Kurosawa's postwar films may thus be read in terms of counter-discourse, in varying degrees of subtlety, but *Rashomon* provides the clearest example in terms of both content and its historical context.

Under the Occupation, *jidai-geki* films were banned as a glorification of the *bushidō* ethic and the feudal system. We have seen how *Men Who Tread on the Tiger's Tail* was banned for its supposedly feudalistic outlook. By making *Rashomon* in the stylistic form of *jidai-geki* in 1950, Kurosawa could be read as testing Occupation censorship.[10] The production of this film in what Ning Wang (1997) has called a context of 'coloniality' shows counter-discourse in the filmic act. James F. Davidson's reappraisal of *Rashomon* reads the film as an example of this kind of counter-discourse, arguing that its imagery and characterisation would have caused Japanese audiences to reflect on the defeat and its aftermath in a way that American audiences would not. Davidson compares the film to its source texts, two short stories by Akutagawa Ryūnosuke, arguing that certain details changed by Kurosawa would have acted as reminders of the war (1972: 125). The film opens at the dilapidated Rashōmon gate to the ancient capital Kyoto, emphasising an atmosphere of ruin and devastation not evident in the original text. The figure of the bandit, too, is changed, so that Tajomaru becomes 'the least Japanese of all the characters, and a sort of incarnation of the *oni*, or ogre, of Japanese folklore, which has often been interpreted as a representation of the foreigner' (ibid.). In the caricature of Tajomaru's 'foreign barbarian', his rape of the elegant Japanese noble-woman acquires an added dimension, reminding Japanese audiences of the conquest of their own nation. Finally, the bleak vision of human nature throughout the film, where all participants lie to some extent and the scrappy, desperate swordfight appears as a travesty of samurai ethics, reflects a feeling that old beliefs and loyalties have died in a defeated nation. The epilogue featuring the woodcutter's decision to save the baby in this reading comes as hope, and a duty for the future, to which Japanese audiences could cling. The film thus points to war and devastation throughout, defying the Occupation censorship which forbade portrayal of the bombing of Japan or the effect it had on the nation.

Another way in which we may read Kurosawa's films as counter-discourse is in their construction of a critique against the Japanese government in postwar, post-Occupation Japan. Kurosawa's use of the Western Other for opposition to the political status quo may be read as an example of what Xiaomei Chen has called 'anti-official Occidentalism' (1995: 8), where constructions of the West are utilised for critique of the prevailing domestic government. One of the strongest examples of Kurosawa's 'anti-official' counter-discourse appears in *Wanu yatsu hodo yoku nemuri (The Bad Sleep Well)* of 1960. That year, the renewal of the US-Japan Security Treaty was set to ensure Japan's status as a shield for the US against East Asian communism in the Cold War, and protest was widespread. At the end of this film the character Itakura cries out that 'All Japan will be fooled again!' As his voice rings out against the backdrop of a ruined munitions factory, the audience focuses on the word 'again'. When was the first time Japan had been fooled? The setting prompts us to conclude that it must have been during World War Two. Yoshimoto points out that there are two possibilities here: Japan was fooled both by its own militaristic government in the nationalistic fervour leading up to the war, and then by the Occupation government which caused a disjunction in Japan's history. But Itakura's cry has another function concerning the contemporary backdrop of protest in 1960: Japan is now being 'fooled again' as the Japanese and American governments are enforcing the security treaty against the will of the Japanese people (2000: 286–7). *The Bad Sleep Well* has often been read for its surface commentary on the corruption inherent in big business, but we may also read Kurosawa's film in terms of counter-discourse, both against the Occupation version of history and against the contemporary Japanese government.

The final component of Chen's model of Occidentalism is the Orient's achievement of self-appropriation through the process of 'constructing its Western Others'. The Western Other rarely appears on screen in Kurosawa's films in the form of a foreign character, unless we count the figure of Tajomaru in *Rashomon*. However, the Western Other underlies the central problematic of Kurosawa's films in his 'obsession' with Japan's modernity, national identity and war memory. Davidson's reading of *Rashomon*, and Yoshimoto's readings of *No Regrets for our Youth* and *The Bad Sleep Well*, emphasise both the sense of conquest and subjugation under an Occidental Other, and also the affirmation and remembrance of a sense of Japanese history which stands counter to that Other. The Western Other is thus always implicitly present. The Western Other may also be read as the technological medium of film, and as the source material upon which some of Kurosawa's films are based. The appropriation of Western film methods and source texts may be seen as Occidentalist use of the West for the director's own purposes. Kurosawa's use of the Western Other as source text brings us back to the issue of adaptation, one of the central problems for critics of Japanese cinema. The following section examines the idea of 'appropriation' of the Western text as an alternative to what Yoshimoto has criticised as 'adaptation discourse' (2000: 258–61).

## Appropriation versus 'adaptation discourse'

Film theory on adaptation has developed far beyond the 'fidelity analysis' that judged a film on its ability to remain true to the original work on which it was based,[11] with most critics now eschewing such hierarchical thinking to argue that the historical, political, semiotic and receptive contexts of any given adaptation must be taken into account to grasp its significance and the motivation for the filmic act.[12] As Dudley Andrew argues, 'we need to study the films themselves as acts of discourse. We need to be sensitive to that discourse and to the forces that motivate it' (1984: 106). But in the case of commentary on Kurosawa's film adaptations of Western source texts we can see persistence in reading the adaptation not only in terms of hierarchy and fidelity, but also in terms of cultural essentialisation. Kurosawa's adaptation of Western literary works for film material is best known through his *jidai-geki* films: *Ran* is based on *King Lear* while *Throne of Blood* is based on *Macbeth*. These two films have attracted much attention in relation to the problem of 'adaptation', in that their *jidai-geki* status has raised questions about 'Japaneseness' in the representation of *Noh* and other Japanese aesthetics through a translated Western script medium. Davis, for example, states that 'the grafting of *King Lear* into a monumental evocation of Japanese history calls the Japaneseness of that history into question' (1996: 244). In contrast, *Donzoko* (*The Lower Depths*, 1957), based on Gorky's play of the same name, and *Hakuchi* (*The Idiot*, 1951), based on Dostoevsky's novel, are frequently overlooked.[13] Yoshimoto believes that critical dismissal of *The Idiot* confirms a certain way of interpreting Japanese cinema, where 'it is only when some uniquely Japanese codes of traditional culture are mixed with great Western originals that Japanese adaptations become worthy of praise and appreciation (for example, the Western reception of *Throne of Blood*)' (2000: 192). Critical reception has certainly privileged *Throne of Blood* and *Ran* over the other films based on Western sources, partly because Shakespeare is seen as greater than Gorky and Dostoevsky. But *Throne of Blood* and *Ran* are also seen as examples of 'Japanese Noh aesthetics' and 'monumental style', while *The Lower Depths* and *The Idiot*, even though based on 'great Western originals', do not incorporate the 'uniquely Japanese codes' of *Noh* and Zen Buddhism beloved of Western critics. Essentialisation thus plays a major role in the reception of films based on Western source texts. When the process of adaptation takes place across cultural boundaries as well as between literary and film media, it seems that critics revert to using a hierarchical structure of the (superior) original Western format versus the Japanese adaptation which is to be judged by Western standards. The implied hierarchy not only posits the original over the adaptation, but also the West over Japan.

Reading Kurosawa in an Occidentalist framework helps to redress and resolve the problems posed by adaptation discourse, as it destroys the essentialising, binary codes of privileged original and powerless adaptation. The film as discursive act implies that power is invested in the 'adaptation' in its political, or counter-discursive, aspect. The adaptation may in fact be seen as privileged, in that it has claimed power over the original through the act of appropriating it. The advantages of this alternative reading may be illustrated by the critical reception of *High and Low*, one of Kurosawa's best postwar social commentaries. Neither the film nor its source text are seen as canonical examples of high Japanese or Western art. The source text is the Ed McBain novel *King's Ransom* (1959). Both the original text and the film adaptation are set in contemporary society. If read in terms of 'adaptation discourse', *High and Low* displays neither the 'unique codes' of Japanese traditional culture nor the 'great Western original', which is probably why it has largely escaped critical commentary. As the novel's title suggests, the plot revolves around the ransom demanded of a business tycoon for the safe return of his chauffeur's son – mistakenly kidnapped instead of his own son. Many have read the film as a simple morality play – does Gondo pay the ransom, thereby ruining his own business chances, for the sake of a child not his own? But *High and Low* also takes issue with a wide range of subjects pertaining to the condition of 'modern Japan'. Not only does the film examine issues of class, wealth and power in a stratified society, but Kurosawa problematises the idea of identity itself in the psychological doubling between Gondo and the kidnapper. *High and Low* functions not only as a commentary on contemporary Japanese society, but also on the fractured nature of the modern individual and ultimately of the nation. Kurosawa has taken the Western source text and used it as the basis for critique directed towards Japan. This use of a Western source text as the basis of social commentary on contemporary Japan may be read as Xiaomei Chen's 'anti-official Occidentalism', appropriating the West for a domestic political purpose.

## Conclusions

Examining Kurosawa's films, and the figure of Kurosawa himself, through the critical lens of Occidentalism, brings a fresh perspective to the question of the text/context relationship in film. The Occidentalist framework is not meant as a monolithic explanation into which every Kurosawa (or Japanese) film may be squeezed, nor is the political aspect of the US-Japan relationship meant to be seen as motivating every Kurosawa film. But the theory of Occidentalism is useful as a tool with which we can understand Kurosawa's filmic act in relation to the Occupation, Japan's rebuilding process, and what Kurosawa may have been doing with his use of *Noh* and *kabuki* sources and *jidai-geki* conventions. The greatest advantage to reading Kurosawa's filmmaking as Occidentalist construction is that it resolves many of the problems inherent in traditional, Orientalist criticism. As we have seen, such a reading bypasses the hierarchical structures of 'adaptation discourse'. Further, the problem of indigenous directors struggling with a foreign medium disappears – the very act of using the technology may be read as agency, appropriation and counter-discourse. This model also resolves one of the apparent contradictions in Japanese cinema studies, that of Kurosawa as the quintessential Japanese director versus the universal '*sekai no Kurosawa*'. In the Occidentalist framework, Kurosawa may be seen as someone who was engaged in 'self-appropriation' – assertion of the power to define a Japanese Self independent of others' definitions – through his problematisation of the national discourse and the idea of 'Japaneseness'. Kurosawa's appropriation of Japanese source texts, especially in his self-reflexive use of *kabuki* and *Noh*, may also be seen as this kind of self-appropriation. At the same time, however, Kurosawa may be seen as 'the world's Kurosawa' because he engaged actively with the Western Other through his appropriation of Western works, methods and filmic techniques. The intertwined nature of so many of Kurosawa's films, based on so many different kinds of source texts, coupled with the self-reflexive consciousness of film as discursive act, gets beyond simple categorisations of 'Japanese' or 'Western' works, 'original' and 'adaptation', the 'universal' and the 'local'. By focusing on the dynamic of appropriation and intertextuality, we can scrutinise our tendency to think in terms of binary structures (East/West, Hollywood/national cinemas), and to focus more on the complexities and historical specificities of world cinema.

The appellation *sekai no Kurosawa* also points to a dynamic interplay of appropriation between and throughout cinematic worlds. Kurosawa's films have been appropriated by the Western film industry in turn, the most well-known example being John Sturges' remake of *Seven Samurai* into *The Magnificent Seven* (1960). While Western directors draw on Kurosawa's films for narratives and action, it is most interesting how the stories are transposed from their original 'exotic Japan' to an equally exotic and distanced locale: *Yojimbo* becomes *Per un pugno di dollari* (*A Fistful of Dollars*, Sergio Leone, 1964) in a Mexican border town, while *Kakushi toride no san akunin* (*The Hidden Fortress*, 1958) becomes one of popular cinema's all-time favourites, set in a galaxy far, far away; the narrative legends of *Star Wars* (1977) have come to represent a kind of universal humanism that seems to take account of the 'mythic factor' in Kurosawa's films. But the emphasis on displacement, the exotic, the liminality of border locations and the vast frontiers of space, raises some interesting questions about the perceived distance between Japan and Hollywood. The transposition of narrative into an exoticised, mythic past or liminal locale perhaps tells us more about the Orientalist perception of Japanese cinema at the time when these films were remade. This chapter has focused on the textual rather than the industrial aspect of appropriation in Japanese cinema. But when we consider that *Kagemusha* and *Ran* were made with American and French backing respectively, and that *A Fistful of Dollars* was an Italian-German-Spanish production, we see that the topic of industrial intertextuality would provide rich grounds for further research into the power structures underlying the discursive acts of such appropriative films.

There is no doubt that Kurosawa will continue to fascinate, not only for the films themselves, but also because the power structures underlying his films, their production and their reception show us the history of the twentieth century at work. This is why Kurosawa cannot be reduced to either a representation of national identity or a universal humanism of 'man in nature', 'man in the world'. The first does not take account of the great scope of appropriative dynamics going on in his work. The second looks only at the social aspect of humanity and ignores the very real political understructure evident in the films. Both ignore the way in which Kurosawa has been received, constructed and appropriated by the (largely American) academic community writing about Japanese film, and what this means in the context of the Occupation and the unbalanced power relationship between Japan and the United States. Neither view addresses the reception of Kurosawa in Europe, especially of *Rashomon* in Venice, in the context of a Europe which could more closely identify with Japan's struggle to rebuild after World War Two. By reading Kurosawa's films and their reception in terms of Orientalist and Occidentalist construction, it becomes possible to integrate the text (filmic act) with its context (structures of political or representational power). By focusing on textual interplay and appropriative dynamics, we may find new ways of overcoming problems of binarism and cultural essentialisation in the study of world cinema.

## Notes

1   *Kabuki* is a popular dramatic form incorporating narrative, dance and song, most associated with the culture of townspeople in the Edo era (seventeenth to nineteenth centuries), while *Nō* drama (usually romanised as *Noh*) developed under the patronage of the shogunate from the fourteenth to sixteenth centuries, and is generally seen as high art; see Inoura & Kawatake 1981.

2   See Miyoshi 1991 and Yoshimoto 2000. Even though Part One of Yoshimoto's book addresses the problem of Area Studies in Japanese film scholarship, he replicates the asymmetrical power structure of Area Studies by couching his discussion in terms of US academia. While there are certainly many academics working on Japanese cinema outside the US, it could be argued that 'Allied' postwar discourse on the Japanese Other and national character has dominated scholarly practice in Britain, Australia, Canada, Europe and elsewhere. For this reason, the 'Area Studies approach' to Japanese film here indicates not only the dominant discourse of US academia but also the approach of any writer who subscribes to Orientalist discursive structures.

3   See Burch 1979. Other good examples are Paul Schrader (1972), Keiko McDonald (1983) and David Desser (1992a; 1992b), who interpret Japanese film in terms of Zen, *bushidō* and *mujō* aesthetics.

4   See, for example, Richie 1972 and 1994, McDonald 1994 and Goodwin 1994.

5   *Ataka* was written by Nobumitsu Kanze in the fifteenth century, while *Kanjinchō* was adapted from the *Noh* play by Gohei Namiki III, in 1840. For a detailed examination of the intertextual references in this film see Yoshimoto (2000: 107–13) and McDonald (1994: 170–80).

6   I use the term 'samurai film' here to emphasise the association of Kurosawa with the samurai spirit made in a particular critical discourse on 'Japaneseness'. The association of Kurosawa with the samurai has been emphasised and reinforced by academic representation, in book titles such as Desser's *The Samurai Films of Akira Kurosawa* (1983) and Stephen Prince's *The Warrior's Camera* (1991), while Audie Bock has named him 'the last samurai' (1988: 60). On the critical implications in using the two terms *jidai-geki* and 'samurai film', see Yoshimoto (2000: 212–22).

7   Yoshimoto notes Kurosawa's play on *jidai-geki* in *Seven Samurai* in particular, with subtle portrayals of the individual in and apart from society; rigorous attention to detail in costume, make-up, sets, props and so on to create a 'realistic' feel to the film; and the portrayal of desperate, violent fight scenes rather than the elaborately choreographed dance-fights of popular *jidai-geki* (2000: 240–5). Yoshimoto suggests that Kurosawa built on the tradition of Yamanaka Sadao and Itami Mansaku, who had also

made satirical, self-aware *jidai-geki* films in the 1930s which questioned convention and genre (2000: 234–5).

8  On Kurosawa's use of the wipe cut and various critics' assessment of this practice see Goodwin 1994: 143–7. On construction in *High and Low* see Yoshimoto 2000: 322.

9  The disjunction between signifier and signified is very strong in the opening shots of *Norainu* (*Stray Dog*, 1949) and *Ikiru* (1952), featuring a panting dog and an x-ray of a stomach, respectively. The visual images, at first presumed to have some meaning in relation to the diegetic space, reveal themselves as either arbitrary or suspect, throwing into doubt the omniscience of the narrator giving the voice-over to the image. This disjunction between image, word and meaning calls attention away from the narrative of the film to its mode of representation, revealing the film as an exercise in rhetoric. Yoshimoto (2000: 148–52) has an interesting reading of the signification of the stray dog in this image. While he argues that the x-ray throws doubt on the omniscience of the narrator in *Ikiru* (2000: 194–5), a more straightforward reading may be found in Desser (1992a: 62–5), although he also argues that the film is fundamentally about truth and its (mis-)representation.

10  *Rashōmon* tested censorship on this point but was not banned, probably because it deviated enough from *jidai-geki* conventions to be seen as a new kind of period drama, while its realistic violence prevented it from being read as a glorification of battle. The overall thrust of the film enquiring into the nature of truth also opened it to a humanist or universalist reading rather than a feudalistic one.

11  On 'fidelity analysis' and the main critical commentaries on it see Whelehan 1999.

12  Some good examples are Andrew 1984, Marcus 1993, Kuoshu 1999 and Whelehan 1999.

13  These two films have been analysed by James Goodwin as case studies of intertextuality in Kurosawa's films (1994: 66–112). However, Goodwin's theoretical approach to semiotic intertextuality draws a strong distinction between intertextuality and adaptation (1994: 11–16), and he is less concerned with the politics of adaptation than with the codes and signs which directly correspond between the film and the literary text. His approach is thus similar in style to that of fidelity analysis. Desser points out that *The Lower Depths* is based more on the influential *Shingeki* (New Theatre) play than on the Gorky original (1992a: 58), which suggests it would be an extremely interesting case study in the dynamics of appropriation operating between Russian and Japanese discursive acts.

## Works cited

Andrew, D. (1984) *Concepts in Film Theory*. Oxford: Oxford University Press.

Bock, A. (1988) 'Japanese Film Genres', in W. Dissanayake (ed.) *Cinema and Cultural Identity: Reflections on Films from Japan, India, and China*. Lanham, New York and London: University Press of America, 53–62.

Burch, N. (1979) *To the Distant Observer: Form and Meaning in the Japanese Cinema*. London: Scholar Press.

Chen, X. (1995) *Occidentalism: A Theory of Counter-Discourse in Post-Mao China*. Oxford and New York: Oxford University Press.

Davidson, J. F. (1972) 'Memory of Defeat in Japan: A Reappraisal of Rashomon', in D. Richie (ed.) *Focus on Rashomon*. Eaglewood Cliffs, NJ: Prentice-Hall International, 119–28.

Davis, D. W. (1996) *Picturing Japaneseness: Monumental Style, National Identity, Japanese Film*. New York: Columbia University Press.

Desser, D. (1983) *The Samurai Films of Akira Kurosawa*. Ann Arbor: UMI Research Press.

____ (1992a) '*Ikiru*: Narration as a Moral Act' in A. Nolletti Jr and D. Desser (eds) *Reframing Japanese Cinema; Authorship, Genre, History*. Bloomington and Indianapolis: Indiana University Press, 56–68.

____ (1992b) 'Toward a Structural Analysis of the Postwar Samurai Film', in A. Nolletti Jr and D. Desser (eds) *Reframing Japanese Cinema; Authorship, Genre, History*. Bloomington and Indianapolis: Indiana University Press, 145–64.

Dissanayake, W. (ed.) (1988) *Cinema and Cultural Identity: Reflections on Films from Japan, India, and China*, Lanham, New York and London: University Press of America.

Freiberg, F. (2000) 'Japanese Cinema', in J. Hill and P. Church Gibson (eds) *World Cinema: Critical Approaches*. Oxford: Oxford University Press, 178–84.

Goodwin, J. (1994) *Akira Kurosawa and Intertextual Cinema*. Baltimore and London: Johns Hopkins University Press.

Inoura, Y. and T. Kawatake (1981) *The Traditional Theater of Japan*. New York and Tokyo: Weatherhill.

Kurosawa, A. (1983) *Something Like an Autobiography*, trans. Audie Bock. New York: Vintage.

Kuoshu, H. H. (1999) *Lightness of Being in China: Adaptation and Discursive Figuration in Cinema and Theater*. New York: Peter Lang.

Marcus, M. (1993) *Filmmaking by the Book: Italian Cinema and Literary Adaptation*. Baltimore and London: Johns Hopkins University Press.

McDonald, K. (1983) *Cinema East: A Critical Study of Major Japanese Films*. London: Associated University Presses.

____ (1994) *Japanese Classical Theater in Films*. London and Toronto: Associated University Presses.

Miyoshi, M. (1991) *Off Center: Power and Culture Relations Between Japan and the United States*. Cambridge, MA and London: Harvard University Press.

Prince, S. (1991) *The Warrior's Camera: The Cinema of Akira Kurosawa*. Princeton: Princeton University Press.

Richie, D. (1972) *Japanese Cinema: Film Style and National Character*. London: Secker and Warburg.

____ (1994) 'The Influence of Traditional Aesthetics on the Japanese Film', in L. C. Ehrlich and D. Desser (eds) *Cinematic Landscapes: Observations on the Visual Arts and Cinema of China and Japan*. Austin: University of Texas Press, 155–63.

____ (1998) *The Films of Akira Kurosawa*. Berkeley: University of California Press, third edition.

____ (2001) *A Hundred Years of Japanese Film: A Concise History*. Tokyo, New York and London: Kodansha International.

Rimer, T. (1994) 'Film and the Visual Arts in Japan: An Introduction', in L. C. Ehrlich and

D. Desser (eds) *Cinematic Landscapes: Observations on the Visual Arts and Cinema of China and Japan.* Austin: University of Texas Press, 149–54.

Satō, T. (1988) 'The Multi-layered Nature of the Tradition of Acting in Japanese Cinema', in W. Dissanayake (ed.) *Cinema and Cultural Identity: Reflections on Films from Japan, India, and China.* Lanham, New York and London: University Press of America, 45–52.

Schrader, P. (1972) *Transcendental Style in Film: Ozu, Bresson, Dreyer.* Berkeley: University of California Press.

Wang, N. (1997) 'Orientalism versus Occidentalism?', *New Literary History*, 28, 1, 57–67.

Whelehan, I. (1999) 'Adaptations: The Contemporary Dilemmas', in D. Cartmell and I. Whelehan (eds) *Adaptations: From Text to Screen, Screen to Text.* London and New York: Routledge, 3–19.

Yoshimoto, M. (1993) 'The Difficulty of Being Radical: The Discipline of Film Studies and the Postcolonial World Order', in M. Miyoshi and H. D. Harootunian (eds) *Japan in the World.* Durham, NC: Duke University Press, 338–53.

_____ (2000) *Kurosawa: Film Studies and Japanese Cinema.* Durham, NC: Duke University Press.

# CHAPTER FIFTEEN

## Consuming 'Bollywood' in the global age: the strange case of an 'unfine' world cinema

Kaushik Bhaumik

I begin by summarising a rather bizarre article by Adam Smith in a recent issue of the *Radio Times* giving details about BBC television's 'Bollywood' season. In this article about 'Bollywood' Smith confesses to not having seen a single Bombay film and goes on to justify his ignorance by pointing out to the very radical difference between Bollywood and the rest of the world. He says, 'the unique thing about Bollywood, as far as I can see, is how hermetically sealed it is'. This interesting observation about Bombay cinema's ambiguous presence amongst inter-or transnational film cultures is then followed by some strange remarks about its lack of influence on anything world cinematic. Good international cinema, according to Smith, is all about cross-pollination and here he rehashes the rather tiresomely predictable celebration of the love-ins between Hollywood and Kurosawa and the French *nouvelle vague*. In contrast to such moments of cross-cultural cinematic dialogue, Smith claims that Bollywood 'for all its sequins and formation hoofing, seems to have had zero influence on anything' (this remark is paraphrased in bold on the centre of the page as the anchoring soundbite for the article). Moreover, Bollywood to him seems to be a plagiarised version of Hollywood. And while Smith appreciates the fact that Bollywood is a lifeline for many and lauds the BBC's efforts to celebrate cultural diversity, for him the totality of Bombay cinema's influence on British or international culture does not go beyond a film season on television. He ends up wondering 'if there's anything of any real or lasting worth' in Bollywood, described here as a 'nation's cinema', if all it could achieve was showings on a television channel at obscure hours. Smith ends the piece by saying that the BBC's tagline of 'lesser known delights' describing the films being shown was apt since Bollywood was 'little known for a very good reason' thus neatly summarising his view of Bombay cinema's position within World Cinema – simultaneous respectable presence and radical isolation (Smith 2004: 45). This chapter would like to explore some of the possible non-articulations of 'Bollywood' in world cinema in the hope of analysing the radical doubts expressed by Mr Smith.

One could begin by saying that Smith's arguments are not representative of the totality of British response to Bombay cinema. Nevertheless they do refer to certain observable contradictions informing this cinema's position within contemporary global film cultures, the principal one being that although Bombay films are shown in considerable numbers in mainstream cinema halls in the West as well as readily available in subtitled video and DVD formats they have not succeeded in attracting non-diasporic Western audiences. However, as will be seen, such contradictions might arise more from the ways in which the category of 'world cinema' has functioned historically rather than, as Smith might want to believe, from the problematic nature of Bombay cinema. A critical analysis of his arguments juxtaposed against an analysis of the historical trajectories informing the reception of Bombay cinema in the West (my analysis of reception is in the main restricted to the UK) will reveal the cultural assumptions informing the formulation of world cinema and therefore reveal it as mediated and constructed through a history of cultural preferences that can sometimes run counter to its avowed aims and objectives. However, it needs to be emphasised that configurations of preferences are historically negotiated and constantly shifting and any analysis restricted to mapping the relational dynamics between the cultural forces animating the field of preferences at a given point in time.

## World cinema and Bollywood

The rub of Smith's article lies in a terminal slippage tucked away in the midst of his expressions of general befuddlement when faced with the phenomenon of 'Bollywood'. This slippage occurs when Smith derives the zero cultural value of Bombay cinema in the context of his talk of mutual cross-pollination between cinemas as giving rise to 'some of cinema's finest films'. One merely needs to note that his discussion about 'fine cinema' through cross-pollination is carried out exclusively in terms of cross-pollinations between Hollywood and the rest of the world (ibid.). Thus Japanese cinema is worth talking of since Western influence on Japanese cinema was matched by the West's admiration for Japanese cinema; Bombay cinema in contrast is merely derivative of Hollywood since the West has not shown its admiration by producing films emulating Bombay film styles. Smith seems to imply that if any good, non-Western filmic norms will be taken up and celebrated by the West, while non-attention on the West's part ensures their worthlessness – a tautology the most strident Western cultural imperialist would be glad to borrow. Such statements about a cinema immensely popular on a global scale mean that at worst Smith is biased against a particular kind of cinema (especially so considering his views are not even based on first-hand experience) or at best he simply cannot recognise Bombay cinema on his radar of cultural experience. One could point out that if not seen, 'Bollywood' *would* remain hermetically sealed forever. Smith's non-recognition of an entire cinema read off its absence in Western cinema becomes a travesty of the very project of World Cinema that has at least as one of its premises the need to facilitate understanding of other cultures through exposure and appreciation on their terms.

To understand the possible reasons for this paradoxical outcome it might be useful to briefly recapitulate the process by which Bollywood came to be part of mainstream world cinema. Here I must emphasise that although 'World Cinema' is also a category in film studies this chapter will forgo discussion about the academic study of World Cinema, firstly for the want of space and secondly because academic or specialist discourses are far more in line with the avowed inclusiveness of World Cinema. The discussion will on the whole stick to an analysis of observable patterns of consumption of world cinema for it is in this context that the ideological operations at work within the category are most visible and felt.

The mainstream movement towards a world cinema took a significant turn in the 1950s with the Euro-American discovery of Japanese cinema alongside the beginnings of the first modernist film movements in postwar Europe. Indian cinema too made its entry almost exclusively through the works of Satyajit Ray. It must be mentioned that within Euro-America, the mainstream discovery of Eastern European and some kinds of Scandinavian cinemas happened under the aegis of world cinema. A key moment for world cinema arose in the 1970s when films from Africa, Asia and Latin America that formed part of a corpus of radical critical national cinemas became fairly staple fare in the repertory cinema houses in Euro-America. The opening of small repertory cinemas played a stellar role in the economics of the crossover of films. The discursive trajectory uniting the diverse flows of cinemas into the West from other parts of the world in this period was the body of cultural values that came to characterise what is now known as art-house cinema.

In the 1990s a new movement in world cinema brought in art-house cinemas from China, Hong Kong and films from various parts of east, southeast and central Asia and most significantly Iran. However, in this period popular films from mainly Hong Kong and Japan and genre films from Euro-America provided the main impetus for world cinema. The entry of popular cinema in this period allowed world cinema to go mainstream and attain substantial economic stability in film markets. Indeed, genre has emerged as the most significant interlocutor for the movement of films across cultures fuelling the current phase of world cinema within the framework of the political economy of global multiculturalism. The political economy of the multicultural weaves in an out of the discursive frameworks articulating genre world cinema, as the consumption of genre cinema substantially and intimately comes to inform the play of postmodern multicultural lifestyles. Preference for films from Hong Kong and Japan consists in the main of an extended list of what Linda Williams (1997) refers to as the body genres – martial arts films, thrillers, horror, chillers and pornography amongst others.

It is in the age of the multicultural global and the movement of popular genre films from the world into the West that 'Bollywood' makes its entry into world cinema. Although genre does not exhaust the meanings of 'Bollywood' in world cinema, the very reduction of a vast array of films to a single name indicates a tendency to accommodate 'Bollywood' in the genre phase of world cinema. Some film scholars have recently taken to describing it as such. According to them, the main generic quality that distinguishes Bombay cinema from all other cinemas is its peculiar mix of melodrama and music.[1]

The movement of popular cinemas into the world cinema mainstream marks its apotheosis. Theoretically it now includes all cinemas. Yet sifting through the list of films on sale one notices that far from being exhaustive world cinema is a category constructed through a process of cultural translation that picks up only that which is familiar or made familiar through particular prisms of interpretation employed in mainstream Western cultural discourses. In what follows I will hope to clarify why 'Bollywood' falls between interpretative stools employed to construct world cinema in practice. The tensions lie between the layers of history that came to constitute world cinema as an economic and cultural phenomenon proceeding implicitly or explicitly through analytical categories employed to classify films such as national, art-house, popular, genre, global and above all 'world'.[2]

## 'Bollywood' in the West

What is striking about Bombay cinema's reception in the West is the fact that it floats uncertainly between various categories of use. The first thing worth emphasising is that this cinema's reputation is not substantially based on a crossover audience for its films, something that Smith refers to. Its emergence as a significant element in Western culture consists of a patchwork of presences in multiple registers of cultural consumption rather than a substantial loyal following for the films themselves. Only amongst the various diasporas, in academia and sometimes in the critical press do the films themselves emerge as cultural artefacts of substantial significance. Efforts are also made by a consortium of governmental, academic and activist institutions dedicated to the promotion of multiculturalism in the West to highlight Bombay cinema as part of cultural programmes aimed at South Asian diasporas. However, such efforts are increasingly mediated through the market that itself actively promotes multiculturalism. Bombay cinema's entry into world cinema proceeds through the interplay of the commercial imperatives of globalisation and the politics of multiculturalism.

The south Asian diasporas have been the single most important catalyst for the mainstream popularity of Bombay films.[3] Although the diasporas have been watching Bombay films for decades it is only in the 1990s that they emerged as a significant niche in the global market for consumer goods mainly through growing numbers and a radical transformation of youth and middle-class cultures through upward social mobility leading to the creation of a substantial market for Bombay films that the Bombay industry could exploit more profitably. From around 1998 when Mani Ratnam's *Dil se...* (1998) entered the UK charts at number six Bombay films have regularly entered the Top 10 lists of bestselling films in the UK. Over time Bombay films have spilt into mainstream cinemas further ensuring a public presence for Bombay films. However, in mainstream cinemas too the audience for Bombay films remains overwhelmingly diasporic. Although Bombay cinema has consistently been the third most successful grosser in the UK behind Hollywood and British films the takings have mainly come from diasporic audiences. Alongside this there has been a steady attempt by cultural agencies to promote multiculturalism through active pat-ronage of diasporic arts. The 2001 Imagineasia season that brought together Bombay cinema amongst other South Asian cinemas with a variety of other cultural and commercial events was the largest event ever to promote South Asian culture in the UK. Over the years the number of Bombay film seasons on UK television has been steadily rising alongside programmes aimed at promoting a better understanding of the films and the industry that produces them (see Kabir 2001).

Mainstream film critical opinion about Bombay cinema in the West has on the whole remained in South Asian hands and barring such isolated instances as the indomitable Richard Corliss' enthusiasm for all things cinematic Western critics are yet to take to Bombay cinema. In his article Smith refers to a friend who, just like himself, wrote about a Bombay film without having ever seen it or any Bombay film for that matter (2004: 45). There is a fringe cult following for Bombay cinema amongst non-diasporic Western audiences that from time to time surfaces on the internet but what its influences are on the overall status of Bombay cinema as world cinema is hard to tell.

Turning to Bombay cinema's crossover presence in the West it needs to be emphasised that it has been substantially built through diverse cultural registers not all pertaining to film. Thus Bombay cinema's music has played a pioneering role in bringing this cinema into the mainstream in the West. Long before films started to be seen by Western mainstream audiences Bombay film music had attained a significant cultural force in experimental music circles where crossover is more prevalent than in the mainstream which was then followed by interest in the films themselves or their fragments. The uncoupling of Bombay film music from the films themselves has gained force over the years, finally hitting the mainstream through Andrew Lloyd Webber's musical, *Bollywood Dreams* (2002). The same could be said about the rising popularity of Bombay *filmi* dancing as part of the recent mass public vogue in the West for exotic dance styles. Here too the diasporas were the first to formulate a subculture of 'Bollywood' dance and on the whole the diasporas have been at the cutting edge of crossover subcultures of music, fashions and lifestyles deriving from Bombay films.

Occidental Orientalism too has had a significant role to play in endorsing Bombay cinema's cause. Through the 1990s Orientalism with respect to things Indian started to get mediated through references to Bombay films as was the case when Madonna took to yoga and then 'expressed her Oriental self' through use of aspects of Bombay cinema, its music and fashions. Although Madonna might not see Bombay films, Bombay cinema becomes the mediator of Orientalism and is in turn endorsed through the elite use of its fragments – songs, dances and fashion. Music videos that isolate song and dance sequences from the films have gone a long way in contributing to the development of 'Bollywood' subcultures of fashion and style.

However, the recent twin successes of *Lagaan* (Ashutosh Gowarikar, 2001) and *Devdas* (Sanjay Leela Bhansali, 2001) amongst a relatively substantial crossover audience in the West ensured that the presence of Bombay films has begun to get felt more palpably in the mainstream. A more substantial dialogue opening up between Bombay and the world is hinted at in the recent use of Bombay film motifs in Terry Zwicker's *Ghost World* (2000) and Baz Luhrmann's *Moulin Rouge* (2001). Here we begin to get an inkling of Bombay cinema as world cinema in the way in which Smith wants it but only in a very limited manner. Bombay cinema's influence on Western culture as globalised culture remains substantial but on the whole spectral. 'Bollywood' floats in the air as a shiny shimmering presence. Films have a substantial following amongst non-diasporic Western women, people interested in India and a fringe film subculture. There are many who consume 'Bollywood' fashions and others who know about its stars, the fashions, the dances, the songs and its vital significance in their neighbours' or friends' lives but not its films. Indeed, to counter Smith's argument about Bombay cinema's zero influence on anything it would have to be said that Bombay cinema's influence on things global and Western does exist but not necessarily in terms cinematic. Smith is at once right and wrong.

## Bollywood and the problems of cultural translation in the age of the global

Bombay cinema in the West can from a certain point of view seem extremely faddish, localised to the club of the global. Yet faced with arguments such as those made by Smith one cannot help but point to the ill-informed brio underlying his own one-man 'formation hoofing' against Bombay films. Indeed, it might be said that such views proliferate in the shadow of the global where cultural practices become globalised yet can still be fenced off from dominant national cultures or fragmented through racial and/or cultural exclusivity – either by design or by habit. Ironically it is Bombay cinema's growing presence in the Western mainstream that occasions articles such as the one written by Smith from a position that seeks to legislate this cinema's entry into the non-diasporic West in terms of the timeless values supposed to be the essence of Western culture. Thus Smith's arguments about Bombay cinema's limited influence on Western culture are worth pondering upon in the context of the politics of world cinema as practised in the West in the era of the global. Why has Bombay cinema failed to get a substantial but more importantly a steadily growing crossover audience? Why has its influence on Western mainstream culture remained spectral to the point that its extra-cinematic impact seems to be more substantial?

One might say that Bombay cinema is the newest popular cinema to enter the world cinema club and it will take time for its influence to become substantial. Hong Kong martial arts cinema did not overnight become a mass entertainment genre in the West. It took almost two decades between Bruce Lee and Jackie Chan to create a genuine crossover audience assuring Hong Kong cinema's presence in the Western cultural mainstream for the foreseeable future. Against this logic of gradual evolution might be posed the intensity of the initial exuberance with which the West embraced Hong Kong cinema and the iconic status of Bruce Lee. Bombay cinema in contrast was smuggled in through the backdoor of diasporic cultures and was soon dismembered and recomposed into a cultural chic leaving the films more or less untouched beyond the diasporas. Moreover, as will be seen its very formal qualities might pose difficulties for the development of a mainstream crossover audience in the West.

If we analyse the history of the world cinema category tendencies towards cultural essentialism in and the extremely limited nature of the West's reception of world cinemas become readily apparent. These two interrelated tendencies of essentialism and limited mainstream comprehension has plagued the development of world cinema both as a commodity and a meaningful cultural category for the West. As will be seen these tendencies determined the shape of world cinema even in the 1990s when popular cinemas finally broke through in an era where film watching was being revolutionised by video and digital media. Concurrently with the expansion in the reach of cinema a new kind of audience increasingly cineaste in nature was beginning to come into place, an audience with eclectic tastes in cinema mainly defined by genre, the independent and the global.

Although theoretically any film outside the Western mainstream qualified for world cinema, entry into the canon was allowed only in a limited number of ways. Despite the avowed liberal premises framing world cinema, in practice cultural essentialism is alive and well in the ways in which the category pans out historically. Needless to say that the cultural framework articulating world cinema is, as for any cinema, ultimately rooted in the economics of film exhibition and distribution, yet when compared to Western cinemas non-Western world cinema has been overwhelmingly dependent on the cultural for its economics. Films from the non-West have in practice always played to limited audiences, a significant barrier to larger audiences being the one posed by language. Genre world films seem to transcend this barrier most consistently possibly because generic action obviates to a certain extent the overwhelming dependence on language for filmic comprehension.

Given the economic realities of world cinema the first portal of entry for non-English language cinemas into world cinema still remains the high national-cultural modernist; cinemas representing national-cultural art-house and radical progressive tendencies have pride of place. Next in line comes the category of popular realist cinemas which has now been extended to include the independent-popular cinemas from Asia and non-mainstream Euro-America. This is followed by genre world cinema that forms probably the most significant world cinema category for contemporary times not least because of its enormous commercial values in the multicultural global. Within this phase there emerges the strange case of 'Bollywood', a world cinema whose career is hard to categorise if only for the reasons delineated in the previous section – a world cinema *qua* cinema fuelled in the main by diasporic consumption while a world cinema *qua* world fragmented by pseudo-generic use by the politics of postmodern multiculturalism. The valorisation of this cinema as generically musical on account of its songs and dances allows consumers to fragment its unity and extract its musical and dance aspects to fuel the crossover postmodern chic of multicultural lifestyles leaving out much of what it has to offer outside of the 'musical'. In action, 'Bollywood' symbolises the reduction of Bombay cinema to a lifestyle accessory – the sequins and formation-hoofing that Smith refers to.

This implicit history of world cinema creates a critical space to speculate upon the possible non-articulations between Bombay and the world. What follows is in substantial measures speculative and a lot of research needs to be done on the reception of Bombay films amongst non-diasporic Western audiences before any firm conclusions can be drawn as regards Bombay films in world cinema. However, the speculations are based on views expressed by non-diasporic Western spectators who watch Bombay films every now and then and end up describing 'Bollywood' as consisting only of musicals, similarly plotted melodramas about tradition and the modern and in other ways that express only a distant interest in the films on account of their non-realism. Bombay films that have invited a substantial crossover audience in the UK have depended for their success upon exotica such as empire, folk-feudal extravaganza or the exotica of the Indian global of weddings. The 'Bollywood' phenomenon remains, as described above, outside the films themselves and although one might say that interest in martial arts films in the US did take advantage of Occidental Orientalism and triggered off a martial arts revolution in the public sphere, the films themselves were over the years watched by exponentially expanding subcultural audiences. My speculations are thus located in a comparative framework testing out the limited audience response I have been able to collect against the histories of various world cinemas entering into the mainstream in the West.

Underlying the aforementioned ambiguities of Bombay cinema's spectral and fragmented presence in Western mainstream culture lies its perceived 'non-realist' and 'multi-generic' qualities that fail to meet the standards of cultural translation employed by the Western mainstream when dealing with non-Western non-mainstream film cultures. Thus audiences primed to see realist or generically pure films as the acme of cinema might find it difficult to take in the totality of Bombay cinema that crosses boundaries of realism and genre effortlessly. Genre world films have gained huge crossover followings and more significantly spawned crossover film productions (even Kurosawa was translated into Hollywood along generic lines). It is hard to imagine Hollywood producing a 'realist' cinema with songs and dances although no cinematic logic *a priori* rules this option out. The perceived 'non-realism' of realist Bombay cinema does not rule out this cinema's powers to articulate cultural experiences – the tensions, ironies and pathos of human life – embodied in a certain register of 'fine' cinema. Politically edgy films do not lose any of their seriousness due to songs and dances nor is the run-of-the-mill version of this cinema texturally any less edgy than a lot of low-budget independent world cinema so dear to Western cinephiles.

Thus to give a possible answer to Smith's views about Bombay cinema's lack of success in producing crossover audiences and films one needs to point out that the category of world cinema has been in practice anchored in viewing practices in the West that has legislated realism or a particular notion of genre as the only viable categories for cinematic comprehension of the Other. The 'world' in world cinema understood as the best cinemas in the world has always stood for the West legislating what is best in other cinemas. Thus European art-house cinema has served as the benchmark for all other art-house cinemas just as the new definition of world cinema Euro-American realist or genre popular cinema serves to decide what 'fine' popular cinema is. The tensions between the 'world' in world cinema understood as the best of world cultures and the world as including all cultures is given direction by the West imposing its own logic by becoming the currency that decides the manner in which the 'best' is extracted from different world cultures. The best the Western mainstream can do with Bombay films is exotica. Indeed, even the crossovers that Smith admires so much are on closer analysis found to have been initiated on extremely unequal terms between the West and the rest of the world and continue to be exploitative of non-Western partner cultures and economies on the whole.

This is not to criticise the postmodern play of the exotic articulating 'Bollywood' in world cinema but to point out that any popular cinema without art-house, realist or genre credentials on the West's terms stands condemned to a marginal position in the mainstream. As a rejoinder to Smith it might be said that to arrive at a genuine recognition of Bombay cinema, a cinema that has nothing to offer to the particularisms guiding the practice of world cinema in the West, the West might need to develop a cultural empathy and an understanding of a different kind of cinema that is lacking at the moment. Calling Bombay films a lifeline for many and worthless in the same breath is as good as saying that consumers of Bombay films (including the South Asian diaspora in Britain) have bad cultural taste. The problem may lie the other way round – in the West's limited comprehension of world cultures.

This may not be the case forever. At the moment beyond an audience watching just the occasional blockbuster or the classics, the 'Bollywood' subculture in the UK amongst Western audiences seems to be restricted mainly to women and young people with an interest in India. There is a substantial following for Bombay films amongst pockets of non-diasporic audiences but these are at the moment not adding up to a film movement capable of energising Bombay cinema in world cinema to bigger things amongst the non-diaspora – culturally and economically. Yet to see Bombay cinema's presence in the West as a fad for the exotic is to miss the crucial actions of globalisation on Bombay cinema. On the one hand Bombay films will continue to be consumed along lines determined by the new cosmopolitanisms spun out by cultural globalisation even if this is substantially restricted to merely a dialogue between the diasporas and Bombay. On the other hand the film industry itself has over the years become desperate to produce crossover films, breathlessly rifling through formula to come up with the magic combination and could come up with the elusive number.

It is hard to predict whether the subculture for Bombay cinema in the Western mainstream will grow substantially – numerically and critically – in the manner for Hong Kong martial arts films. Moreover the situation might differ in the US from the UK. The limited crossover success of *Monsoon Wedding* (Mira Nair, 2001) that was produced in the West but paid tribute to Bombay film style points towards a cultural dynamic of globalisation that holds out the possibilities for crossover audiences for films about the global cultures of South Asian immigrants. There is always the possibility that Bombay cinema's potential as a 'musical' might connect with the revival of the genre in Hollywood that seems to be under way (evident from Luhrmann's tribute to 'Bollywood'). More substantial engagements with the rules of Bombay cinema are difficult to imagine but cannot be entirely ruled out. Of course the economics of global Hollywood increasingly dependent on tax savings through world cinema might come to play the most important determining role in shaping Bombay cinema in world cinema.

The irony is that even an art-house film such as *Monsoon Wedding* rather than represent the radical possibilities embodied in the histories of Bombay cinema articulates itself around a face of globalising India that the West wants to see – a culture of colourful and tuneful weddings. Bombay cinema itself seems to be still in the main dedicated to turning out 'unfine cinema' of saucy action films and comedies for its time-tested core audiences – the globalising disadvantaged classes who make up probably the largest audience for a cinema other than Hollywood's thus showing up this cinema's significance in cultural globalisation but from below. Ironically, this goes back to one of the horizon of expectations originally embodied in the world in world cinema – a world articulated around the experiences of the disadvantaged. However, the world articulated by Bombay film audiences is created on their terms and not on those of the global bourgeoisie. This is not to celebrate the hegemony of 'Bollywood' in non-Indian contexts but to point out the ironies that reside in the histories of world cinema.[4]

## Conclusion

The greatest influence that 'Bollywood' in world cinema has had is on Bombay cinema itself. Entry into the club of world cinema has reconfigured the economic framework of the industry. It has also given the industry confidence to claim respectability as an 'authentic' cinema representative of Indian values. Indeed, an awareness of the perception of Bombay cinema seen as an inferior version of Hollywood informs the recent move by the Bombay film industry to contest being called 'Bollywood'. As Bombay films have found popular international attention, elicited interest from Hollywood and gained acclaim amongst elements of the cultural elite of the West the industry has decided to exert its uniqueness by refusing to accept any comparisons with Hollywood. According to them any comparison with Hollywood is bound to place Bombay cinema in a position of inferiority, copies being by definition inferior products of plagiarism rather than original imagination. Although the industry itself had promoted the image of Bollywood in the 1980s to legitimise its position with respect to Indian audiences just as it was emerging from decades of critical opprobrium from the middle classes for its non-realism (measured in the main against Hollywood realism), by the 1990s the industry no longer needed to do so with the arrival of a new generation of middle-class audience that was willing to evaluate Bombay cinema more positively on its own terms.

The coming of age of Bombay cinema in world cinema has resulted in a remarkable expansion in industry's economic and cultural power at home and abroad. The expansion of Bombay cinema's influence on the culture of consumption began in the 1990s with the onset of globalisation under the aegis of policies of economic liberalisation in India. The diaspora played a crucial role in constructing material cultural practices in shapes and colours borrowed from Bombay cinema. Bombay cinema's cultural prestige expanded exponentially with the West beginning to see Indian culture substantially through the prism of Bombay films now endorsed as 'Bollywood'. This in turn has informed the ways in which Bombay cinema aspires to itself become 'Bollywood', seeing itself as 'fine' cinema in the mirror of the seal of approval bestowed by the West.[5]

However, a substantial strand of Bombay cinema fuelling such globalisation of Indian mass culture is articulated around some of the most conservative cinema ever produced in Bombay, films that promote consumption of lifestyles that strengthen the stranglehold of repressive traditions on Indian culture, traditions that are in turn projected as India's unique contribution to the world. Certain cultural commentators who resist Bombay cinema being called 'Bollywood' not only display a cultural pride about Bombay cinema as 'authentically' Indian but also articulate this pride in films through a celebration of repressive tradition as the essence of Indian culture, a move given respectability by the West's play on the Orientalist glamour of 'Bollywood' weddings. Ironically, much of this glamour is amongst sections of contemporary Indian middle classes the new crucible for rearticulating repressive tradition within and through the global. Thus 'Bollywood' lives on as a marketing catchphrase to define a cultural chic and above all as a sign of global with-it-ness pragmatically contested and promoted by Indian entrepreneurs and cultural commentators depending on the context of enunciation.

And herein lies the true irony of Smith's comments about Bombay cinema – that while Smith refuses to watch Bombay films, his bullying others to fit into the values of 'fine cinema' stands a good chance of inadvertently egging Bombay cinema further towards problematic cultural hierarchies and practices of 'Bollywood' as world cinema. World cinema it may become, but for which world(s)?

## Notes

1   For the politics of diasporic reception of Bombay cinema, see Mishra 2002; see also Dwyer 2000.
2   For a description and analysis of world cinema categories, see Crofts 1998.
3   For an analysis of the reception of Bombay cinema amongst the diasporas, see Mishra 2002.
4   There are indications that 'Bollywood' is beginning to be resisted in Africa on account of its hegemonic hold over market niches at the expense of regional cinemas.
5   For an analysis of Bombay cinema in the era of economic globalisation, see Dwyer 2000.

## Works cited

Crofts, S. (1998) 'Concepts of National Cinema' in J. Hill and P. C. Gibson, *The Oxford Guide to Film Studies*. Oxford: Oxford University Press, 385–94.

Dwyer, R. (2000) *All You Want is Money, All You Need is Love: Sex and Romance in Modern India*. London: Cassell.

Kabir, N. M. (2001) *Bollywood: The Indian Cinema Story*. London: Channel 4 Books.

Mishra, V. (2002) *Bollywood: Temples of Desire*. London: Routledge.

Smith, A. (2004) 'On Bollywood', *Radio Times*, 7–13 August.

Williams, L. (1997) 'Film Bodies: Gender, Genre and Excess', in B. K. Grant (ed.) *Film Genre Reader II*. Austin: University of Texas Press, 140–58.

# INDEX